War's Glorious Art

One to destroy is murder by the law
And gibbets keep the lifted hand in awe

To murder thousands

goes by a specious name

War's glorious art

And gives immortal fame.

(Edward Young, 1685–1765)

D1600156

Saipan ("Baby taken from near cave") Life 1944. W Eugene Sm

An Insect

Writing, I crushed an insect with my nail
And thought nothing at all. A bit of wing
Caught my eye then, a gossamer so frail

And exquisite, I saw in it a thing
That scorned the grossness of the thing I wrote.
It hung upon my finger like a sting.

A leg I noticed next, fine as a mote,
"And on this frail eyelash he walked," I said,
"And climbed and walked like any mountain-goat."

Then in my heart a fear
Cried out, "A life – why, beautiful, why dead!"
It was a mite that held itself most dear,
So small I could have drowned it with a tear.

(Karl Shapiro)

~~SECRET~~

July 17, 1945

A PETITION TO THE PRESIDENT OF THE UNITED STATES

Discoveries of which the people of the United States are not aware may affect the welfare of this nation in the near future. The liberation of atomic power which has been achieved places atomic bombs in the hands of the Army. It places in your hands, as Commander-in-Chief, the fateful decision whether or not to sanction the use of such bombs in the present phase of the war against Japan.

We, the undersigned scientists, have been working in the field of atomic power. Until recently we have had to fear that the United States might be attacked by atomic bombs during this war and that her only defense might lie in a counterattack by the same means. Today, with the defeat of Germany, this danger is averted and we feel impelled to say what follows:

The war has to be brought speedily to a successful conclusion and attacks by atomic bombs may very well be an effective method of warfare. We feel, however, that such attacks on Japan could not be justified, at least not unless the terms which will be imposed after the war on Japan were made public in detail and Japan were given an opportunity to surrender.

If such public announcement gave assurance to the Japanese that they could look forward to a life devoted to peaceful pursuits in their homeland and if Japan still refused to surrender our nation might then, in certain circumstances, find itself forced to resort to the use of atomic bombs. Such a step, however, ought not to be made at any time without seriously considering the moral responsibilities which are involved.

The development of atomic power will provide the nations with new means of destruction. The atomic bombs at our disposal represent only the first step in this direction, and there is almost no limit to the destructive power which will become available in the course of their future development. Thus a nation which sets the precedent of using these newly liberated forces of nature for purposes of destruction may have to bear the responsibility of opening the door to an era of devastation on an unimaginable scale.

If after this war a situation is allowed to develop in the world which permits rival powers to be in uncontrolled possession of these new means of destruction, the cities of the United States as well as the cities of other nations will be in continuous danger of sudden annihilation. All the resources of the United States, moral and material, may have to be mobilized to prevent the advent of such a world situation. Its prevention is at present the solemn responsibility of the United States—singled out by virtue of her lead in the field of atomic power.

The added material strength which this lead gives to the United States brings with it the obligation of restraint and if we were to violate this obligation our moral position would be weakened in the eyes of the world and in our own eyes. It would then be more difficult for us to live up to our responsibility of bringing the unloosened forces of destruction under control.

In view of the foregoing, we, the undersigned, respectfully petition: first, that you exercise your power as Commander-in-Chief, to rule that the United States shall not resort to the use of atomic bombs in this war unless the terms which will be imposed upon Japan have been made public in detail and Japan knowing these terms has refused to surrender; second, that in such an event the question whether or not to use atomic bombs be decided by you in the light of the considerations presented in this petition as well as all the other moral responsibilities which are involved.

DECLASSIFIED
NND 730039
By _____ NARS, Date _____

The July 17, 1945 Petition to President Roosevelt by Dr Leo Szilard and 67 fellow scientists from the atomic project.

Former President Truman at the Truman Library in 1959.

When Mercy Seasons Justice

The quality of mercy is not strained. It
droppeth as the gentle rain from heaven
Upon the place beneath. It is twice blessed:
It blesseth him that gives and him that takes.
'Tis mightiest in the mightiest. It becomes
The thronèd monarch better than his crown.
His scepter shows the force of temporal power,
The attribute to awe and majesty
Wherein doth sit the dread and fear of kings,
But mercy is above this sceptered sway.
It is enthronèd in the hearts of kings.
It is an attribute to God himself.
And earthly power doth then show likest God's
When mercy seasons justice.

(William Shakespeare, *The Merchant of Venice*)

Something Special

The Reverend Mr Tanimoto got up at five o'clock that morning. He was alone in the parsonage, because for some time his wife had been commuting with their year-old baby to spend nights with a friend in Ushida, a suburb to the north. Of all important cities in Japan only two, Kyoto and Hiroshima, had not yet been visited in strength by "*B-san,*" or *Mr. B,* as the Japanese, with a mixture of respect and unhappy familiarity, called the B-29. And Mr Tanimoto, like all his neighbors and friends, was almost sick with anxiety.

He had heard uncomfortably detailed accounts of mass raids on Kure, Iwakuni, Tokuyama, and other nearby towns; he was sure Hiroshima's turn would come soon. He had slept badly the night before, because there had been several air-raid warnings, almost every night for weeks, for at that time the B-29s were using Lake Biwa, northeast of Hiroshima, as a rendezvous point, and no matter what city the Americans planned to hit, the Superfortresses streamed in over the coast near Hiroshima.

The frequency of the warnings and the continued abstinence of *Mr. B* with respect to Hiroshima had made its citizens jittery; a rumor was going around that the Americans were saving something special for the city.

(John Hersey, *Hiroshima*)

"'Oh! The B-29 dropped something white,' said someone, and I looked up through the window to see a plane and something falling from it. Just then a terrible pain, as if I had been struck by a wet leather whip." – A Zuroku A-Bomb drawing by a survivor, Hiroshima Peace Museum.

Neighbors Break Bonds of Friendship

A world where right spells wrong,
and wrong spells right!
So many wars! So many shapes of crime!
The plough despised! the ploughmen reft away!
The widowed fields unkempt!
The sickle's curve melted
to mold a sword blade's stiff straight edge...
Neighbors break bonds of friendship,
take up arms,
The wicked war god rages everywhere.

(Virgil, *Georgics I sos.11*)

Paper Tiger

The atom bomb is a paper tiger which
the United States reactionaries use to
scare people. It looks terrible but in fact it isn't.

(Mao Zedong)

Hiroshima Nagasaki

An Illustrated History, Anthology, and Guide

"Those who are not shocked when they first come across quantum theory cannot possibly have understood it."
– Niels Bohr

Hiroshima, August 6, 1945.

ODYSSEY BOOKS & MAPS **ODYSSEY EDGE**

Distribution in the USA by W.W. Norton & Company, Inc. 500 Fifth Avenue,
New York, NY 10110, USA
Tel: (800) 233-4830; Fax: (800) 458-6515; www.wwnorton.com

Odyssey Books & Maps is a division of Airphoto International Ltd.
1401 Chung Ying Building, 20–20A Connaught Road West, Sheung Wan, Hong Kong
Tel: (852) 2856 3896; Fax: (852) 3012 1825
E-mail: magnus@odysseypublications.com; www.odysseypublications.com
Follow us on Twitter – www.twitter.com/odysseyguides

Hiroshima Nagasaki: An Illustrated History, Anthology, and Guide, First Edition
ISBN: 978-962-217-860-1
Library of Congress Catalog Card Number has been requested.
Copyright © 2015, published by Airphoto International Ltd.

Executive editor: Jeremy Tredinnick
Managing editor: Sam Inglis
Odyssey Edge: George Baily
Associate editor: Neil Art
Publicity Contact: mbisbee.beek@gmail.com

Cover Designer: Alex Ng Kin Man
Designer: Au Yeung Chui Kwai

Production by Twin Age Ltd.
Printed in Hong Kong

Hiroshima
Nagasaki

An Illustrated History, Anthology, and Guide

Let the People know the Facts and
the Nation will be Safe

– Abraham Lincoln

Magnus Bartlett • Robert O'Connor

with

Sam Inglis and George Baily

CONTENTS

"Two forces rule the universe, gravity and light." – Simone Weil
Nagasaki, August 9, 1945.

"The giant pillar of smoke rose rapidly in the sky, creating a thundercloud that piled on itself as it spread. Within its billows, orange, red, blue sparks shot in all directions like streak lightning. As this bizarre configuration expanded, it shaped itself into a mushroom." – A Zuroku A-Bomb drawing by a survivor, Hiroshima Peace Museum.

ACKNOWLEDGMENTS & THANKS

No book like this is a solo effort, and many people stepped up to help it come into being. In Hiroshima, Steve Leeper jumped at the chance to help, and a thousand thanks are due for his efforts in getting us in touch with Mayors for Peace. We'd also like to thank Hiroko Nakamoto of Gateway to World Peace and Aaron Tovish and Yasuyoshi Komizo of Mayors for Peace. Also due thanks are Shoko Mizuki of the Hiroshima Museum of Art and especially Director Kenji Shiga of the Hiroshima Peace Memorial Museum, as well as his curatorial staff.

In Nagasaki thanks are due to Matsuo Koki of the Nagasaki Peace Sphere, Natsu Sueyasu and Kenji Odawara at the Nagasaki City Tourism Office, and Satoshi Ohori at the Museum of History and Culture.

We'd like to thank Chiyoko Iwanami of CSA Inc. and Manami Okazaki, both in Tokyo; the Hon. Wilfred Mohr, Consul General of the Netherlands in Hong Kong; Artur K. Wardega, S.J. of the Matteo Ricci Institute in Macau; Junzo Sawa of The English Agency in Tokyo; Shogo Yamahata in Tokyo, and Victor Boggio of Action Language Academy in Nagoya.

Throughout this book we use photographs and artwork owned by various institutions, and we would like to show our gratitude to the many people at these institutions for helping us in making these images available to the public in our book. We couldn't have done it without them.

We'd also like to thank the staff at various libraries who let us peruse their collections and scan items. Of note are those in the Ryerson and Burnham Library at the Art Institute of Chicago, the Ronald William Library of Northeastern Illinois University, the Joseph Regenstein Library of the University of Chicago, and the Richard J. Daley Library of the University of Illinois at Chicago.

Within the Odyssey office our thanks go to Cecilia Lee, Au Yeung Chui Kwai, Sam Inglis and later Jeremy Tredinnick and Neil Art for making sure it looked good. Associates of Odyssey like Margarita Delgado, Roger Brumhill, George Bailey and others also contributed much needed feedback, reassurance and facilitated connections with crucial people. My thanks to all of these and the many others – too many to mention – who contributed in one way or another.

The Authors, June 2015

Prologue

"Hiroshima is contaminated with radiation. It will be barren of life and nothing will grow for 75 years."

— attributed to Dr. Harold Jacobson, August 7, 1945

"Over everything up through the wreckage of the city, in gutters, along the river banks, tangled among tiles and tin roofing, climbing on charred tree trunks, was a blanket of fresh, vivid, lush, optimistic green; the verdancy rose even from the foundation of ruined houses. Weeds already hid the ashes, and wild flowers were in bloom among the city's bones."

— John Hersey, *Hiroshima*, first published by *The New Yorker*, Aug 31, 1946

The world changed instantly and irrevocably on a clear Monday morning, August 6, 1945. People were arriving at work in the Japanese city of Hiroshima when a new secret weapon unleashed its power 1,900 feet (579 meters) above a hospital. The city center was obliterated and in less than an hour, 80,000 people were dead. Three days later, a similar weapon would drop on a tennis court in the Nagasaki area of Urakami, 1,640 feet (500 meters) from the largest Catholic church in East Asia. The two bombs are to this day the most powerful weapons ever used in war.

Hiroshima and Nagasaki crumbled, but what they were before August 6 and August 9, 1945 didn't entirely disappear. Dr. Jacobson's quote was widely printed in the international media, but the following spring, hundreds of trees in Hiroshima and Nagasaki that had been charred and broken sprouted new shoots, leaves and branches, as noted by Hersey. These trees still live, and the two cities have rebuilt. Their civic leaders became advocates for peace and the abolition of nuclear weapons, summed up in the plea "never again."

"Never again," the phrase many people utter when they leave museums concerning the Holocaust, Apartheid, both World Wars and other sites that memorialize horrific acts by man. Their purpose, like the Hiroshima Peace Museum and the Nagasaki Atomic Bomb Museum, is to show what happened, in order that these events may never happen again.

The bombs, and the ensuing surrender and occupation of Japan fundamentally changed the country and erased many ideas of the past. For more than 2,000 years, the Japanese worshipped their Emperor as a living god (*Arahitogami*), descended from the first emperor, Jimmu, who journeyed from Kyushu to the Nara basin and founded what became Japan. According to legend Jimmu's great-grandfather Ninigi, grandson of Amaterasu the sun goddess, descended to Earth from Heaven carrying the three sacred treasures of Japan: the sword *Kusanagi*, the mirror *Yata no Kagami* and the jewel *Yasakani no Magatama*.

The public is invariably shown warfare through sanitized coverage, with the explanation always being that some images are too graphic and disturbing. This book will show images that are graphic and disturbing – they are meant to be. All too often people do not see the true reality of war, and this allows them to be more accepting of war when it happens.

The world knew what had happened to Hiroshima and Nagasaki by 1950, but the belief that future threats could be placated with these powerful weapons led the United States, the Soviet Union, Britain, France and China to build and test additional and increasingly powerful nuclear weapons. India, Pakistan, Israel and North Korea have tested nuclear weapons of their own. The radiation and fallout from such tests have destroyed ecosystems, deformed infants and afflicted thousands of people with sickness and disease. Even if they are never used in war again, nuclear weapons cause death and unimaginable suffering.

This book sets out to introduce the reader to what Hiroshima and Nagasaki were before the bombings, particularly their role in the history of Japan. It will also take a brief look at 20th-century physics and its *reductio ad absurdum*, atomic weapons. It is intended to provoke discussion and to better inform the world about what happened in the centuries leading up to those three fateful days in 1945 and the aftermath of that defining moment of the last century.

For those wishing to travel to these important historic locations, this book also provides useful information regarding the cities and nearby places significant to this story. The best history is the kind one can experience personally. We want people to visit these cities and see the triumph of their being rebuilt from total destruction. We'll give brief histories of each of these, in the hopes that a traveler can experience what the city has to offer beyond the Peace Park.

This book will also illustrate, using recently released documents, that there is no set consensus on many aspects of the dropping of the atomic bombs. Many prominent politicians at the time, even as they publicly proclaimed the bombings were necessary, had private (and not-so-private) doubts about using them. The official story and the rationale that Americans have largely accepted for decades is not clear cut and deserves to be re-examined in light of what we now know.

The reader will be introduced to rarely seen documents, photographs and, most powerful of all, illustrations of the bombing. There is a wide range of extracts from literature and art to show the history of the two cities and how artists – especially from the West – have interpreted this sometimes otherworldly island nation.

At the beginning of the 20th century we knew next to nothing about the atom. By 1945, we had acquired the knowledge to not only destroy two cities, but to build weapons so powerful that they could wipe out most life on our planet. By the end of the century the Cold War, which had precipitated the development of these weapons, was on hold, and efforts were started to reduce the number of nuclear weapons. Our book is timely as tensions rise between the nuclear powers, especially the United States and Russia over the situation in Crimea, and between China and Japan over the latter's reinterpretation of its constitution to allow for collective self-defense, and China's assertion of certain air-space rights.

Efforts to rid the world of nuclear weapons have been slow, mainly because politicians in each of the nuclear powers – the United States, Britain, France, China, Russia, India, Pakistan, Israel and North Korea – all claim that having these bombs is both a "useful deterrent" and "necessary," even as the biggest threats to their national security have changed from nation states to lone-wolf fanatics with bombs hidden in their clothes. Rampant poverty, global warming and pandemics have also emerged as threats to the security of nations and like nuclear weapons, these dangers affect everyone, regardless of race, creed, caste, or class.

However, despite the heavy subject matter, we will show the more positive sides of each city – pilgrimages like this don't always have to be somber, and to use Samuel Johnson's line, "the use of traveling is to regulate imagination by reality, and instead of thinking how things may be, to see them as they are."

The realization of truth can be hard sometimes, but it can also be regenerative. We hope this book brings people closer to the truth of what happened, and helps them to gain a better understanding of the issues faced then and now.

Our book is dedicated to the innumerable needless dead of the 20th century and those living who strive for a more just, peaceful world. It is dedicated to the people of Hiroshima and Nagasaki, who count both within their numbers.

"The force from which the sun draws its power has been loosed against those who brought war to the Far East." – President Truman August 6, 1945

Dear President Obama

Greetings. We realize that the invitation we are making to you here probably cannot be "taken up" so long as you are the President; our invitation, that you visit Hiroshima and Nagasaki, would have to be at the Japanese Government's invitation and this is not likely to materialize before you complete your term in office. Unfortunately, influential members of the government in Tokyo are loath to give encouragement to the large number of Japanese who oppose the government's move towards a more muscular foreign policy, and it appears that a visit to either city by an incumbent President would send a powerful signal of solidarity to the many Japanese "peaceniks" who prefer their nation remain committed to a pacific foreign policy. Thus, domestic politics make your visiting of either of the bombed cities in 2015 or 2016 highly unlikely - we can hope for miracles but must plan for their not materializing.

We trust you will not find this primer for your eventual visit too scrappy. We have attempted to put together a manual which will encourage you, and many others, to come to these two unique cities and see for yourself how they have literally risen from the ashes.

We must apologize to the mayors of both cities for not approaching them to make their own invitations, but things grind slow at city halls the world over; we hope they will forgive us and will appreciate our efforts to promote visits, including by pilgrims, to their respective cities. Furthermore, this book represents our humble contribution to the Mayors for Peace agenda, which successfully brings together thousands of communities around the world with a common interest in a nuclear-free world - but which until now has not successfully engaged the "Crucial Four."

To have a significant impact, the initiative must engage the paramount leaders of Japan, China, Russia, and America, in the context of long-term stability in the aptly named Asia Pacific region.

Ideally Prime Minister Abe would issue the invitations, with both mayors' signatures beside his, to coincide with the 2016 anniversaries - the 71st - of the bombs in Hiroshima and Nagasaki. They are only three days apart, so it ought to be possible for both President Xi Jinping and President Vladimir Putin to set aside three or at most four days next August; and you, Mr. President, entering the last six months of office, would have the necessary flexibility to arrive a little earlier and perhaps leave a little later.

We have the dream that you, together with Presidents Xi and Putin, hosted by Japan's Prime Minister, would leverage these exceptionally symbolic venues to signal to the world that the past has passed and that it is truly time to move forward to meet the new global challenges that require we no longer be haunted by the dismal delinquencies of the 19th and 20th centuries.

In doing this you would prove that, despite the magnitude of these problems, it is not only possible for four great nations to come together, but mandatory. Simply meeting together in either nuclear city will obviate the need for politically awkward apologies, nice though that would be; the sincere intent of their respective leaders to put aside past differences is, we believe, the first and most important step.

Sincerely yours,

Guns and rosaries: Henry the Navigator's maritime missions struck not just gold and ivory but human cargos too, at first bound for European markets, later for the Americas especially Brazil. Note, Cueta appears as Scuta, opposite today's Straits of Gibraltar.

The Usual Booty

The Portuguese armada stormed the fortress at Cueta on August 24, 1415, in a one-sided battle. Well armed and armored, and supported by a contingent of English archers, they overwhelmed the Muslims, who were reduced to hurling rocks. Within a day the Portuguese crusaders had taken the Infidel stronghold and provided Prince Henry with his moment of glory. Only eight Portuguese had been killed, while the city streets were piled with Muslim bodies. By afternoon the army had begun sacking the city, and the spiritual rewards of killing the Infidels was supplemented by more worldly treasure.

This occasion gave Henry his first taste of the dazzling riches of Africa. For the loot in Cueta was the freight delivered by the caravans that had been arriving there from Saharan Africa in the south, and from the Indies in the east. In addition to the prosaic essentials of life – wheat, rice, salt – the Portuguese found exotic stores of pepper, cinnamon, cloves, ginger, and other spices. Cuetan houses were hung with rich tapestries and carpeted with Oriental rugs. All in addition to the usual booty of gold, silver, and jewels.

(*The Discoverers* – Daniel J. Boorstin)

These Were Staggering Numbers

Not far from my boarding house, between large waterfront boulders and thick vegetation, one can see the remnants of calcified walls ruined by time and salt. These walls and all of Goree in fact are infamous. For 200 years, perhaps even longer, the island was a prison, a concentration camp, and a port of embarkation for African slaves being sent to the other hemisphere, to north and south America and the Caribbean.

According to various estimates several million, 12 million, perhaps 20 million young men and women were deported from Goree. These were staggering numbers in those days. The mass abductions and deportations depopulated the continent... for years on end, uninterruptedly, columns of people were driven from the African interior to where Dakar lies today, and from there were convoyed to this island; some died of hunger, thirst and disease whilst awaiting the ships meant to transport them across the Atlantic.

(*Travels with Herodotus* – Ryskard Kapuscinski)

CHAIN REACTION

An apology nevertheless. I cannot speak for my co-author Robert, whose grandfather was one of the signatories of the letter of July 17, 1945 to President Truman, so I'll make a "General Apology" on behalf of all those who share with me remorse for one or more crimes against humanity, or human rights abused in some way, related in this all too brief history and guide. But I need a lot of help; here is Reinhold Niebuhr:

"The sin of self-righteousness is not only the final sin in the subjective sense but also in the objective sense. It involves us in the greatest guilt. It is responsible for our most serious cruelties, injustices and defamations against our fellow men. The whole history of racial, national, religious and other social struggles is a commentary on the objective wickedness and social miseries which result from self-righteousness."

And help from another quarter:

"Be compassionate like your Father, do not judge and you shall not be judged, do not condemn and you will not be condemned, forgive and you shall be forgiven, give and you shall receive."

However I, and some others, fail repeatedly in heeding either Christ's or Niebuhr's simple plea. Nor for that matter do we follow either President George Washington's sentiments or reflect sufficiently carefully on the words of Richard Young (penned a hundred years earlier than Washington's), who lament the paradox of mass murder (as in war, even in a *righteous* war), in that after a certain point, the more victims there are in any outrage the less the outrage signifies, beyond involuntary gasps of statistic-related amazement.

So my proxy apology, token as it may be, is as much for my own inclinations to self-righteousness, as it be for my sense of a shared responsibility for my ancestor's depredations. If that seems strange, kindly put it down to what I call the Simone Weil Effect:

"For already here below we receive the capacity for loving God and representing Him to ourselves with a complete certainty as having the substance of a real, perfect and infinite joy. Through our fleshly veils

[Continued on page 29]

A Race of Pirates and Highwaymen

On my next trip to the United States I went with a group of American friends to visit the Indians of New Mexico, the city-building Pueblos. "City" however, is too strong a word. What they build are in reality only villages; but their crowded houses piled one atop the other suggest the word "City" as do their language and their whole manner. There for the first time I had the good fortune to talk with a non-European, that is to a non-white.

He was a chief of the Taos pueblos [not much more than 200 miles from the Trinity site], an intelligent man between the age of 40 and 50. His name was Ochwiay Biano ("Mountain Lake"). I was able to talk with him as I have rarely been able to talk with a European. To be sure he was caught up with his world just as much as a European is in his, but what a world it was!

"We have men-stealers for ministers, women-whippers for missionaries, and cradle-plunderers for church members." – Frederick Douglass

Isaac Cruikshank's illustration of abuse of a 15-year-old aboard a slaver's ship, as Captain Kimbers reveals "the inhumanity of dealers in human flesh."

John Gast's 1872 painting *American Progress*, portrays the "Spirit of the Frontier", with colonists, protected by the Lady Columbia, gliding across the prairie into the American heartland, driving before them the Native Americans and their bison.

In talk with a European, one is constantly running up on the sand bars of things long known but never understood; with this Indian, the vessel floated freely, on deep alien seas. At the same time, one never knows which is more enjoyable: catching sight of new shores, or discovering new approaches to age-old knowledge that has been almost forgotten.

"See," Ochwiay Biano said, "how cruel the whites look. Their lips are thin, their noses sharp, their faces furrowed and distorted by folds. Their eyes have a staring expression: they are always seeking something. What are they seeking? The whites always want something; they are always uneasy and restless. We do not know what they want. We do not understand them. We think they are mad."

I asked why he thought the whites were all mad. "They say they think with their heads," he replied.

"Why of course. What do you think with?" I asked him in surprise.
"We think here," he said, indicating his heart.

I fell into a long meditation. For the first time in my life, so it seemed to me, someone had drawn for me a picture of the real white man.

It was as though until now I had seen nothing but sentimental prettified color prints. This Indian had struck our vulnerable spot, unveiled a truth to which we are blind.

I felt rising within me like a shapeless mist something unknown yet deeply familiar. And out of this mist image upon image detached itself: first Roman legions smashing into the cities of Gaul, and the keenly incised features of Julius Caesar, Scipio Africanus, and Pompey. I saw the Roman eagle on the North Sea and on the banks of the White Nile. Then I saw St Augustine transmitting the Christian creed to the Britons on the tips of Roman lances, and Charlemagne's most glorious forced conversions of the heathen: then the pillaging and murdering bands of the Crusading armies. With a secret stab I realized the hollowness of that old romanticism about the Crusades.

Then followed Columbus, Cortes, and the other conquistadors who with fire, sword, torture, and Christianity came down upon even these remote pueblos dreaming peacefully in the Sun, their Father.

I saw too the peoples of the Pacific islands decimated by firewater, syphilis, and scarlet fever carried in the clothes the missionaries forced on them.

It was enough. What we from our point of view call colonization, missions to the heathen, spread of civilization, etc, has another face – the face of a bird of prey seeking with cruel intentness for distant quarry, a face worthy of a race of pirates and highwaymen. All the the eagles and other predatory creatures that adorn our coats of arms seem to me to be apt psychological representatives of our true nature.

(*Memories, Dreams, Reflections*, C.G. Jung with Amelia Jaffe)

we receive presages of eternity which are enough to efface all doubts on the subject. There is only one time when I know nothing of this certitude any longer. It is when I am in contact with the affliction of other people, those who are indifferent or unknown to me as much as the others, perhaps even more, including those of the most remote ages of antiquity.

This contact causes me such atrocious pain and so utterly rends my soul that as a result the love of God becomes almost impossible for me for a while. It would take very little more to make me say impossible. So much so that I am uneasy for myself. I reassure myself by remarking that Christ himself wept foreseeing the horrors of the destruction of Jerusalem. I hope he will forgive my compassion."

The magnificent Simone Weil died at the age of 34 while working for Charles de Gaulle's Free French in London in August 1943, less than a month before my birth. My English family came from Bristol, in the 17th and 18th centuries the slaving capital of Britain. My Scottish blood is from Dundee shipbuilders who, along with other shipyards, built vessels for the opium trade. Be that as it may, Simone Weil is on a quite different plane to most mortals; her *cri de coeur* resonated for me from the first time I came across her writing, just as did Kurosawa Akira's *The Seven Samurai*, which opened my 11-year-old eyes to the fact that not all Japanese were *Banzai*-screaming suicide pilots; and Spencer Tracy's wonderful performance in John Sturges's movie *Bad Day At Black Rock*, when I learned that Japanese GIs had fought with the US Army in the European Theatre. Rather later, re-watching Kurosawa's *Rashomon* I started to understand that truth is not always an absolute, that each of our so-different perspectives can, for want of a better word, "drive" truth.

Was Emperor Hirohito's uncle-by-marriage Prince Asaka Yasuhiko a prime culprit in the December 1937 atrocities at Nanking, and were his troops supercharged with methamphetamines? Did the otherwise brilliant James F. Byrnes, who came within a hair's breadth of succeeding FDR to the Presidency, and who determined perhaps more than anyone else that the atomic bombs be used without prior demonstration, really say, earlier in his exalted career, that lynching was necessary to hold "in check the Negro in the south," and also allegedly say "rape is responsible, directly and indirectly, for most of the lynching in America"? Such disturbing questions rose again and again whilst we were assembling this "primer" publication; so many wars, so many shapes of crime mark the "Via Dolorosa" (literally "Way of Grief" or "Way of Suffering") that ultimately led to the atomic bombing of Nagasaki - by many reckonings Asia's most Christian city.

Guns and rosaries

I first visited Nagasaki in 1974, intrigued by the idea of the Jesuit missionary Francis Xavier having arrived in Japan a surprising 400 years earlier than I (which I found rather annoying!). I knew it had once been decimated by an atomic bomb, but at the time I was more interested in the fact that Christianity had taken hold here so very long ago, leap-frogging from Portugal via Africa's Slave Coast, around the curiously named Cape of Good Hope, via Goa, Malacca, and once-charming Macao, so very far from its Mediterranean cradle. I was impressed to learn that in spite of that distance - or perhaps because of it - very large numbers of the Japanese converts to Christianity had died for their new faith, either as individuals or en masse in various rebellions during the brief period before the remaining faithful went underground to practice their belief in secret.

As for the Nagasaki bomb, I recall no evidence of it at all - the sharp ridges that form spurs down the city's valley had provided limited shelter for some of the citizens and their homes, but by no means all. I got to meet *hibakusha*, survivors of the blast, but back then felt no compulsion to learn more about the bombing, I was trying get to grips with the culture of medieval Japan. Also, at that time we were all preoccupied by President Nixon's Watergate denouement, as well as the course of the about-to-be-lost American war in Vietnam.

Casus Belli all over again

Forty years later, in the early months of 2014 the international media was full of accounts of what seemed to be another Asian war about to begin. The extreme tension between Japan and China over the disputed territorial waters in and around the East China Sea seemed to make a collision between both countries' fighter jet-jocks almost inevitable - *Top Gun*, but now deadly serious. Having a long-established affection for the people of both countries I felt the need to acquaint myself better with what I understood to be the sources of the resurgent bitterness which, when combined with both countries' now dangerous over-dependence on imported oil, make for another catastrophic clash. Terrible things happened between China and Japan in both the late 19th Century and the early-mid 20th Century, but then China had no nuclear weapons, and Japan certainly did not have an American "shield."

Casting around my bookshelves, the first book I picked up was Jonathan Schell's *The Fate of the Earth*; as is too often the case, bought years before then neglected. I was especially riveted by his description of the potential results of a 20-megaton bomb detonated above New York - little wonder we are almost all in denial of such a likely scenario.

A disgrace to the British flag

A year or too earlier I had been shocked and, I must add, shamed by the scholarly Maurice Collis's *Foreign Mud*: the breathtaking gall of the British government who took up arms on behalf of the East India Company as well as independent British firms (American traders too) dedicated to the opium trade on the China coast. The fact that they often shipped thousands of Bibles, translated into Chinese, adds to the irony. When the Qing Emperor's Manchu officials demurred, the young Queen Victoria's Royal Navy - the strongest in the world, and armed with the first steamers to be seen in Asia - forced open not only Canton for trade but the entire Chinese coast. Whilst the immediate loss of Chinese life was not on the scale of the subsequent wars with Japan, a great deal of innocent Chinese and Manchu blood was spilt. More serious from the geopolitical angle were the Unequal Treaties that concluded the Opium Wars at Nanking in 1842 and then at Tientsin in 1858.

Just imagine, for it is a close parallel, that the Chinese Navy sailed up the Hudson River and bombarded New York and Boston until the American government agreed to the import of Chinese "ice"!

These two Unequal Treaties are for us the most significant place in the chain reaction that led, via the first Sino-Japanese War, to the invasion of China by the Japanese within a century of sustained British assaults on Chinese sovereignty. The Japanese, too, felt entitled to a

[Continued on page 36]

Following pages: *"Unless men are blinded by faction they cannot shut their eyes to the fact that we are engaged in a war without just cause, that we are endeavoring to maintain a trade [opium] based on unsound principles, and to justify proceedings which are a disgrace to the British flag."* – Sidney Herbert, Member of Parliament

Above: The signing and sealing of the Treaty of Nanking, the first of the "Unequal Treaties" on August 29, 1842. In the wake of China's defeat in the First Opium War representatives from the British and Qing

empires negotiated aboard the British warship *Cornwallis* (painted by John Platt, engraved by John Burnett).
Below: *Attack on Manhattan*, a painting by Chesley Bonestell imagining a catastrophic bombing of New York.

And They Will Want a Slice of Ours

In my opinion the true and healthy constitution of the State is the one which I have described. But if you wish also to see a State at fever-heat, I have no objection. For I suspect that many will not be satisfied with the simpler way of life. They will be for adding sofas, and tables, and other furniture; also dainties, and perfumes, and incense, and courtesans, and cakes, all these not of one sort only, but in every variety; we must go beyond the necessaries of which I was at first speaking, such as houses, and clothes, and shoes: the arts of the painter and the embroiderer will have to be set in motion, and gold and ivory and all sorts of materials must be procured.

True, he said.

Then we must enlarge our borders; for the original healthy State is no longer sufficient. Now will the city have to fill and swell with a multitude of callings which are not required by any natural want; such as the whole tribe of hunters and actors, of whom one large class have to do with forms and colors; another will be the votaries of music – poets and their attendant train of rhapsodists, players, dancers, contractors; also makers of diverse kinds of articles, including women's dresses. And we shall want more servants. Will not tutors be also in request, and nurses wet and dry, tirewomen and barbers, as well as confectioners and cooks; and swineherds, too, who were not needed and therefore had no place in the former edition of our State, but are needed now? They must not be forgotten: and there will be animals of many other kinds, if people eat them.

Certainly.

And living in this way we shall have much greater need of physicians than before? Much greater. And the country which was enough to support the original inhabitants will be too small now, and not enough?

Quite True.

Then a slice of our neighbours' land will be wanted by us for pasture and tillage, and they will want a slice of ours, if, like ourselves, they exceed the limit of necessity, and give themselves up to the unlimited accumulation of wealth? That will be inevitable. And so we shall go to war, Glaucon. Shall we not?

Most certainly, he replied.

(Socrates, on the Origin of War)

China, the Cake of Kings and Emperors [from French magazine *Le Petit Journal*, 1898].

slice of the Chinese pie, but whilst the British and other Western powers wanted mostly tea, silk, and porcelain, the Japanese wanted oil and ore, and the Shinto version of *lebensraum* (literally "living space", a concept used by the Nazis to justify their brutal expansionism).

Iris Chang's landmark book, *The Rape of Nanking*, is an exceptionally distressing account of the terrible weeks that followed the collapse of the defense of the Chinese Nationalists' capital, established there in 1927. This came almost immediately after the fall of Shanghai after four months of bitter fighting in and around the great port city where the Nationalist Kuomintang army took a heavy toll of the Japanese attackers before falling back, some to defend Nanking. However, no meaningful defense took place, and Generalissimo Chiang Kai-shek effectively abandoned his capital. It was a mean and vengeful Japanese force that stormed into Nanking in December 1937.

Again, our dismaying contention that it was the British government's self-serving behavior in 19th Century China that was the principal rationale for subsequent Japanese depredations. And to reinforce their case, as the 19th Century drew to a close, the Japanese witnessed the French seize Indochina, followed by the US seizing the Philippines, whilst Russia and Germany staked their own regional claims.

That Chiang Kai-shek and his nemesis, Mao Zedong, were unable to unify their forces to fight this copycat imperial power is a tragedy as great in magnitude as anything we can recall elsewhere in China's tumultuous history.

One of the Communist and Nationalists' successes had been to greatly reduce opium dependency. Ironically, the decline in the consumption of opium by the Chinese coincided with a new, and ongoing, addiction for oil, for gasoline to fuel China's own industrial revolution. Yet a far greater craving for oil was in Japan, which produced as much oil in a year at home as the US did in a day - peculiarly, over 50 percent of Japan's oil needs came from America throughout the 1930s. American oil fueled the sophisticated and highly mechanized Japanese war machine, (initially in Manchuria, where Japan had gone in search of oil, coal, ores, and markets for her goods), which required large amounts of gasoline as it drove south

[Continued on page 39]

Mao on the Long March, 1935.

War can only be abolished through war, and in order to get rid of the gun it is necessary to take up the gun.
(Mao Zedong)

As long as war is regarded as wicked it will always have its fascination. When it is looked upon as vulgar it will cease to be popular.
(Oscar Wilde)

The best among the poor are never grateful, they are ungrateful, discontented, disobedient and rebellious. They are quite right to be so.
(Oscar Wilde)

The sky cannot have two suns.
(Chiang Kai-shek)

In the early days of the Russian Revolution in 1917, I was completely in sympathy with it. I felt that it established a new era in the history of the modern world. I was so overwhelmed by it that, if people made any unfriendly comment, I would vigorously defend it. If people condemned the Communist party, I would speak in its defense.
(Chiang Kai-shek)

Chiang Kai-shek.

I am not competent to judge how long this war may last, but this I can say, that a war more unjust in its origin, a war more calculated in its progress to cover this country with permanent disgrace, I do not know and have not read of.

(William Gladstone, a future British prime minister, at the outset of the First Opium War)

Top: The infamous opium trade (*The Illustrated London News*, December 8, 1883).
Bottom left: By WWI Japan was dangerously dependent on American oil (Tokyo Art Directors Club).
Bottom right: A cover of satirical magazine *Puck* in April 1901 showing "Columbia's Easter Bonnet," taking a shot at America's maritime manifest destiny (courtesy of the Library of Congress).

into the Chinese heartland; likewise at sea the Imperial Navy's battle fleet would soon be devouring oil voraciously.

The European colonial powers, together with the US, had for a short time allowed the Japanese into their exclusive "Club," impressed by the way the Japanese, unlike the Chinese, had so rapidly industrialized. They had thrashed the Russians in Manchuria, and devastated the Czar's fleet in the Tsushima Straits, close to where Kublai Khan's Mongolian marines, intent on invading Japan, were defeated 700 years earlier by successive typhoons known as "divine winds," the original *Kamikaze*.

But the Western Club was growing uneasy; the disruptive Japanese were mimicking their colonial manners far too closely, in China they were taking over the traditional markets formerly dominated by Western manufacturers (from clothing to machine tools), the Japanese had far less distance to ship, and their costs were significantly lower.

This unease increased greatly after the USS *Panay* was sunk by Japanese aircraft in the Nanking campaign, and forward-thinkers saw a clash of civilizations was inevitable. However, the oil lobby and Western businesses not adversely affected by the Japanese, or even benefitting, put a brake on any inclinations to draw a line in the sand after Nanking; the British too were anxious to avoid confrontation, distracted as they were by Hitler in Europe. Indeed within nine months of the Nanking Massacre, Neville Chamberlain would sign the Munich Agreement to appease the Nazis.

Thus the Western democracies lost two opportunities (in close succession) to show sufficient resolve to corral the totalitarian menaces, compromised as they were by a fear of Bolshevism, which was seen by many at the time as being an even greater threat than the Germans and Japanese with their extreme varieties of nationalism.

The Nanking Massacre however would come back to haunt not only the Imperial Japanese Army but countless innocent Japanese. The theatre commander in Central China in December 1937 was the ailing General Matsui Iwane. Iris Chang recounts how Iwane confronted the officers commanding the occupying Japanese troops, including Prince Asaka Yasuhiko, after he, Iwane, realized what horrors had already taken place

[Continued on page 43]

At the Yata Conference: Winston Churchill, Franklin Delano Roosevelt and Joseph Stalin, February 1945.

This Otherwise Superhuman Being

And the wonderful thing is that three-quarters of the population of the world imagine that Churchill is one of the Strategists of History, a second Marlborough, and the other one-quarter have no idea what a public menace he is and has been throughout this war!
It is far better that the world should never know, and never suspect the feet of clay of this otherwise superhuman being. Without him England was lost for a certainty, with him England has been on the verge of disaster time and again... Never have I admired and despised a man simultaneously to the same extent. Never have such opposite extremes been combined in the same human being.

(Field Marshal Alan Francis Brooke, 1st Viscount Alanbrooke KG, GCB, OM, GCVO, DSO & Bar, was a senior commander in the British Army)

Total War

I have nothing to offer but blood, toil, tears and sweat.
We have before us an ordeal of the most grievous kind.
We have before us many many long months of struggle and suffering.
To ask what is our policy, I say it is to wage war, war by land sea and air,
War with all our might and with all the strength God has given us.
To wage war against the monstrous tyranny never surpassed before
In the dark and lamentable catalogue of human crime,
That is our policy. To ask what is our aim,
I can give the answer in one word, it is Victory.

(Prime Minister Winston Churchill, May 13, 1940)

From left: Vyacheslav Molotov, Soviet Minister of Foreign Affairs, James F. Byrnes, Secretary of State, and Anthony Eden, British Foreign Secretary.

Without Prior Warning

Mr. Byrnes recommended, and the Committee agreed, that the Secretary of War should be advised that, while recognizing that the final selection of the target was essentially a military decision, the present view of the Committee was that the bomb should be used against Japan as soon as possible; that it be used on a war plant surrounded by workers' homes; and that it be used without prior warning.

(The Interim Committee Meeting's log from June 1, 1945)

Killing the Chicken to Scare the Monkey
殺 雞 儆 猴

I do not recall the exact date, but after the close of one of the formal meetings Truman informed Stalin that the United States now possessed a bomb of exceptional power, without, however, naming it the atomic bomb.

As was later written abroad, at that moment Churchill fixed his gaze on Stalin's face, closely observing his reaction. However, Stalin did not betray his feelings and pretended that he saw nothing special in what Truman had imparted to him. Both Churchill and many other Anglo-American authors subsequently assumed that Stalin had really failed to fathom the significance of what he had heard.

In actual fact, on returning to his quarters after this meeting Stalin, in my presence, told Molotov about his conversation with Truman. The latter reacted amost immediately. "Let them. We'll have to talk it over with Kurchatov and get him to speed things up."

I realized that they were talking about research on the atomic bomb.

It was clear already then that the US Government intended to use the atomic weapon for the purpose of achieving its Imperialist goals from a position of strength in "the cold war." This was amply corroborated on August 6 and 8 [sic]. Without any military need whatsoever, the Americans dropped two atomic bombs on the peaceful and densely populated Japanese cities of Hiroshima and Nagasaki.

(Georgii Konstantinovich Zhukov, *The Memoirs of Marshal Zhukov*, New York, Delacorte Press, 1971)

Multiplying Millions

"It is our manifest destiny to overspread the continent allotted by Providence for the development of our yearly multiplying millions."

(John L. O'Sullivan in 1845. O'Sullivan was a Jacksonian Democrat and advocate, columnist, and editor famed for coining the term "Manifest Destiny") in the city prior to his own arrival: "Everything has been lost in one moment," Iwane said. Indeed it was - the war in the Pacific that would begin almost exactly four years later at Pearl Harbor was in some ways lost long before it started, or rather, the way it was lost was to be dictated, perhaps unconsciously, by American memories of the butchering at Nanking.

Surrounded by workers' homes

In wars up to and including World War I (WWI) the casualties were usually for the most part military personnel, but with the end of that terrible war the rules of engagement began to fray. Counter-insurgencies in colonial wars had frequently meant significant civilian deaths - "keeping the natives to heel" and so on - but with the Spanish Civil War civilian death tolls rose as Russian and German advisors helped the respective sides. The bombing of Guernica, immortalized by Picasso, was but a dress rehearsal for Wieluń, Poland on September 1, 1939, when twice as many civilians died in a morning. Warsaw, too, whilst being bombed almost continuously for the whole of September, would lose almost 1,000 citizens a day to the Luftwaffe's Heinkels, Messerschmitts, Dorniers, and the terrifying Stuka divebomber.

France, Holland, then the UK would receive similar punishment for winning WWI, an oversimplification no doubt but there is painful truth in the fact that the victorious allies, in the aftermath of the curiously named "Great War," unimaginatively imposed the most draconian Peace terms on a humbled Germany, terms that made it all too easy for the Nazi Party to get enough of the public behind Adolf Hitler, 10 years later, to engineer Hitler's becoming German Chancellor.

War with all our might

Growing up in London in the 1950s it was impossible not to feel warmly towards Winston Churchill, whatever one's parents' political affiliations, so it is dismaying to have to recast one's ideas of childhood heroes long treasured. Churchill was almost certainly the only alternative to defeat and Nazi occupation, but to him - and many of those who surrounded him, to say nothing of the majority of the armed forces and indeed most British civilians - that meant waging "Total War," fighting fire with fire. Hamburg and Dresden are Exhibits A and B: in July 1943, over

40,000 citizens went up in smoke within a week in Operation Gomorrah, the destruction of almost the entire city of Hamburg:

"Some people who tried to walk along, they were pulled in by the fire, they all of a sudden disappeared right in front of you... You have to save yourself or try to get as far away from the fire, because the draught pulls you in."

Dresden was spared till February 1945, but then, in three days of intense bombardment by the RAF and the USAAF, between 20,000 and 30,000 would die. Both cities, and many others similarly visited, certainly had numerous war-related plants and/or were important to military logistics, and therefore needed to be struck. Unfortunately the extreme inaccuracy of most bombing raids gave the planning committees back in England cause to broaden the scope of attack, and soon it became the intention to destroy workers' homes too.

Yet, when the Army Air Force came within striking distance of Japan, there was at first an effort made to focus on military and factory targets only, as in the early stages of the air war in Europe. This would change, because the accuracy of "precision bombing" had not greatly improved. When General Curtis LeMay took over command of the air war above Japan, he would order area bombing of 67 cities; a month after the destruction of Dresden, in the biggest hit of all - Operation Meetinghouse - LeMay's armadas of B-29s would burn the heart out of Tokyo (but somehow fail to level the Imperial Palace). As in Germany, these Japanese cities would be torched in the knowledge that there would be very large numbers of mostly civilian casualties in the conflagrations triggered by a deadly cocktail of high explosives leavened with phosphorous, magnesium, and napalm.

In the run-up to the dropping of the two atomic bombs, Barton J. Bernstein's *The Atomic Bomb Reconsidered* stands out for us as the most convincing easily digested retrospective. Of an earlier vintage still, Herbert Feis' masterful quartet - *The Road to Pearl Harbor*, *The China Tangle*, *Churchill-Roosevelt-Stalin*, and *Between War and Peace* - is representative of authorship that was sufficiently close to the events and the players to have a special authenticity.

[Continued on page 54]

A New Relationship of Man to the Universe

On May 28, 1945, physicist Arthur H. Compton, a Nobel laureate and member of a special scientific panel advising the high-level Interim Committee newly appointed to recommend policy about the bomb, raised profound moral and political questions about how the atomic bomb would be used. "It introduces the question of mass slaughter, really for the first time in history," he wrote. "It carries with it the question of possible radioactive poison over the area bombed. Essentially, the question of the use . . . of the new weapon carries much more serious implications than the introduction of poison gas."

Compton's concern received some independent support from General Marshall, who told Secretary Stimson on May 29 that the A-bomb should first be used not against civilians but against military installations – perhaps a naval base – and then possibly against large manufacturing areas after the civilians had received ample warnings to flee. Marshall feared "the opprobrium which might follow from an ill considered employment of such force." A graduate of Virginia Military Institute and a trained soldier, Marshall struggled to retain the older code of not intentionally killing civilians. The concerns of Compton the scientist and Marshall the general, their values so rooted in an earlier conception of war that sought to spare noncombatants, soon gave way to the sense of exigency, the desire to use the bomb on people, and the unwillingness or inability of anyone near the top in Washington to plead forcefully for maintaining this older morality.

On May 31, 1945, the Interim Committee, composed of Stimson, Bush, Harvard President James Conant, physicist and educator Karl T. Compton, Secretary of State designate James F. Byrnes, and a few other notables, discussed the A-bomb. Opening this meeting, Stimson, the aged secretary of war who had agonized over the recent shift toward mass bombing of civilians, described the atomic bomb as representing "a new relationship of man to the universe. This discovery might be compared to the discoveries of the Copernican theory and the laws of gravity, but far more important than these in its effects on the lives of men."

Directed by Stimson, the committee was actually endorsing terror bombing – but somewhat uneasily. They would not focus exclusively on a military target (the older morality), as Marshall had recently proposed, nor fully on civilians (the emerging morality). They managed to achieve their purpose – terror bombing – without bluntly acknowledging it to themselves. All knew that families – women, children, and, even in the daytime, during the bomb attack, some workers – dwelled in "workers' houses."

(Barton J. Bernstein, *The Atomic Bombings Reconsidered*, Foreign Affairs)

Was it Justified?

If then the use of the bomb was not essential, was it justified – justified, that is, as the surest way, in combination with other measures, to bring about the earliest surrender? That is the hardest question to answer, harder now than it seemed to be at the time of the decision.

It may be contended with assurance supported by history that no justification for the use of the bomb is needed, since the accepted ruling attitude sanctions the use of any and all weapons in war except any banned by explicit international agreement. Did not every one of the contending nations strive its utmost to invent and produce more effective weapons: faster planes of greater bomb capacity, new types of mines, rockets, and buzz-bombs; and were not each and every one brought into action without ado or reproach? Almost all professional military men, and probably almost all men in uniform in 1945, would then have denied that any justification was needed and would still dispose of the subject in the same way.

"Although 2,550 kamikaze planes had been expended, there were 5,350 of them still left, together with as many more for orthodox use and 7,000 under repair or in storage; and 5,000 young men were training for the Kamikaze Corps."

Above: Schoolgirls on Kyushu wave farewell to a kamikaze pilot in 1945.

Opposite: Off the coast of Okinawa, the USS *Bunker Hill* burns fiercely after being hit by two kamikaze planes in quick succession, setting fire to the fully fueled aircraft on her deck; miraculously she did not sink.

They might add, as well, that the decision to use the bomb was not really important; that the measures of permanent significance to mankind had been taken when physicists learned to split the atom, and when scientists and engineers and builders succeeded in embodying the energy of the fissured atom in a bomb: and that after these were achieved, it made little or no difference if this novel weapon was used against Japan, since it would certainly be used in the future time unless nations renounced war. Or if it were not, other equally dreadful threats would remain: chemical or biological ways of bringing death; and these were already in secret arsenals of nations.

The source of restraint lies in fear of consequences; fear of the fact that the enemy will use the same terrible weapon. This was why neither side used poison gas in the war. When humane feeling is allied to such fear it may command respect, and even those striving to win a war may recognize that "virtue is to abstain even from that which is lawful."

Our right, legal and historical, to use the bomb may thus well be defended; but those who made the decision to use it were not much concerned over these considerations, taking them for granted. Their thoughts about its employment were governed by one reason which was deemed imperative: that by using the bomb, the agony of war might be ended most quickly, and many lives be saved. It was believed that thousands, probably tens of thousands, of lives would have to be spent in the continuation of our air and sea bombardment and blockade, victims mainly of Japanese suicide planes.

In spite of its confidence in ultimate success, the assailant force felt vulnerable, because of grim and agonizing experience. Since the desperate kamikaze attack began, suicide planes had sunk 34 American ships, including three aircraft carriers, and damaged 285 (including 36 carriers of all sizes and sorts, 15 battleships, 15 cruisers, and 87 destroyers). It was reliably known that the Japanese were assembling thousands of planes, of all kinds and conditions, to fling against the invasion fleet and the troop-carrying ships.

According to Samuel Elliot Morison, in mid-August "Although 2,550 kamikaze planes had been expended, there were 5,350 of them still left, together with as many more ready for orthodox use and 7,000 under repair or in storage; and 5,000 young men were training for the Kamikaze Corps" (*Atlantic Monthly*, October 1960). This is a much higher estimate of actual usable Japanese air strength than others I have seen, but I leave the task of confirming or contradicting it to military historians who are better acquainted with all the Japanese records.

Thus if it proved necessary to carry out the plans for the invasion, the losses might run to hundreds of thousands. Our allies, it was reckoned, would suffer a corresponding loss of life – the men in the naval and air groups of the British Commonwealth, if they had to engage in amphibious operations in Southeast Asia; and the soldiers in the Red [Soviet] Army [one wonders why Mr Feis omits mention of the Chinese armies – Communists and Nationalists are unremarked here] if they had to fight on until they smashed the Kwantung Army in its last stand in Southeastern Manchuria and Korea.

But the people who would have suffered most, if the war had been carried on much longer and if their country was invaded, were the Japanese. One American incendiary air raid on the Tokyo area in March 1945 did more damage and killed and injured more Japanese than at Hiroshima. Had the war continued, even greater groups of American bomber planes would have hovered over Japan, consuming their land and its people with blast and fire, leaving them no place to hide, no chance to rest, no hope of reprieve. A glance at the charts kept in the Headquarters of the US Strategic Air Force at Guam, with its steeply ascending record of bombing flights during the summer of 1945 and scheduled for the next month or two, leaves visions of horror of which Hiroshima is only a local illustration.

(Herbert Feis, *Japan Subdued*, Princeton 1961)

An American B-San ("Mr. B") flying over Osaka; note Osaka Castle beneath the plane's extreme right engine.

It Had Needed No Atom Bomb to Crush Japan

I was off by plane to visit MacArthur's command in the Philippines in July, when news reached us that the air force could now make direct flights between China and the Pacific commands. I flew on to Okinawa for the last days of the mop-up and saw bulldozers pushing the sun-dried bodies of dead Japanese off newly built roadways as if they were garbage. I flew back to Manila and woke to hear that we had dropped an atomic bomb on Japan. The news came on the armed forces radio while I was shaving, on a day of terminal madness and joy. My instinct was to hurry to my post in Chunking, but first I wanted to talk to MacArthur himself.

He received me two days after the bomb dropped, the day he himself had been briefed for the first time on the bomb by Karl Compton of MIT. After some pleasantries of reacquaintance he got right to the bomb, no longer roaring as he used to roar. "White," he said, "White, do you know what this means?" "What Sir?" I asked. It meant, he said, that all wars were over; wars were no longer matters of valor or judgement, but lay in the hands of scholars and scientists. "Men like me are obsolete," he said, pacing back and forth. "There will be no more wars, White, no more wars."

With that assurance I was off again, back to the mainland, up to Chunking to find out how the surrender was being taken, lingered in Chunking for a few days, then decided the story was elsewhere. I flew back to Manila to hedge-hop to Okinawa, whence I hoped our plane could make it to Tokyo Bay, where, apparently, the Japanese were about to surrender...

It was a short flight, three hours on bucket seats. The sentiment of the men was simple: "Don't trust the sons of bitches;" and no one slept, the men fingering and plucking at their guns, opening them, cleaning them again and again as combat troops always do before action. We were flying underneath an overcast and dawn seeped in at six. Below we could make out the tips of the volcanic islands that lead to Tokyo Bay. Our plane rocked in a rain squall, bobbed about, then slipped into a patch of sun. And there in the morning sun, stretching as far as the eye could see in the inner arms of Tokyo Bay, was Halsey's Third Fleet – flattops and battleships, cruisers and destroyers, more ships than anyone had seen in one place, or is ever likely to see again. Then to the left, in the distance, a gray, unmistakable perfect mountain cone, Fujiyama, so lovely one's eyes had to caress its slopes and flanks.

"Then to the left, in the distance, a gray unmistakable perfect mountain cone." – Theodore H. White, 1945 B-29s fly past Mount Fuji.

Then the surf breaking on sand shores below, the green rice fields, nothing moving on any road, and down to the landing at Atsugi, which is 22 miles southwest of the Imperial Palace and perhaps 12 miles from Yokohama...

The city was dead. So apparently was Japan. It had needed no atom bomb to crush Japan; the B-29s had already done it with their fire bombs, killing more by far, than both the atom bombs did. The atom bombs had been essential only as a pretext for the Japanese to give up the idea of their eternal invincibility. But the fire bombs had already wiped out the vitality of the nation. I felt no shame at that moment at the slaughter of Japanese, either by fire bomb or by nuclear fission: I had cowered under their bombs, under their machine guns, seen the victims they had savaged with knife and bayonet and club. And they had bombed my country first. Revenge is a dry form of satisfaction; but the dryness was clean to my taste, even though I could not bring myself to hate the stooped and forlorn people on the street.

This was no cloistered surrender, as had been the surrender of the Germans at Reims, three months earlier. MacArthur wanted everyone there and the world to watch. The enlisted men who had fought the war, the sailors and marines, found what space they could, and very few of the *Missouri's* crew could have remained below; sailors in their dress whites sat with their legs dangling over the long gray barrels of the 16-inch guns, on which they perched; they hung from every line and rope. This would be a sight to tell their children, to tell their grandchildren. None of us knew then that this was the last war America would cleanly, conclusively win. We thought it was the last war ever...

At eight minutes past nine on September 2, 1945, Douglas MacArthur emerged from a cabin and took the curse off the savage moment. MacArthur could always savor a moment and this one was worth savoring. If television had been available then he would have delighted in displaying himself to it. He was the master of the Pacific. He had spent some time composing his remarks, and what emerged was a mixture of Lincoln's Gettysburg Address with phrases plucked from the William McKinley school of American rhetoric. Out of respect, I shall quote the Lincolnian phrases not the McKinley purple.

His hands quivered as he read his text and we listened, "We are gathered here... to conclude a solemn agreement whereby Peace may be restored... Nor is it for us here to meet... in a spirit of distrust, malice or hatred. But rather it is for us both victors and vanquished, to rise to that higher dignity which alone befits the sacred purposes we are about to serve... It is my earnest hope... that from this solemn occasion a better world shall emerge out of the blood and carnage of the past – a world founded upon faith and understanding – a world dedicated to the dignity of man and the fulfillment of his most cherished wish – for freedom, tolerance and justice... as Supreme Commander for the Allied Powers, I announce it my firm purpose... To proceed in the discharge of my responsibilities with justice and tolerance, while taking all necessary dispositions to insure that the terms of surrender are fully, promptly and faithfully complied with."

Here MacArthur looked directly at the Japanese and intoned:
"I now invite the representatives of the Emperor of Japan and the Japanese Government, and the Japanese Imperial General Headquarters to sign the instrument of surrender at the places indicated."

(Theodore H. White, *In Search of History,* Harper & Row, 1978)

"A glance at the charts kept in the Headquarters of the US Strategic Air Force at Guam, with its steeply ascending record of bombing flights during the summer of 1945 and scheduled for the next month or two, leaves visions of horror of which Hiroshima is only a local illustration." – Herbert Feis

A mother and son amidst the devastation of nuclear war (photo by Alfred Einstadt).

Down to earth

The single most outstanding publication relating to the on-the-ground effect of either of the A-bombs remains John Hersey's admirably short, shrapnel-sharp *Hiroshima*. If you only read one book before you travel there, this is the one. Read it "away from the madding crowd;" read it twice, and imagine you are Mrs Kamia, anxious that your husband see his daughter one more time...

As we hope is self-evident, the remit of this volume, this preliminary sketch for a planned "Pacific Quintet" of books, is to present as best we can (with our limited resources) testimonies that might help in the painful process of international reconciliation between firstly China and Japan, then between both those countries and the United States, not yet forgiven for variously backing Chiang Kai-shek, winning the war, or using the "new weapon." Reconciliation too between Korea and Japan, and between the US and Russia, together with overarching reconciliation between all these countries most dear to us, and their neighbors in the broadest sense.

Our planet is far too fragile now to be effectively protected from our collective material excesses without a coming together of the magnitude of the Marshall Plan rolled out globally, scientifically, technologically and dare I say, spiritually:

No Man is an Island

No man is an island entire of itself, Every
man is a piece of the continent, A part of
the main. If a clod be washed away by the sea,
Europe is the less, as well as if a promontory were,
As well as if a man or of thy friend's
Or of thine own were.
Any man's death diminishes me,
Because I am involved in mankind,
And therefore never send to know for whom the bell tolls,
It tolls for thee.

(John Donne, 1572–1631)

We Should Take Nothing for Granted

A vital element in keeping the peace is our military establishment. Our arms must be mighty, ready for instant action, so that no potential aggressor may be tempted to risk his own destruction...

This conjunction of an immense military establishment and a large arms industry is new in the American experience. The total influence – economic, political, even spiritual – is felt in every city, every statehouse, every office of the federal government. We recognize the imperative need for this development. Yet we must not fail to comprehend its grave implications. Our toil, resources and livelihood are all involved; so is the very structure of our society. In the councils of government, we must guard against the acquisition of unwarranted influence, whether sought or unsought, by the military-industrial complex. The potential for the disastrous rise of misplaced power exists, and will persist. We must never let the weight of this combination endanger our liberties or democratic processes. We should take nothing for granted. Only an alert and knowledgeable citizenry can compel the proper meshing of the huge industrial and military machinery of defense with our peaceful methods and goals so that security and liberty may prosper together.

(President Dwight D. Eisenhower's
"Farewell Address to the Nation" on January 17, 1961)

Southern barbarians arrive in Japan (Nagasaki Museum of History and Culture).

昭和二十年八月六日十二時頃、ぞくぞく続く避難者のなかに

若き母親のみじめな姿　避難の途中で子供を死なせ

頭からすっぽり黒い布をかぶた　どうで捨ったのか荒縄で

死んしみを背負って　炎天下　言い足を引きつり去った

死んしみを背負って

何處を目ざして　行ったのでしよう　楽々園海老橋附近

He Loved Our Baby So Much

Just before dark, Mr Tanimoto came across a twenty-year-old girl, Mrs Kamai, the Tanimotos' next-door neighbor. She was crouching on the ground with the body of her infant daughter in her arms. The baby had evidently been dead all day. Mrs Kamai jumped up when she saw Mr Tanimoto and said, "Would you please try to locate my husband."

Mr Tanimoto knew her husband had been inducted into the army just the day before; he and Mrs Tanimoto had entertained in the afternoon, to make her forget. Kamai had reported to the Chugoku Regional Army Headquarters – near the ancient castle in the middle of the town – where some four thousand troops were stationed. Judging by the many maimed soldiers Mr Tanimoto had seen during the day, he surmised that the barracks had been badly damaged by whatever it was that had hit Hiroshima. He knew he didn't have a chance of finding Mrs Kamai's husband, even if he searched, but he wanted to humor her. "I'll try," he said.

"You've got to find him," she said, "He loved our baby so much. I want him to see her once more."

(John Hersey, *Hiroshima*)

———————●———————

"The young mother's baby had died as they fled. She had covered it with a black cloth and tied it to her back with a straw rope she found somewhere. She dragged herself along under the scorching sun. I wondered where she was going." – A Zuroku A-Bomb drawing by a survivor, Hiroshima Peace Museum.

The most beautiful and most profound experience is the
sensation of the mystical. It is the sower of all true
science. He to whom this emotion is a stranger, who can
no longer wonder and stand rapt in awe, is as good as
dead. To know that what is impenetrable to us really exists,
manifesting itself as the highest wisdom and the most
radiant beauty which our dull faculties can comprehend only
in their primitive forms – this knowledge, this feeling is at
the center of true religiousness.

(Albert Einstein)

Twenty Megatons

A description of the effect of a one-megaton bomb on New York City gives some notion of the meaning in human terms of a megaton of explosive power, but a weapon that is more likely to be used against New York is the 20-megaton bomb, which has 1,600 times the yield of the Hiroshima bomb.

The Soviet Union is estimated to have at least 113 20-megaton bombs in its nuclear arsenal... since the explosive power of the 20-megaton bombs greatly exceed the amount necessary to destroy most military targets, it is reasonable to suppose that they are meant for use against large cities. If a 20-megaton bomb were air burst over the Empire State Building at an altitude of 30,000 feet, the zone gutted or flattened by the blast wave would have a radius of 12 miles and an area of more than 450 square miles, reaching from the middle of Staten Island to the northern edge of the Bronx, the eastern edge of Queens, and well into New Jersey, and the zone of heavy damage from the blast wave (the zone hit by a minimum of two pounds of overpressure per square inch) would have a radius of 21.5 miles, or an area of 1,450 square miles, reaching to the southernmost tip of Staten Island, north as far as southern Rockland County, east into Nassau County, and west to Morris County, New Jersey.

The fireball would be about 4.5 miles in diameter and would radiate the thermal pulse for about 20 seconds. People caught in the open 23 miles from ground zero, in New Jersey, Long Island and southern New York State would be burned to death. People hundreds of miles away who looked at the blast would be temporarily blinded and would risk permanent eye injury... The mushroom cloud would be 70 miles in diameter. New York City and its suburbs would be transformed into a lifeless, flat, scorched desert in a few seconds."

(Jonathan Schell, *The Fate of the Earth*, 1982)

———————●———————

Adam and Eve, painted by Lucas Cranach the Elder (Staatliche Museen, Zu Berlin PK).

First Contacts and Early Power Struggles

Conquistadors of the Orient

For millennia the Japanese had no written language, and their history was passed down orally, from generation to generation, in the form of story-telling. The stories were finally written down 1,200 years after Emperor Jimmu had allegedly founded Japan. Until the Meiji Restoration, historians treated these storied events as literal history, but as scholarship turned its attention to these texts, and developments progressed in archaeology and historiography, they were treated less like history and more like myth.

Today, most scholars do not believe that Jimmu existed, and there are some (mostly Chinese) scholars who say he may have been the revered Chinese explorer Xu Fu, who set sail to find the "Elixir of Immortality" in 219 BCE (Before Common Era). He returned without it, claiming there was a giant sea monster blocking his path. He was sent a second time with archers to kill the creature and never returned. Some scholars contend that Xu Fu landed in Japan and helped turn it from the hunter-gatherer society it had been into an agrarian society.

When the Japanese language was first committed to paper, it was written in Chinese characters out of necessity (the *kanji* writing system is still used in Japan along with *kana*). During the Nara period (710-794 CE, or Common Era), the aristocracy modeled itself after Tang China. The remains of the capital, Heijo-kyo and other related sites, are now housed in museums in the city of Nara, Nara Prefecture. The court sent emissaries to Tang China and many Japanese studied at Buddhist monasteries in China.

Japan also received many Chinese ideas from the kingdoms of the Korean Peninsula. Buddhism was first introduced to the nation through gifts sent by the Emperor of Baekje in 552 CE. In 660 CE, Japan and China fought their first recorded battle, the Battle of Baekgang (known as the Battle of Kakusukinoe in Japan). Fought on the Korean Peninsula, two opposing Korean kingdoms – Baekje and Silla, were supported by Yamato Japan and Tang China, respectively. Silla triumphed over Baekje, and for many centuries this was Japan's worst defeat and one of its few attempts to exert military power on foreign shores.

But while Japan didn't succeed in exerting military power beyond the home islands, it was successful at repelling two attempted invasions in very quick succession. In 1260, Kublai Khan, grandson of Genghis Khan, was declared the Great Khan of the Mongol Empire, which at the time extended from Korea in the east to Syria in the west. The Goryeo Dynasty in Korea reaffirmed its status as a vassal of the empire, as it had regularly been to previous dynasties, though it was governed autonomously and required to pay an annual tribute to the Mongols.

In 1264 Kublai moved his capital to Dadu (Beijing), and two years later planned to make Japan part of his growing empire. In his self-titled book *The Travels of Marco Polo* the famed Venetian merchant traveler describes Japan thus:

"Zipangu is an island in the eastern ocean, situated at the distance of about fifteen hundred miles from the mainland... Their religion is the worship of idols. They are independent of every foreign power, and governed only by their own kings. They have gold in the greatest abundance, its sources being inexhaustible, but as the king does not allow of its being exported, few merchants visit the country, nor is it frequented by much shipping from other parts. To this circumstance we are to attribute the extraordinary richness of the sovereign's palace, according to what we are told by those who have access to the place. The entire roof is covered with a plating of gold, in the same manner as we cover houses or more properly churches, with lead... So vast, indeed, are the riches of the palace, that it is impossible to convey an idea of them... Of so great celebrity was the wealth of this island, that a desire was excited in the breast of the Grand Khan Kublai, now reigning, to make the conquest of it, and to annex it to his dominions."

Kublai sent emissaries to Japan to persuade them to become vassals, as Goryeo was, and to pay tribute to the Khan or risk invasion. The emissaries left empty-handed. The Khan sent emissaries again in 1268, 1269 (twice), 1271 and 1272, all of them unsuccessful.

Consequently, in 1274 Kublai sent an armada of 900 ships carrying between 33,000 and 41,000 Mongol, Chinese and Korean soldiers and sailors to Japan with the intention of invading it, launching from the Korean port of Masan, and according to Marco Polo, Quanzhou and Hangzhou. Along with the men, the ships carried relatively modern weapons like composite bows, poisoned arrows and early forms of grenades and fire arrows, predecessors of cannons, that used gunpowder as

"Of all the warriors of the clan, I, Suenaga will be the first to fight from Higo." – Takezaki Suenaga
The samurai Takezaki Suenaga of Kyushu charges through a hail of arrows, seeking to break the Mongol-Yuan forces at the First Battle of Hakata Bay.

their fuel, which the Japanese called *teppu* ("iron wind"). The ships were built by experienced Korean shipwrights, and the fleet was mobilized by Kublai's son-in-law, King Chungnyeol.

The fleet leap-frogged from China and Korea to Tsushima then the Iki islands before landing in Hakata Bay (now Fukuoka) on the island of Kyushu on November 19, 1274, 17 kilometers from the regional capital of Dazaifu. The Japanese samurai were caught by surprise and were not prepared to deal with such a large, well-armed force – their long, thin swords snapped when they tried to pierce the leather armor used by the Mongols.

A storm persuaded the Mongols to anchor their fleet at sea rather than rest them on the shore and run the risk of being marooned in Hakata Bay. As many as 200 ships were anchored at sea and these were sunk in the typhoon that descended on them; the majority of the horde, who had stayed on the ships, were all drowned.

The Khanate tried to invade Japan a second time in 1281, this time with a force of 142,000 Chinese, Mongols and Koreans in 4,400 ships. It would be the largest amphibious assault in history until D-Day on June 6, 1944, when 156,000 British, American and Canadian troops landed on the beaches of Normandy in 6,939 ships.

The Japanese had heavily fortified Hakata Bay and were much better prepared to deal with the larger forces. In the interim, the samurai had armed themselves with the *katana* (a sword with a curved blade that is longer than 60cm/23 inches), which could better pierce Mongol armor. The Korean ships launched first, capturing Tsushima and Iki; Chinese ships from Ningbo joined the rest at Hirado in July and the combined fleet sailed for Hakata Bay.

Mirroring the previous invasion, however, a typhoon swept through the area, fortuitously sinking much of the Mongol fleet. The Japanese refer to this second typhoon as "divine wind," or *kamikaze*.

Wokou pirates

For two centuries the *wokou* pirates ruled the East China Sea. The first wokou set up bases on Tsushima, Iki and the Goto Islands, near the Strait of Korea (these are all now part of modern Nagasaki Prefecture). In 1372, Korean civil servant and poet Jeong Mong-ju went to Kyushu to negotiate the quashing of the troublesome pirates. The military leader of Kyushu, Imagawa Sadayo, promised aid in stopping the pirates. In 1405, Shogun Ashikaga Yoshimitsu punished 20 captured pirates by boiling them in a cauldron.

In 1419, Korea invaded Tsushima with a fleet of 227 ships and 17,285 soldiers. They cut a swath of destruction across the island, before negotiating a peace treaty with the So clan, who ruled the island, in 1420. Piratical raids dropped considerably afterwards, but the pirates did not disappear entirely. In 1555 Shandong's defense forces, led by Qi Jiguang, led a counterattack against the pirates, with decisive victories at Cengang in 1558 and Taizhou in 1559. Jiguang's forces, as well as those of Yu Dayou and Tan Lun, defeated the remains of the pirates on the island of Nan'ao in September 1565.

Yu Dayou's son Yu Zigou became an admiral in the Chinese navy. He led the successful effort in 1624 to remove the Dutch from the Pescadores Archipelago, just off Taiwan, but in 1628 he was killed by the Chinese merchant and pirate Zheng Zhilong.

Zheng was born in Fujian and became a merchant, first in Macau, then in Nagasaki. While in Macau, he was baptized as a Catholic and took the name Nicholas Gaspard. In Nagasaki, he met a Japanese woman, Tagawa Matsu, and had a son with her named Zheng Chenggong, better known as Koxinga. Zhilong eventually joined the Ming Navy, rising to the rank of "Admiral of the Costal Seas," and he and his family resettled in Fujian.

"Let your losses at least teach you, that your power here cannot be compared to a thousandth part of mine." – Koxinga

The Dutch Fort Zeelandia, on Formosa, is relinquished to the Wokou pirate-lord Koxinga.

The routes by which Wokou privateers navigated, raided and traded along the Asian coastline. Their hunting grounds expanded southwards in the 1540s, stretching from Korea to Vietnam.

Koxinga followed in his father's footsteps and became a merchant and pirate. When the Ming Dynasty collapsed, his father defected to the Qing Dynasty, while Koxinga remained loyal to the Ming, whose remnants had fled to Formosa. Zheng was executed in 1661 for his son's resistance to the Qing Dynasty. That same year, Koxinga's forces attacked the Dutch settlement of Fort Zeelandia on the southeast coast of Taiwan. The Dutch departed and Koxinga established the Kingdom of Tungning, intending Taiwan to be a base from which to launch an invasion of China and restore the Ming Dynasty. Koxinga died suddenly in 1662 at the age of 37. His son Zheng Jing ruled Tungning until his death in 1681, and in 1683 Qing troops invaded Taiwan.

European contact

For the three centuries after the two failed Mongol invasions, Japan had minimal contact with the outside world, and that was often negative. The wokou pirates would plunder the Japanese, Korean and Chinese coasts from their island fastnesses, while the Kyushu *daimyo* (feudal lord) reaped rewards in plunder and manpower by turning a blind eye to the piracy.

However, on August 25, 1543 a Chinese junk washed ashore on Tanegashima Island. Among her crew were two Portuguese merchants. These merchants were of immense interest to the local population, so much so that they were given an audience with the Lord of Tanegashima, Tokitaka. Neither side could understand each other, but on board was a Ming scholar named Goho, who acted as a translator. The two sides wrote their initial communications in the sand.

"Swift as the Wind, Silent as a Forest, Fierce as Fire and Immovable as a Mountain." – Sun Tzu
Mounted samurai take to the battlefield at Kawanakajima, under the banner of Daimyo Takeda Shingen, the "Tiger of Kai."

The two Portuguese had a variety of gifts from the West that impressed Lord Tokitaka, but the ones that most impressed him were the muskets they had brought. A contemporary account (quoted from *A History of Japan* by James Murdoch) told it thus:

"Hereafter, the guns will be the most important arms, therefore decrease the number of spears per unit, and have your most capable men carry guns." – Daimyo Takeda Shingen
Matchlock *ashigaru* stabilize their firearms using ropes, to ensure their accuracy when firing at night.

"They had in their possession an object, which was about two or three shaku in length. As for its shape, it was straight on the outside with a passage inside, and made of a heavy substance. Even though its inside was hollow, its bottom end was closed. There was an aperture at its side, through which fire was applied. Its shape could not be compared with anything else. When used, some mysterious powder was put into it and a small lead pellet was added. At first, a small white target was set up on a bank. When it was discharged, the man gripped the object with one hand, straightened his posture and squinted with one eye. When there upon fire issued from the opening, the pellet always hit the target squarely. The explosion seemed like lightning and the sound like rolling thunder. All bystanders covered their ears... One shot from this object can make a mountain of silver crumble and break through a wall of iron. Someone with aggression in mind toward a neighboring country would lose his life instantly when hit. Needless to say, this also holds for the deer that ravage the rice just planted. The many ways this object can be used in the world cannot possibly be counted."

Shimazu Takahisa, the Daimyo of Satsuma, heard of this strange weapon and purchased firearms from the Portuguese, eventually ordering the local smiths to make their own.

The exact identity of the two Portuguese traders has never been confirmed, and various famous traders like Fernão Mendes Pinto claimed to be on the ship when they were not. Katsushika Hokusai, in his manga sketchbook, gave their names as "Murashukusha" and "Krishitamota."

Crusading Christian: Francis Xavier

The Portuguese arrived during what is called the Sengoku ("belligerent country") period of Japanese history. The heads of state – the Emperor, the official head of state, and the Shogun, the leader of the military (the title literally translates as "commander") – had little control over the local daimyo (warlords), who fought endless feudal wars amongst themselves. That era would come to an end when Oda Nobunaga, assisted by Toyotomi Hideyoshi and Tokugawa Ieyasu, fought a series of campaigns that culminated in the unification of the country by 1615.

Fernão Mendes Pinto was probably not one of the two Portuguese who washed up in Tanegashima, despite his claims, but he most definitely arrived in Japan in 1549 with a missionary from Navarre who had been sent to Asia by Pope John III several years earlier. His name was Francis Xavier, the first Jesuit missionary to Japan.

The Society of Jesus had been founded by St. Ignatius of Loyola and was officially

"In this life, we find our greatest comfort living in the midst of danger, that is, if we confront them solely for the love of God." – St Francis Xavier"
(Kobe City Museum/DNPartcom)

"We are now like so many statues among them, since they speak and talk much about us, while we, not understanding their language, are mute." – St Francis Xavier

St Francis Xavier and his faithful companion Anjiro (Kobe City Museum/DNPartcom).

created by a papal bull issued by Pope Paul III in 1540. Members, known as Jesuits, took vows of poverty, chastity, and obedience to the Pope. Xavier had been one of the first members of the society and was its first missionary in Asia. He traveled east through the growing Portuguese Empire where he evangelized extensively. He arrived first in Portuguese Mozambique, in 1542, then Goa where he stayed for three years. He then evangelized in Malacca, a former state of the Malay Peninsula, Indonesia and Canton. While in Indonesia he met a Japanese exile named Anjiro, who converted to Catholicism and was christened Paulo de Santa Fe.

With Anjiro as his interpreter, Xavier arrived at Kagoshima on August 15, 1549. He met with Shimazu Takahisa, who received him cordially and allowed him to evangelize, but in 1550, under pressure from Buddhist monks, Takahisa forbade his subjects from converting to Christianity under penalty of death. That same year, the Portuguese were granted trading rights on the island of Hirado, now a part of Nagasaki Prefecture, by the local daimyo Matsura Takanobu.

Xavier traveled to Hirado that year, journeying with Anjiro to his family home in Yamaguchi. He traveled farther to Kyoto where he hoped to meet with the Emperor, but he failed to get an audience and returned to Yamaguchi.

Xavier preached extensively in Japan and learned very quickly that any Western missionary heading to Japan should be well prepared. Not only were the Japanese ready to debate theological points of Christianity, but they were also curious about the Western world – his audiences were especially impressed by the news Xavier brought of Western astronomy.

In a letter to Goa dated November 5, 1549, Xavier wrote:

"They are the best race yet discovered and I think among non-Christians their match will not easily be found. Admirable in their social relationships, they have an astonishing sense of honor and esteem it above all things. In general they are not wealthy people, but neither among nobles or plebeians is poverty regarded as a disgrace. A very poor noble would not dream of marrying a woman not of his own class, however wealthy she might be, for he thinks he would lose his honor by doing so and he esteems honor far above riches, which is something, so far as I know, that cannot be said of Christian peoples.

The peoples of Japan are full of courtesy in their dealings with one another. They set great store by weapons, and nobles and plebeians alike always carry sword and dagger from the age of fourteen. They will not endure to be treated slightingly or addressed in contemptuous terms. The ordinary people hold the the military class [samurai] in great respect, and they for their part glory in serving their lord [daimyo] on whom they greatly depend, not, I think, from fear of anything he could do to them, but because it would mean loss of honor to fail in duty to him.

They are a moderate people as regards food, but they indulge a good deal in an intoxicating liquor made from rice [sake], as the vine does not grow in Japan. They never play games of chance, considering them to be a form of theft and therefore highly dishonorable. Swearing is little heard and when they do swear it is by the sun. A good proportion of the people can read and write, which is a great help towards helping teach them quickly the prayers and things of God.

They are monogamists and they abominate thieving and punish robbers invariably with death. Of all the peoples I have seen in my life, Christians included, the Japanese are the most vigorously opposed to theft, and there are few robbers in the country. They are a well-meaning people and very sociable and anxious to learn. They take pleasure in hearing of the things of God especially such as they can understand, and they have no idols made in the shape of beasts, but believe in men of ancient times, who, as far as I can make out, lived as philosophers.

Many Japanese love the sun, others the moon [Shinto]. They like to be appealed to on rational grounds, and are ready to agree what reason vindicates is right. In my view the ordinary people commit fewer sins and are more obedient to reason than those they call Bonzes and regard as their spiritual fathers. The bonzes are addicted to unnatural vice, and readily admit it, for it is so notorious and well known to everybody that men and women of every condition take it for granted and show no abhorrence of it. Still, the laity are very pleased to hear us denounce this abominable sin."

"Whoever does not comply with this order will, in the case of clergy, be evicted from our territory, and in the case of ordinary citizens, merchants or hooligans, receive severe punishment."
– Mori Motonari

The martyrdom of Saint Sebastian, painted during the Sengoku Period in Japan.

The Jesuit missionaries brought paintings of the Madonna and other religious figures with them from Rome to illustrate their points. These also served as gifts to the various leaders, including the daimyo of the Awari Province (now Nagoya), Oda Nobunaga. In 1551 Nobunaga began a decades-long campaign to unify Japan under a single ruler and the Jesuits were caught up in the struggle.

Nobunaga tolerated Christians and was combative with Buddhists, something the Jesuits praised him for in their reports. Some even claimed he converted to Christianity, but this is not the case – Nobunaga's tolerance of Christianity was a political move, since the missionaries were foils for his Buddhist enemies.

After two years in Japan, Xavier judged his work in Japan to be successful, and decided to return to India. In 1552 he headed for China, but died of a fever on Shangchuan (Shangchuandao or St. John's Island) while waiting for permission to enter. His body was moved to Malacca, and from there to the Basilica of Bom Jesus in Goa. Pope Gregory XV canonized him as St. Francis Xavier 70 years later in 1622.

Nagasaki: from nothing to nucleus

Hirado had been a leading center of trade in Japan, both legitimate and illegitimate, for centuries. Japanese, Korean and Chinese pirates traded their goods at Hirado and the ruling Matsura clan reaped huge profits from these sales. When the Portuguese set up trade in Kyushu, they needed a developed trading center and Hirado suited their purpose.

"At which time came to us many boats and we suffered them to come aboard, being not able to resist them, which people did us no harm, neither of us understanding the one the other." – Pilot William Adams
A Portuguese carrack, known locally as a *kurofune* or "Black Ship," due to its covering of protective pitch (Kobe City Museum/DNPartcom).

The daimyo of Hirado, Matsura Takanobu (known to the Portuguese as Taqua Nombo), along with fellow Kyushu-based daimyo, saw the enormous profits to be made and allowed the Portuguese to trade and to evangelize. Matsura privately opposed the religion, however, and with the endorsement and support of the region's Buddhist monks, expelled all Jesuits from his domain in 1558.

By that time, the Portuguese had monopolized trade between China and Japan, making handsome profits for themselves as intermediaries by marking up the goods each side wanted from the other.

In 1561 the Jesuits were keen to move their mission, as fewer and fewer converts were coming into the fold, and Matsura was proving to be difficult to deal with. The Portuguese decided to move their trading base to a more prosperous port. Their prayers were answered by Omura Sumitada, the daimyo of Shimabara, who opened the port of Yokose-ura (north of modern-day Saikai) to them. Omura and Matsura were great rivals who competed for trade, both legitimate and illegitimate.

Omura welcomed the Portuguese into his domain, granting them very generous concessions – they were exempt from paying taxes, as were those who traded with them, they were free to build churches and he ordered Yokose-ura to be expanded. Omura and his retainers converted to Christianity in 1563, forcing the faith on his subjects, not only demanding they convert, but also burning down Buddhist and Shinto shrines. In revenge, an illegitimate son of Omura led an uprising and burned down Yokose-ura in the late 1560s. By 1571, however, Omura had opened the alternate port of Nagasaki to the Portuguese.

Until that time Nagasaki had been nothing but a small, inconsequential fishing village. Now it grew rapidly as Portuguese traders moved their operations there. Omura, meanwhile, was facing opposition from another daimyo, Ryuzoji Takanobu, who gained territory in the nearby Hizen domain (now a part of Nagasaki Prefecture).

The Omura family did not submit to Ryuzoji and held fast at their castle, 30 kilometers northeast of Nagasaki. Omura ran out of money and ended up borrowing from the church, mortgaging the taxes collected from the villages in his domain. In return, the Portuguese gave him modern weapons like guns, bullets, and gunpowder. In 1578, Omura successfully repulsed an invasion and, on June 9, 1580, he ceded Nagasaki to the Society of Jesus in perpetuity. When the mortgage came due, he defaulted, and the villages of Yamazato, Urakami and Fuchi were added to the Jesuits' holdings.

By 1580 there were an estimated 130,000 Christians in Japan, most concentrated on the island of Kyushu (unsurprisingly), where the Portuguese missionaries had full control of Nagasaki port.

The Tensho Embassy

In 1579, Jesuit missionary Alessandro Valignano arrived in Nagasaki from Macau, with the intention of solidifying the Society of Jesus's influence in the country. During his time there, the port of Nagasaki was handed over to the Jesuits and was established as a major trading post. However, the Superior General of the Jesuits, as well as the Pope, were uneasy about the Jesuits taking on such a role and ordered the missionaries to cease mercantile activity. Valignano and his colleagues ignored these requests.

In 1581, Valignano made a proposal to send an embassy of Japanese Christians to Europe to ease the fears in Rome, to support their cause and to introduce the country to the crowned heads of Europe. The embassy was underwritten by three Christian daimyos including Omura Sumitada, the daimyo who gave Nagasaki to the Jesuits. They chose four young *kirishitan* noblemen to lead the embassy.

"I have always found things in this country so altered and changed from what they were when I left them that when I returned I could find scarcely a trace of what I had seen and left at my departure." – Visitor Alessandro Valignano

The members of the Tensho Embassy (Top, from left to right: Julião Nakaura, Father Mesquita, Mancio Ito. Bottom, from left to right: Martinho Hara, Miguel Chijiwa).

The four emissaries, Mancio Ito, Martinho Hara, Miguel Chijiwa and Julião Nakaura, left Nagasaki on February 20, 1582. They arrived in Lisbon over two years later, on August 11, 1584, have stopped at numerous Portuguese territories along the way. Valignano had hoped to accompany the embassy to Europe and propose some of his ideas on the future of Japan to European powers; however, he was ordered to stay in Goa.

The embassy met with King Philip II of Spain, the Grand Duke of Tuscany Francesco de' Medici, Pope Gregory XIII, and Pope Sixtus V, who succeeded Gregory in 1585. The Vatican made the four men Knights of the Golden Spur. Gregory was intrigued by the Japanese noblemen and endorsed the Jesuits' activities in Japan. The embassy also lobbied to establish a Bishop of Japan, at Nagasaki, which was also granted.

The mission returned to Nagasaki in 1590. They met with Hideyoshi in Kyoto and were admitted as Jesuits on July 25, 1591, the first Japanese members of the Society. Unfortunately, as we will see in the following pages, the Christian's lot in Japan soon changed. Marinho Hara was forced to leave Japan for his Christian beliefs in 1614, and died in Macau in 1639. Julião Nakaura was martyred in 1633 for refusing to renounce Christianity.

Hiroshima: harbor to hub

Like Nagasaki, Hiroshima began as a humble fishing village before outside forces gave it importance. The nearby island of Itsukushima (Miyajima) for many centuries served as the center of activity in the region, with many samurai visiting the famous shrine on the island. The Ota River Delta, where the modern city of Hiroshima now stands, contained five quiet villages called Gokamura.

Things began to change in the 1570s with the growth in influence of the Mori clan, who ruled Aki Province (now the western half of Hiroshima Prefecture). The Mori clan was centered in Koriyama Castle in what is now Nara Prefecture. Under Mori Motonari the clan defeated its old rivals and took over the Izumo

"Although a single arrow is easily breakable, three arrows together are hard to break at the same time. When the three of you unite your strength, it will be hard for your enemies to defeat you." – Daimyo Mori Terumoto

and Suo provinces (now the Shimane and Yamaguchi Prefectures, respectively). Motonari is most famous for a lesson he taught to his three sons: He gave each of them an arrow and instructed them to break it. They did so, easily. Then he gave them three arrows bundled together and instructed them to break it... they could not. This event probably did not actually happen, but the lesson is powerful, and is still taught to Japanese children today: one acting alone will break easily, but three united are unbreakable. (According to another legend, an inscription on Motonari's grave bears his motto: "*Hyakuman Isshin*," –"Union is Strength.")

Motonari's eldest son Takamoto succeeded him as head of the clan in 1557 (Motonari remained as advisor). The clan's longtime rivals the Ouchi clan were seen as weak in 1560, so the Mori moved to conquer their land. However, in 1563, during their conquest of Ouchi lands, Takamoto died suddenly of food poisoning. With Takamoto's death, his son Terumoto was selected as Motonari's heir. In reality Motonari, as advisor, wielded the true power of the clan until his death in 1571. It was then that Terumoto was able to take full control, and Hiroshima's fortunes would blossom.

During this time Oda Nobunaga was fighting his own grand campaign to unite all of Japan, and end the feudal wars that defined the Sengoku period. He continued his campaigns until being assassinated by one of his generals in 1582, and was succeeded by his loyal general (and former sandal bearer) Toyotomi Hideyoshi.

In 1586, Terumoto mobilized his forces to assist Hideyoshi in attacking Kyushu. By the following year, all warlords opposed to Hideyoshi had been subjugated. Terumoto thus became one of the five most powerful daimyo in Japan, and at the height of his power could summon a force of 120,000 samurai.

In 1589, Terumoto moved his base of power to the more strategic Ota River Delta, near Gokamura. There he built a castle that would serve as the center of political and economic power in the region, naming it after a combination of the Mori family patriarch Oe no Hiromoto, and Fukushima Motonaga, who helped decide the site of the castle: Hiroshima.

Korean campaigns and the Council of Five Elders

Diplomatic relations between Korea and Japan had been strained for centuries, largely due to the wokou pirates raiding Korea's coast. Diplomatic relations between the two nations were cut off in 1555, and Qi Jiguang led a series of successful campaigns against the pirates in the Chinese coastal provinces of Zhejiang and Fujian.

Before the campaign to conquer Kyushu, Hideyoshi informed Terumoto that he planned to use Kyushu as a launching point to invade first Korea, then Ming China. He planned to install a Japanese Emperor in Peking and open trade with India. The So clan, who ruled Tsushima, acted as mediators and sent letters to Korea asking for diplomatic relations, but Korea rejected these gestures.

Hideyoshi drew up plans to invade Korea in 1590, and assembled an army of 225,000 on Kyushu (A.L. Sadler in *The Maker of Modern Japan* puts this figure at 270,570) in preparation for the invasion. On May 23, 1592, the first invasion force left Tsushima for Korea. At first the invading army was successful, capturing the capital Hanseong (now Seoul) in June, and Pyongyang the following month. However, Korea used the centerpiece of its navy, the *Panokseon*, to sink much of the Japanese navy, which had more ships, and when in 1593 Ming China intervened, Japan was forced into a stalemate.

Western Honshu and Kyushu were the launching and receiving points for foreign interaction. As such, these regions played a key role in the modernization of Japan, and allowed Christianity to flourish.

In 1595 Hideyoshi appointed his two-year-old son, Hideyori, to succeed him. To ensure his succession, he appointed the five most powerful daimyo to cooperate in the governance of the country. He hoped, no doubt, that the equilibrium of power among the lords would ensure that each kept the others under control, until Hideyori could assume his position as shogun. The five elders were:

- Ukita Hideie, Daimyo of Bizen and Mimasala provinces (now Okayama Prefecture)
- Maeda Toshiie, Daimyo of Kanazawa (now Ishikawa and Toyama Prefectures)
- Uesugi Kagekatsu, Daimyo of the Aizu and Echigo provinces (now Niigata and Fukushima Prefectures)
- Mori Terumoto, Daimyo of the Choshu domain (now Hiroshima and Yamaguchi prefectures)
- Tokugawa Ieyasu, Daimyo of Edo (now Tokyo)

Despite distrusting his motives, and fully aware of his lust for power, Hideyoshi appointed Ieyasu to the council. The mistrust was mutual, as Ieyasu had supported

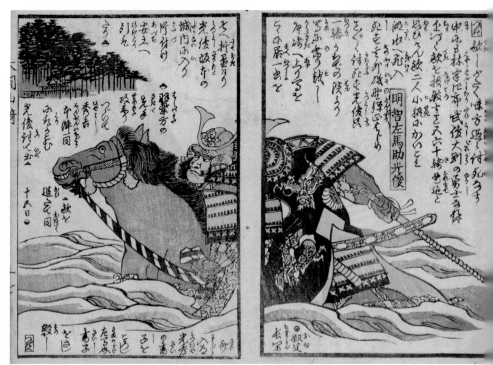

"I have never fought without conquering and when I strike I always win. Man cannot outlive his hundred years, so why should I sit chafing on this island?" – Daimyo Toyotomi Hideyoshi

Oda Nobukatsu – the son and heir of Oda Nobunaga – against Hideyoshi when Nobunaga had been assassinated. The other four daimyo had supported Hideyoshi in his campaigns to unite Japan, providing hundreds of thousands of samurai for his successful campaigns to capture Kyushu, as well his invasion of Korea.

A wind change for Westerners

Hideyoshi had been tolerant of Christianity for most of his reign, but that changed with the arrival of the Spanish ship *San Felipe* in 1596, which had been traveling between Acapulco and Manila when it ran aground at Urado Bay. The local daimyo, Tadayoshi, ordered the ship broken up and its cargo seized and divided between the central and local treasuries. The captain, a Portuguese sailor named Landecho, protested forcefully and sent two officers to Osaka to make their case to Hideyoshi in person.

The crew tried to intimidate Tadayoshi by producing a map of the world showing Spain's holdings, which at that time stretched from California to Argentina. Tadayoshi asked how Spain had got hold of so much land, and the captain explained that the Empire sent missionaries into the lands they wished to conquer. When the population accepted Christianity, troops would be sent in mixed with the missionaries, with Landecho allegedly concluding that "our kings have not much trouble accomplishing the rest."

Upon hearing this Hideyoshi was furious, and his animosity towards the Jesuits intensified. He issued an edict banning missionaries, fearing they might incite a peasant revolt. He also removed Nagasaki from Jesuit control. But while the Jesuits reduced their activities, Franciscans and Dominicans continued to preach to the commoners.

Less than a month after the *San Felipe* was wrecked, Hideyoshi ordered the execution of all missionaries remaining in Japan. A list of Christians in Osaka and Kyoto was drawn up and scores were arrested. Twenty-six of them were taken to Nagasaki, the largest Christian city in Japan, where they were hung on crosses and lanced to death on February 5, 1597. Among these were Paulo Miki, who joined the Jesuits in 1580, the first Japanese member of any Catholic order, and St. Philip of Jesus, from Mexico City, who had been on the *San Felipe* when it ran aground (he had been on his way to the Ecumenical See in Manila). Of those killed 20 were Japanese converts, five were Spanish and one was from Portuguese India. Pope Pius IX canonized all 26 martyrs in 1864, and St. Philip of Jesus is now the patron saint of Mexico City.

Peace talks with the Koreans and Chinese continued for some years, but broke down in 1597. The failure of the Korean campaigns weakened Hideyoshi's influence as well as his health, and on his deathbed in 1598, Hideyoshi ordered a withdrawal of Japanese forces.

As the 16th century came to an end Japan was entering a new period of change, and its clear cultural contrasts with other countries are highlighted in a letter written in 1599 by Padre Alexandro Valignano, successor to Francis Xavier in Japan:

"The Japanese have rites and customs so different from those of other nations that it looks as if they studied of set purpose to be unlike any other race on earth. It can safely be said that Japan is a world the reverse from Europe. Hardly in anything do their ways conform to ours. They eat and dress completely differently... Their obsequies, their language, their way of doing business, their manner of sitting down, their buildings, their domestic arrangements, their medicine, their education of their children, and every mortal habit of theirs are so unlike ours as to go beyond description or understanding.

What I could not get over in all this was that a people so utterly unlike ourselves should yet be so highly civilized. Even their feelings and natural tastes are so much our opposites that I would hardly dare asset it had I not lived long among them.

For instance we hold white to be a joyous color, but with them it is the color of mourning and sorrow and when they want to celebrate and be merry people they put on black or purple, our mourning colors. As of the eye so of the ear. Our instrumental and vocal music offends their sensibility, and their music, which they love, is an absolute torment for us to listen to. Again, we take off our hats or sombreros and stand up to greet a visitor, but they remove their shoes and sit down, considering it the gravest discourtesy to receive anyone standing... The way they eat is equally astonishing, neatly and elegantly with much composure, and their table service like their clothes is always immaculately clean. They do not use napkins, and have no knives, forks or spoons, but only two little sticks with which they manipulate the food so dexterously and cleanly that, though they never touch anything with their hands, not so much as a crumb falls from the plate to the table. Until a foreigner gets the knack of this he has many tribulations at his Japanese dinner."

(From *St Francis Xavier* by James Brodrick, S.J.)

*"Burned in their mothers' armes, criing out 'Jesus receve their soules'... the rest beheaded & cutt in peeces &
cast into the sea in sackes at 30 fathom deepe."* – Richard Cocks, Overseer of the English factory at Hirado
Kirishitan martyrs were tortured, burned, beheaded, and crucified by the Tokugawa regime for hundreds
of years. Twenty-six were publicly brutalized in 1597, and a further 188 were similarly martyred between
1603 and 1639.

Japan-China relations

During the 1590s, when Hideyoshi was planning his assault on Korea, he realized that many of the Chinese traders in Nagasaki were of fighting stock. Thinking that, as foreign subjects he might be able to employ them in his envisaged campaign on the mainland, he offered them generous and unprecedented freedoms, even allowing them to marry Japanese women. His generosity paid off, and many Chinese joined Hideyoshi as mercenaries in his attempted conquests of Korea, whilst his favorable treatment attracted Chinese trade to Nagasaki.

Traders were only allowed to operate officially at Nagasaki, but some of them defied this restriction. The daimyo of Kagoshima, in fact, often requested their presence in defiance of the shogunate. Shinchi had as many as 10,000 traders in residence and, at its peak, it even had its own judicial system. China's primary exports to Japan were sugar and cotton, which could not be produced locally, and were thus highly sought after.

Another prized commodity from the mainland were books. Japan was hungry for knowledge of the outside world, a symptom of its isolation, and this hunger was sated mainly by foreign literature. Imported Chinese texts were a rarity, and would only become well known outside of Nagasaki if they were reprinted and distributed by publishers in other cities. An official would inspect every book – going through each page – to make sure there were no offensive (ie Christian) passages.

> *The carp wind was blowing strong when the first Chinese junks arrived;*
> *Now our guildhalls stand wall-to-wall with rich merchants' mansions.*
> *Besides fighting to buy snowy cotton and sugar white as frost,*
> *The Japanese all ask about the latest bestsellers from China!*
>
> Huang Zunxian, written in the 1870s

This Sino-centric altruism, enhanced during the 1590s, extended into the next century in large part because the Chinese were Asians, and were thus seen as racially closer to Japanese.

An example of the East-West disparity could be seen in Maruyamamachi, Nagasaki, one of the largest prostitution quarters in Japan. In 1723, it was patronized by as many as 20,000 Chinese and a mere 270 Dutch. Reflecting the pro-Chinese attitude, the prices charged in the red-light district were highly disparate. A Chinese patron could expect a charge of 5 *momme* of silver (one momme equaled roughly four grams), whilst it cost 60 momme of silver for a Dutchman.

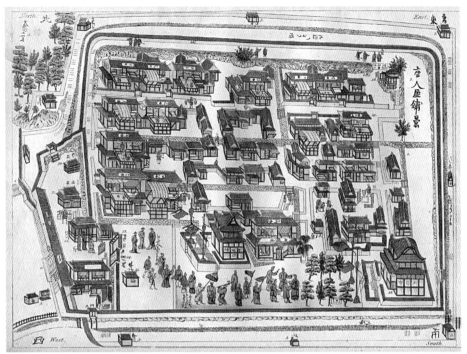

"I will make a leap and land in China and lay my laws upon her. I shall go by way of Korea and if your soldiers will join me in this invasion you will have shown your neighborly spirit. I am determined that my name shall pervade the three kingdoms." – Daimyo Toyotomi Hideyoshi

Illustrated map of Shinchi, created by Isaac Titsingh during his tenure as VOC Ooperhoofd in the 1780s.

In 1629 the Kofukuji Temple was built in Nagasaki. Like the nearby temples of Sofukuji and Fukusaiji, it is dedicated to the Chinese goddess of the sea, Matsu. Today, these remain important temples in the Obaku school of Zen Buddhism. In 1654, Ingen Ryuki (his Chinese name was Yinyuan Longqi) arrived in Nagasaki from Fujian and began teaching at the three temples. Japanese students came to study under him and persuaded him to stay in Japan; Ingen moved to Kyoto in 1661 where he established the Manpukuji temple, the head temple of the Obaku sect.

Officially, Ming China did not have a trade policy with Japan. It was reluctant to establish one due to the problems it had with the wokou, who it had often suspected were privateers in the employ of Japanese daimyo. Traders who ventured into Japanese waters did so against Ming decrees, and many found their way to a variety of Japanese ports, trusting that their unpredictability would allow them to evade officials. China finally lifted its ban on maritime activities in 1684, in part so it could control the Pescadores (Penghu) islands, which until that year were governed by Zhu Shugui, the last claimant of the Ming throne, which had been overthrown four decades earlier.

"Look upon the wrath of thy enemy. If thou only knowest what it is to conquer, and knowest not what it is to be defeated; woe unto thee, it will fare ill with thee." – Shogun Tokugawa Ieyasu

Panels depicting the 1600 victory of the Tokugawa forces against the disaffected daimyos at Sekigahara.

THE TOKUGAWA SHOGUNATE AND DUTCH EXPANSION

When Toyotomi Hideyoshi died in 1598 at the age of 61, Tokugawa Ieyasu, a member of the Council of Five Elders, swiftly began to engineer an alliance of daimyo who had been dissatisfied with Hideyoshi and his allies. A year later Maeda Toshiie died, leaving Ieyasu the undisputed regent of Hideyoshi's young son and successor; Ieyasu was now the most powerful daimyo in Japan. On his deathbed, Toshiie said: "I don't care about the next world, what I am worried about is what I leave behind in this. Hideyori is young… when I die I fear for his interests. I wonder if there will be anyone to stand by him."

In response to the ascendance of the Tokugawa clan, two other members of the Council of Five Elders, Uesugi Kagekatsu and Mori Terumoto, rallied other disillusioned daimyo against Ieyasu, and the two sides met on October 21, 1600 at Sekigahara, in what is now Gifu Prefecture. Ieyasu and his allies prevailed and he was subsequently appointed Shogun in 1603, a title that imbued more political power than that of the Emperor. Ieyasu moved the Shogunate capital from Kyoto to his center of power in the small fishing village of Edo (now Tokyo). This event is considered the beginning of the Edo Period (also known as the Tokugawa Period) of Japanese history.

Terumoto, on the losing side at the Battle of Sekigahara, lost Hiroshima Castle, and the Choshu Domain, over which he had dominion, shrank significantly. The provincial capital was moved accordingly, from Hiroshima to Hagi in modern Yamaguchi Prefecture.

Hiroshima Castle was turned over to Fukushima Masanori, an ally of Shogun Ieyasu. Masanori stayed in the castle until 1619 when Ieyasu's third son and successor, Hidetada, accused him of poor governance, and he was removed and replaced by Asano Nagaakira, the daimyo of the Wakayama domain. His descendants would be the daimyo of the Hiroshima Domain until the feudal system was dismantled in 1871.

Right: "Coming before the king, he viewed me well, and seemed to be wonderfully favorable. He made many signs unto me, some of which I understood, and some I did not." – Pilot William Adams
A cartouche from William Adams' map of Japan, depicting his first meeting with Shogun Ieyasu in 1600.

The coming of the Protestants
and the Dutch East India Company

In 1600, the Dutch ship *Liefde* (translating as either "Love" or "Charity") reached Japan. It had set out from Rotterdam with five other ships two years before to trade for silver in South America. However, it ran aground off the east coast of Kyushu, near present-day Usuki in Oita Prefecture. Local Portuguese Jesuit priests claimed the vessel was a pirate ship and called for the crew to be crucified. The Pilot Major, Englishman William Adams, and second mate Jan Joosten van Lodensteijn were presented to the Shogun Ieyasu, who questioned them extensively on European affairs and their intentions.

Ieyasu was intrigued by their knowledge of ships, and especially impressed when Adams produced a map of the route they had taken – across the Pacific Ocean through the Straits of Magellan. He promptly ordered them to steer the rotted *Liefde* to Edo Bay, where it subsequently sank.

In 1604, Ieyasu asked Adams and his crew to help build Japan's first Western-style ship, under the supervision of his admiral of the navy, Mukai Shogen. Using local carpenters, the crew designed and helped build an 80-ton ship, which was used to survey the Japanese coast. They were subsequently commissioned to build a 120-ton ship, which the Shogun greatly approved of. As a reward, Adams became the official interpreter and advisor on foreign affairs to the Shogun, though this meant he was not allowed to leave Japan.

Two members of the crew were given permission to leave Japan in 1605, in order to invite the recently formed Dutch East India Company to trade with Japan. On March 20, 1602, the Dutch Empire had established the Dutch East India Company (in Dutch it was rendered Vereenigde Oostindische Compagnie or VOC), with the remit to assist merchants competing in the spice trade. At the time,

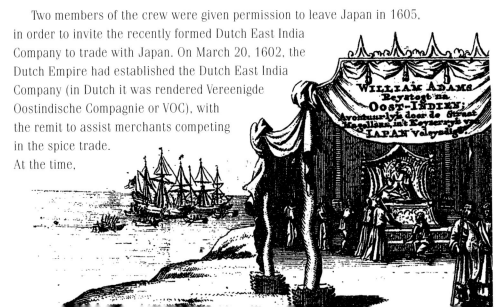

the Portuguese and Spanish dominated the routes. The Protestant Dutch Republic had separated from Catholic Spain in 1581, a year after the Portuguese and Spanish kingdoms were united under Philip II. The Iberians had been using the ports of Antwerp and Rotterdam to unload spices and other cargo from the East, but after Dutch independence, they migrated to ports in what are now Italy and Germany.

"W'th two of his brothers and 3 or 4 of his uncles besides many noblemen of his kindred, all w'ch look for presentes or else it is no living amongst them." – Richard Cocks, Overseer of the English Factory at Hirado

The diplomatic exchange as a Japanese procession greets Dutch traders outside Edo.

As a result, Dutch merchants were cut off from the profitable spice trade. In 1596, therefore, Dutch explorers determined that Batam, on the island of Java, could be a lucrative alternative to the Portuguese and Spanish trading posts, which had previously maintained Europe's spice stocks. The Dutch subsequently set up outposts in present-day India, Indonesia and Japan, to compete directly with the Portuguese and Spanish.

Over the course of the 80-year Dutch War of Independence, Dutch traders also engaged in privateering and armed clashes with Portuguese traders across Asia. By the end of the conflict Portuguese trading outposts at Malacca, Ceylon and Nagasaki had all been captured by the Dutch.

The VOC is notable for issuing the first corporate stock in the world and founding the oldest stock exchange in the world at Amsterdam (now a part of Euronext). A useful innovation was added to the VOC's arsenal in 1608, when the first refracting telescope was invented. The telescope became a prized gift in the East, where there was a deep curiosity about Western scientific discoveries. Many Japanese prints depict Dutchmen looking through telescopes.

The VOC set up a factory in 1609 at Hirado, the same island on which the Portuguese had started their trading operations in Japan 59 years earlier. The first ship to export goods from Japan arrived in Holland in 1610, carrying nearly 10,000 porcelain items, though it is thought that these were Chinese porcelain rather than Japanese.

In an effort to maintain their superior position with the Japanese officials, the Portuguese spread rumors that the Dutch were really pirates. The Dutch promised that a ship would come each year, but in 1610 the Spanish sank their fleet off the coast of Playa Honda (now Botolan) in the Philippines. The VOC's Japanese outpost was not as profitable as it could have been, since the Dutch, unlike the Portuguese, didn't have trade hubs in China. (The major Dutch operations in the Far East were concentrated in Batavia, now Jakarta.) The Dutch therefore tried to take Macau from the Portuguese in 1622 – they had raided Macau in 1601 and 1603 – and attempted to open ports in Fujian using military force that same year. Both attempts were unsuccessful.

On June 12, 1613, the English ship *Clove* landed at Hirado. John Saris, the ship's captain, met with Ieyasu and, aided by Adams, established a factory for the British East India Company (EIC). The Shogun and Adams suggested putting it at Uraga, at the entrance of Edo Bay, but Saris was determined to install it on Hirado, where the Dutch factory was. Saris departed at the end of the year and left Richard Cocks in charge of the factory. Adams signed on as an employee, largely working as an

"Yow shall understand that the Hollanders have here an Indies of monney, for out of Holland is noe need of silver to come into th'Est Indies, for in Japan is much silver and gold to serve for the Hollanders to handell."
– Pilot William Adams

The factory of Hirado or Firando was situated to the northwest of Nagasaki.

advisor. Unfortunately, the goods imported from the British Empire were considered inferior to those of the Dutch, and the factory was bankrupt by 1623.

In 1619, the Dutch and British Empires signed the Treaty of Defense, which regulated trade in the East Indies and allowed them to collaborate in breaking the Spanish-Portuguese monopoly on trade in the Pacific. However, each side frequently accused the other of underhanded tactics to gain advantage in local markets. This reached fever pitch in 1623, when 20 men, 10 of them employees of the EIC, were tortured and executed by VOC agents in Amboyna (Ambon Island, part of the Spice Islands in Indonesia) over accusations of treason, for colluding to assassinate the provincial governor. Twenty-five years later, the incident served as one of the pretexts for the first Anglo-Dutch War.

Meanwhile, in an effort to curb the wakou pirates who still presented a threat to trade in the late 16th and early 17th centuries, first Hideyoshi and later the Tokugawa Shoguns issued "Red Seals" to feudal lords interested in foreign trade. This helped facilitate legitimate trade between Japan and other ports around East Asia, from the Philippines, Macau and Vietnam to Thailand, Malacca, Indonesia, and even India.

"In Japan is much silver and gold to serve for the Hollanders to handell wher they will in th'Est Indies allwaies provided for their commodeties, viz. rawe silk and pepper, w'th other commodetyes, and to excuse the reason best, lead, and such like is in Japan marchaundiz allwaies redy money." – Pilot William Adams

From 1604 to 1639, Japan sent an average of ten Red Seal ships out per year (the Portuguese sent one ship to Japan each year and the Dutch sent three). The Red Seal ships were given to Japanese traders such as Yamada Nagamasa, who became the head of a Japanese settlement at Ayutthaya in Thailand, eventually rising to becoming governor of the Nakhon Si Thammarat. Nagasaki magistrate Murayama Toan used Red Seal ships to attempt an invasion of Taiwan in 1616, but the fleet was dispersed by a typhoon.

Red Seal ships were also issued to Westerners. William Adams used such a ship to trade in Siam (Thailand) and Cochin China (Vietnam). His second mate on the *Liefde*, Jan Joosten, was also given command of Red Seal ships that he used to trade in Siam. This system ended after the Shogunate introduced *Sakoku* and isolated the country from the outside world.

Anti-Christian edicts, martyrdom, and rebellion

The Emperor has always been the head of state in Japan, but true political control was wrested from the theocratic ruling class and held by the Shogunate from the 12th century until 1867. Like the Emperor, the Shogun derived much of his power from familial descent. Minamoto no Yoritomo established himself as the first Shogun in 1192, and future shoguns, including Tokugawa Ieyasu, claimed descent from him.

Ieyasu abdicated in 1605 to allow his son Hidetada to ascend to the position, a common practice at the time. However, Ieyasu maintained influence over the government until his death in 1616, and it was he who signed the 1614 edict that expelled Christians from Japan, and forbade the religion in the country. Many Christians went into exile, but roughly 30,000 remained in the archipelago, hiding their faith and living in seclusion.

Shogun Hidetada now ordered his daimyo to increase their efforts to eradicate Christianity. Between 1614 and 1622 a minimum of 434 Christians were publicly executed, tortured or died in prison. The "Great Martyrdom" in Nagasaki on September 10, 1622, saw 55 Christians burned alive – a spectacle witnessed by up to 150,000 bystanders.

"Ther be many Christians by reason of the Jesuites, w'ch be many in this lande, and Fraunciscanons, havinge many churches in the lande." – Pilot William Adams

The Kirishitan strongholds of Japan, circa 1585, as reported to the Jesuits' headquarters. The suggestion that Christianity was so rampant is improbable.

During this period of religious purging, in 1615 the Shogunate sent a trade delegation, the Keicho Embassy, to meet with the monarchs of Europe and discuss commerce. They were received courteously, but the Catholic sovereigns were troubled by the reports of suppression of Christianity in Japan, and ultimately proved to be unhelpful. The delegation met with Pope Paul V, who similarly expressed concern at the anti-Catholic stance of the Shogunate.

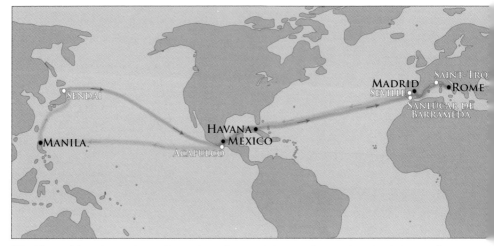

"Should any of these three make it to Rome, do not be too quick to trust them or champion their cause." – Jesuit Father Peter Kibe, January 12, 1618

The journey undertaken by Hasakura and his companions, from Sendai, in the domain of the Date, through Central America, across to Spain, France, and Italy. They returned via a similar route, visiting Manila before returning home.

In 1616, Osaka was besieged by the Shogun, who eliminated the Toyotomi clan for fear of retribution by future generations. Upon learning his forces were vanquished, Hideyori, Hideyoshi's son and designated successor, retreated and committed seppuku along with his wife and retainers. One of Ieyasu's allies in this campaign, Matsukura Shigemasa, received Hizen Province, and the Arima clan who ruled it were removed – the clan had converted to Christianity, as had many of their subjects.

Two years later, the Shogun issued an order saying only one castle would be allowed per province. Shigemasa dismantled his two castles and began constructing the Shimabara Castle, 58 miles east of Nagasaki. To raise the funds to finish it, taxes were levied upon the peasants, who faced intensified work with diminished rewards. The persecution of Christians continued, but in 1621 Shigemasa began to take excessive measures against them, hoping to extend the hegemony of the Shogunate. Unrest began to build amongst the masses.

Shogun Hidetada, meanwhile, was striving to repair relations between the Shogunate and the Emperor. As part of this reconciliation, his daughter Kazuko married the Emperor Go-Mizunoo, and they had a daughter who became the Empress Meisho. Hidetada himself abdicated in 1623, but like his father he continued to enforce punitive anti-Christian policies, banning Christian literature, forcing Christian daimyo to commit *seppuku* (ritual suicide), and executing Christians who refused to renounce their faith.

"Emperour will banish all Spaniardes and Portingall howseholders out of Japon... to prevent entertayning of padres." – Richard Cocks, Overseer of the English Factory at Hirado

The priest Father Marcelo Mastrili bows to his fate, upon Mount Uzen, near Nagasaki.

The next Shogun, Iemitsu, issued edicts restricting foreign trade to the Chinese and Dutch at Nagasaki. He also forbade Japanese nationals from leaving the country on penalty of death, at the same time reaffirming his predecessors' dictates banning Christianity, and enacted a system by which someone could prove that they were not Christian, such as forcing them to stamp on an image of Jesus.

When Shigemasa died in 1630, his son Katsuie succeeded him, persevering with his father's hard anti-Catholic stance, as well as maintaining high taxes. In 1637 the populace rose up; first local ronin began plotting his assassination, and following a number of provincial uprisings, 30,000 rebels, led by 16-year-old Amakusa Shiro (known as "Heaven's Messenger"), gathered at Hara Castle, the former headquarters of the Arima clan.

Katsuie, backed by the Shogun, besieged the rebels with a force exceeding 100,000 soldiers. After four months of conflict, up to 40,000 Christian men, women and children had been killed, while the Shogunate alliance lost more than 10,000 men. When the costly Shimabara rebellion finally came to an end, Katsuie was removed from his post for allowing insurrection to foment within his territory, and sent to Edo for further investigation. As a result he was beheaded, on August 28, 1638 – the only daimyo to die in this way, by Shogun dictate, during the Edo Period.

Sakoku: the chained state

The Shogunate suspected that the Portuguese had incited, or assisted, the rebels at Shimabara, so in 1639 it issued an edict known as *Sakoku* that forbade Portuguese from entering the country. Any Portuguese ships that approached Japan were to be destroyed, and all crew members beheaded.

By the time they were removed, the Portuguese had already been restricted to the artificial island of Dejima, built just off the coast of Nagasaki. Dejima was built

"One of the fairest and lardgest harbours that eaver I saw." – Richard Cocks, Overseer of the English Factory at Hirado

An illustrated map of Nagasaki, produced by Dutch residents in the 18th Century.

in 1634 by order of the Shogun to separate the Portuguese from the Japanese and prevent the spread of Christianity.

As well as removing the Portuguese the Sakoku edict also banned trade with the West, with the exception of the Dutch, who now gained control of Dejima. Japan effectively closed the door to the outside world; the only crack left open was the fan-shaped island, 2.2 acres in area, within Nagasaki Harbor.

For 200 years Japan remained virtually closed off from the world. Few went in, none came out. Its trading ships only docked in Japanese ports, and the ships it built could not travel long distances. The only outlet to the world was the port of Nagasaki, and the two artificial islands built for foreign ships – Shinchi for the Chinese, Dejima for the Dutch.

The Dutch at Dejima

Having assisted the Shogunate in suppressing the Christian rebels at Shimabara, and having maintained a steady supply of gunpowder and cannons, the Dutch had affirmed their relationship with Japan. Despite being Christian, the predominantly Protestant republic was comparatively lax in its approach to evangelizing – the only active Protestant missionaries at that time were with the Massachusetts Bay Colony, on the other side of the world.

When the Portuguese were expelled from Dejima, Nagasaki lost much of its prosperity. The city's citizenry subsequently petitioned the Shogun to allow the Dutch to fill the void. The Shogun consented, and the Dutch trading post was moved from Hirado to Dejima. Noting the Shogunate's swift and irrevocable shunning of Portugal for their perceived slights, the VOC made sure its employees did nothing to upset their hosts. Francois Caron, the 12th VOC Opperhoofd in Japan, told new arrivals, "do not indulge in extravagances and never show anger."

"When it rains on the Portuguese, the [Dutch East India] company gets splattered too." – François Caron, Opperhoofd of the Dutch factory at Hirado

A Nagasaki-e painting of a Dutchman posed at Dejima.

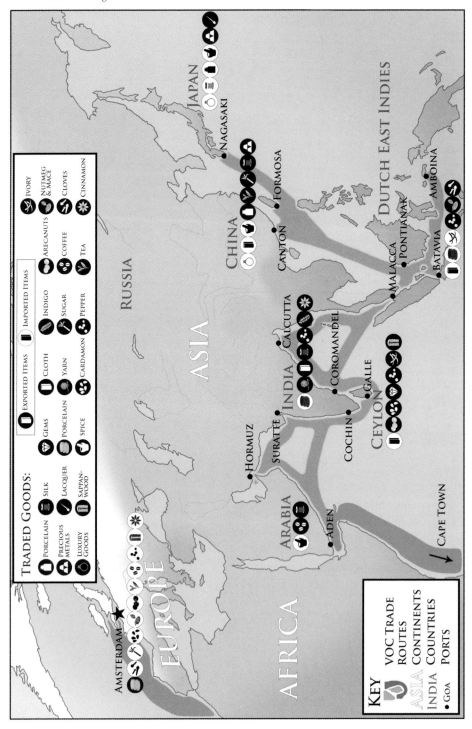

On the high seas, the Dutch were not above piratical behavior. In the northern China Sea, they attacked ships, regardless of nationality, plundered their goods and sold the spoils to their Japanese counterparts. Through such methods they gained and secured a monopoly on the oceanic routes between Portuguese-owned Macau and Nagasaki. Now, not only could they sell their own goods to Japan for a handsome profit, but they also had dominion over the conveyance of Japanese goods to China and Europe. The company's maritime prowess allowed it to accrue exorbitant wealth. By 1637, its overall value amounted to 78 million Dutch guilders, equivalent to US$7.4 trillion today.

Whilst internationally the company grew exponentially, its Japanese trade faced severe restrictions. Maintaining its beneficial trade policies with China, the Shogunate permitted up to 30 Chinese merchant ships to trade in Japan each year. The Dutch, conversely, were limited to five ships per year in 1671, under Tokugawa Tsunayoshi. By 1713, Tokugawa Ienobu had it reduced to two.

For the first few decades in Dejima, knowledge from the West was highly controlled. Dutch traders were ushered annually to a meeting with the Shogun, in Edo, where they were obliged to detail the goings-on in the outside world. The only texts permitted were those related to medical and nautical subjects. Japanese translators would translate only sanctioned works, but many Dutch traders sold books as part of "private trade" – that is trade conducted on their own, separate from the company transactions. Through this underhanded method the Japanese got hold of their first books from the West.

"I esteem our Japon trade alltogether unprofetable yf wee procure not tradde into China" – Richard Cocks, Overseer of the English Factory at Hirado

Representatives of Chinese, Japanese and Western merchants gather to discuss trade in the archipelago.

Opposite: "A company of rich userars whoe have gotten all the trade of Japon into their owne handes." – Richard Cocks, Overseer of the English Factory at Hirado

The maritime routes controlled by the Dutch East India Trading Company (VOC) in the 1600s. After capturing a number of key strategic ports, many formerly Portuguese, the Dutch gained a monopoly over regional oceanic trade.

In 1720, Shogun Tokugawa Yoshimune relaxed the ban on Dutch books, and students from around the region came to Nagasaki to study *rangaku*. This variously translated as "Dutch learning" or "Red-hair learning." The Japanese started to learn Dutch and began translating and interpreting books from The Netherlands.

The artistic bridge: Nagasaki-e, Ranga painting, and literature

During the Edo Period, printmakers in Nagasaki made a handsome profit producing artworks (*Nanbanbijutsu*) depicting Nanban ships, foreigners, and Dejima. Several publishers like Toshimaya, Yamatoya, Bunkindo, Bunsaido and Hariya produced

hundreds of prints. Most Japanese would never see a "red-haired barbarian" in person, and consequently these prints were widely sold as curios.

The prints were called *Nagasaki-e* (literally "Pictures of Nagasaki"). The local print industry tapered off when alternate ports were opened for trade, and their monopoly was compromised. Similar prints, depicting Westerners,

Opposite page: *"I am a nightingale, you are a plum blossom. If I had my way some time, would not the blossoms be my perch anyway...?"* – Shibata Hanamori

A Nagasaki-e depicting a Dutch couple, dressed in finery, meeting outside an enclosed, manicured blossom tree.

Below: *"On pain of corporal punishment, no decent women are allowed to come to us."* – Francois Valentijn

A ranga painting of two Westerners staring out across the harbor. Painted by Shiba Kokan in the 1790s (Kobe City Museum/DNPartcom).

were made in Yokohama after the Treaty of Kanagawa opened the port in 1854. These prints, called *Yokohama-e*, are prized by print collectors due to their rarity. Nagasaki-e, harking back to the late 16th Century, are even more rare.

Artists closely studied books on painting techniques from the West. Some included these new Western techniques in their work, incorporating shadows, perspective and painting the sky blue – thus distinguishing their work from traditional *nihonga* ("Japanese-style paintings"). In 1773, the rangaku scholar Hiraga Gennai was brought to what is now Aki Prefecture to advise the daimyo Satake Yoshiatsu on copper mining. The two men were both artists who incorporated Western techniques in their work, and they created the Akita Ranga School of painting. That same year, Gennai met Shiba Kokan, a printmaker who specialized in *ukiyo-e* ("floating world") prints, and Kokan was influenced by Gennai to create prints in this style.

Englebert Kaempfer (1651-1716) was one of the first German scholars to visit Japan. His book *A History of Japan*, published posthumously in 1727, was the chief source of Western knowledge about the country for decades.

His odyssey began in 1681, when he was commissioned by the Government of Sweden to establish a consulate in Isfahan, Persia (present-day Iran). He arrived in the city in 1684, but a year later his peers in the Swedish legation returned

"It is one globe in miniature. When the people of these islands, mutually traversing considerable distances by water and land, entertain friendly relations and trade with each other, they already have the pleasure of roaming around and seeing exceptional sights throughout the whole of the country." – Shizuki Tadao Englebert Kaempfer's exquisite map of the Nagasaki-Kokura highway, circa 1691.

home, and Kaempfer joined the VOC as a surgeon, spending the subsequent four years traveling across Persia. In August 1688 he sailed for Batavia, reaching the Dutch colony in 1689, and traveling onwards to Japan in 1690. After two years in

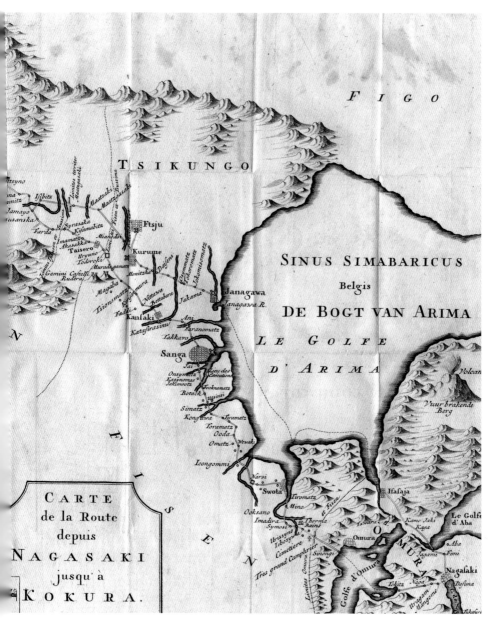

Japan he returned to The Netherlands, gained his Doctorate of Medicine and began publishing his manuscripts, mostly on plant and animal life in the places he had visited.

In life, despite his extensive travels and laudable, diligent research, Kaempfer was unable to publish the majority of his works. It was only after his death, in 1716, that his papers were purchased by Sir Hans Sloane, then president of the Royal College of Physicians and a collector, who had the works translated into English by his librarian, John Gaspar Scheuchzer. Upon his own death in 1753, Sloane bequeathed his library, and objects collected during his illustrious career, to the British people. These possessions formed the foundation of the British Museum, which opened in 1759.

"Think of me as often as I think of you, when one or another of your herbs speaks to me in your stead."
– Carl Linneaus in a letter to Carl Thunberg

A sample of the Japanese lady slipper (*Cypripedium japonicum*), collected and described by Thunberg, courtesy of Uppsala University.

Some European scholars headed to Dejima to discover what little they could about Japan. Carl Thunberg, a Swedish physician and botanist, traveled to Dejima and exchanged his expertise in Western medicine for plant specimens. He catalogued a vast array in his book *Flora Japonica*, published in 1784. It was the first compendium of knowledge in the West of Japanese plant life, identifying more than 250 species of flora and fauna. Thunberg is sometimes called the "Japanese Linnaeus." A fitting title, as Thunberg studied under and was one of the heralded "apostles" of Carl Linnaeus, the father of modern taxonomy, at Uppsala University.

Katsuragawa Hoshu, a student of Thunberg, was a leading rangaku scholar who co-authored a translation of a Western anatomy textbook, the first of its kind in

Japan. Hoshu's younger brother, Morishima Churyo, published a humorous volume *Sayings of the Dutch*, which detailed various discoveries in the West, like hot-air balloons, microscopes and static electricity.

The Tale of the Forty-seven Ronin

In 1619, Asano Nagaakira, the daimyo of Wakayama, was made the daimyo of Hiroshima. He moved to Hiroshima Castle and his descendants would rule the area until feudal titles were abolished in 1871. The Asano clan came to prominence with Nagaakira's father Nagamasa, Hideyoshi's close advisor and brother-in-law. In addition to Hiroshima, the clan also ruled the adjacent domains of Bingo and Aki, but it is probably most famous for its role in one the best-known samurai stories, the Tale of the Forty-seven Ronin.

In 1701, Daimyo Asano Naganori of Aki and Daimyo Kamei of Tsuwano were asked to prepare a reception for the Emperor at Edo Castle. Kira Kozuke-no-Suke Yoshinaka, a powerful official under Shogun Tsunayoshi, offended the pair during their preparation because they neglected to bribe him. Asano weathered his insults, but Kamei prepared to kill Kira to avenge his insults. However, seeking to avoid conflict Kamei's retainers quickly bribed the insolent Kira, who then treated Kamei more politely but continued to insult Asano, finally calling him a country boor with no manners. Asano could no longer restrain himself and attacked Kira, drawing his dagger and stabbing him.

Kira's wound was not serious, but violence of any kind was not permitted within Edo Castle, and Asano was ordered to commit seppuku. His lands were confiscated, his family members were made destitute and his retainers were made *ronin* (masterless samurai).

Forty-seven of Asano's retainers plotted revenge, taking on the role of workmen to familiarize themselves with the layout of Kira's household. After two years of planning, the ronin killed Kira in revenge, cutting off his head and laying it on their former master's grave as an offering. They were then arrested and ordered to commit seppuku for the crime of murder.

Following page: *"Since ancient times, in both China and our land alike, it has been contrary to the way of the warrior to leave one's enemy at peace."* – The ronin Otaka Gengo's farewell letter, written prior to taking part in the massacre
A depiction of the 47 ronin taking their revenge upon Kira Yoshinaka and his household.

AN ISOLATED NATION

America on the horizon

The first American to set eyes on Japan was a whaler and naval officer from Wareham, Massachusetts named John Kendrick. Kendrick became a mariner through whaling, joining the Continental Navy in 1777, at the height of the Revolutionary War. Throughout the war he disrupted the Royal Navy and traveled to Europe to enlist the support of the French and Spanish navies in America's War of Independence. He was captured by the British in 1779, and soon thereafter released, in a prisoner exchange. After the war he returned to the whaling business and, in 1787, was given command of the ship *Columbia Rediviva* and the sloop *Lady Washington* on a voyage of discovery and trade.

The expedition was financed by a group of investors from Boston. They learned that Captain James Cook (the famous English explorer who mapped much of the Pacific Ocean) was involved in the lucrative sea otter pelt trade in the Pacific Northwest during his third and final voyage, and were determined to share in the spoils. The *Columbia Rediviva*, and her tender *Lady Washington*, became the first American vessels to pass through the Straits of Magellan, and eventually reached the Pacific Northwest, where the Russians and British were actively involved in the fur trade.

Robert Gray, the captain of the *Lady Washington*, was given command of the *Columbia Rediviva* from Kendrick, and sailed to Macau via the Sandwich Islands in 1790. He then returned to Boston, making the ship the first American vessel to circumnavigate the globe.

Above: *"Having met with a terrible typhoon off the coast of Japan, he had on account of damages... given up all hope of proceeding to America until the following spring."* – Captain Bishop of *The Ruby*
The *Columbia Rediviva* forging a path through broiling seas in a typhoon.

Kendrick, meanwhile, took the *Lady Washington* to Macau, where the sloop was upgraded to a brigantine. He turned the vessel towards Japan in March 1791, accompanied by the ship *Grace*, captained by Scotsman William Douglas. The pair reached Japan on May 6, 1791, where Kendrick tried to make trades, but was turned away after a week of negotiations. He and Douglas then went to the Bonin archipelago, south of Japan, where they parted ways.

In 1794, Kendrick and two British vessels assisted Kaeokulani, Chief of Kauai (modern Hawaii) in an unsuccessful invasion of Oahu. On December 12, 1794, off Honolulu, the British ship *Jackal* fired a 13-gun salute for the *Lady Washington*, but one of the cannons was loaded with real ammunition and it killed Kendrick as it smashed through the ship's hull.

To avoid capture by the British, the annual Dutch ship from Batavia to Nagasaki in 1797 was an American ship, the *Eliza*, which flew an American flag and was piloted by New York native Captain William Stewart. The ship completed the same journey in 1798, but it sank shortly after leaving Nagasaki Harbor. The ship for the 1799 trip was another American ship, *Franklin*, from Boston, piloted by Captain James Devereux. Captain Stewart returned to Japan aboard the *Eliza* in 1800, which he'd renamed *The Emperor of Japan*. The Dutch confiscated his cargo as contraband and sold it to recover the debt he owed for the repairs to *Eliza*.

More American ships came to Nagasaki in the following years: the *Massachusetts* of Boston in 1800, then the *Margaret* of Salem in 1801, the *Samuel Smith* under Captain G. Stiles in 1802, and the *Rebecca* of Baltimore in 1803. The ship *America* arrived in Nagasaki in 1806 and *Mount Vernon* in 1807. Captain Stewart returned to Nagasaki in 1803 aboard the *Frederick*, but was unable to sell any cargo.

Dutch decline and Russian interest

After the fourth Anglo-Dutch War (1780-1784), the VOC was in dire financial straits. It was finally dissolved on December 31, 1799. From then on, trade at Dejima was handled directly by the Batavian Republic, which had replaced the Dutch Republic in 1795.

The Batavian Republic lasted until 1806, when Napoleon installed his younger brother, Louis I, as the King of Holland. The English were determined to destroy the Dutch-French monopoly of trade in the South Seas, and their naval forces fought against the Dutch fleet during the Napoleonic Wars. To protect their cargo from seizure by British ships, Dutch traders chartered American ships to transport their goods from Batavia to Nagasaki. Once they reached Japanese waters, the crew hoisted the Dutch flag and fired the required gun salutes as they sailed into port.

On July 8, 1799, the Tsar chartered the Russian-American Company ostensibly for a fur trading enterprise. His true purpose, however, was to expand Russian territory eastward. In 1803, the company financed the first circumnavigation of the globe by a Russian ship, which launched from St. Petersburg in August 1803, under Adam Johann Ritter von Krusenstern. The primary remit of the expedition was to report on company activities, as it had an active fur trading operation in what is now Sitka, Alaska, partially secured by the company's new director Alexandr Baranov. The secondary objective of the expedition was to establish trade and diplomatic relations with Japan and China, brokered by fleet commander Nikolai Rezanov.

"They carried to Japan about two hundred prime sea otter skins but the Japanese knew not the use of them." – Sailor John Hoskins

Putiatin and his crew pose with the Russian Imperial flag.

The expedition reached Nagasaki in September 1804, but the Russians failed to endear themselves to their hosts. In his book about the expedition, Captain von Krusenstern recalled:

"Everyone knows the insulting jealousy which is observed towards strangers in Japan; we had no right to expect a more favorable treatment than other nations; yet, as we had an ambassador on board, who was sent merely with assurances of friendship by the monarch of a powerful empire bordering upon these people so suspicious in their politics, we hoped not to be received unfavorably.

Although we certainly expected to be allowed more liberty than the Dutch enjoy here, we found ourselves greatly mistaken. This trifling freedom, which can only be called so when compared with our confined state on board the ship, and which appeared to us at first so despicable that we should have rejected it with scorn, if it had been offered to us on condition that we should demand no more; even his little was entirely denied us, and the time of our stay here was literally a confinement, from which the ambassador was no more exempted than the meanest sailor in the ship."

The expedition was resigned to leaving empty-handed in April 1805, and arrived back in St. Petersburg in 1806. During their stay, Nagasaki printmakers, who had always been fascinated by Europeans or "red-headed barbarians," made a series of engravings of the intrepid Admiral Rezanov and Captain von Krusenstern, which were subsequently widely distributed in Japan.

The printmakers in Nagasaki had earlier made a host of engravings of Dutchmen, and the Western inventions they brought, and these sold widely in Japan. Especially popular were prints of the first Western ladies to set foot in Japan: Titia Bergsma, wife of the VOC's Hirado Opperhoofd (Factory Director) Jan Bloemhoff, and her servant Petronella Muns. The two of them arrived on Dejima in July 1817, when Jan Bloemhoff replaced Hendrik Doeff as Opperhoofd. His one-year-old son Johannes also accompanied them.

Western women and children were not permitted in Japan, but the *bugyo* (Governor) of Nagasaki, Matsuyama Naoyoshi, made an exemption on July 16, 1817. However, the Shogun, Tokugawa Ienari, refused to sanction residency permits for Bergsma and Muns, who were ordered to leave Nagasaki on December 4, 1817. By this time local printmakers had made almost 500 engravings of them.

On October 4, 1808, the HMS *Phaeton* entered Nagasaki Harbor flying a Dutch flag in the hopes of ambushing Dutch ships. When Dutch representatives approached the ship they were taken hostage and

"Their Way of Marriage is truly correct. Once a man is married he does not mix with other women, nor does a wife meet other men. Mutually they observe the love between husband and wife and have no affection for others." – Ando Shoeki

A Nagasaki-e depicting Titia Cock-Blomhoff and her wet-nurse, Petronella Muns, holding baby Johannes.

Captain Fleetwood Pellew demanded that the port provide supplies for the ship's crew, firing on Dejima to make sure the demands were met. When Captain Pellew learned that Dutch ships would not be coming, that they had arrived earlier in the year, he ensured his ship was resupplied, and departed within two days.

The incident with the HMS *Phaeton* prompted the Shogun Tokugawa Ienari to issue an edict saying all foreign vessels, except for Dutch and Chinese ships, should be driven away from Japanese shores, and any foreigners who set foot ashore would be put to death.

When France occupied The Netherlands during the Napoleonic Wars, Britain used the conflict to take possession of Dutch colonies. After the British invaded Java in 1811, Dejima was the only place in the world to fly the Dutch flag, on the insistence of Opperhoofd Hendrik Doeff. In 1815 the Conference of Vienna restored The Netherlands, and Britain returned those colonies that it had claimed, with the exception of Guyana and the Cape Colony (now South Africa). Doeff was later decorated by The Netherlands for his loyalty.

"Lend me your arms, fast as thunderbolts, for a pillow on my journey." – A haiku composed by Hendrik Doeff
A vignette of Opperhoofd Hendrik Doeff, painted by Kawahara Keiga.

"A garish flag, to be the aim of every dangerous shot." – William Shakespeare
The Dutch flag stands out proudly against Nagasaki harbor, in a painting by Kawahara Keiga.

Following in the footsteps of Thunberg and Kaempfer, Philipp Franz von Siebold became Dejima's resident scientist in 1823, and like his predecessors, he contributed significantly to Japanese knowledge of the West. Siebold had been inspired by Alexander von Humboldt's landmark travels to South America at the turn of the century, and desired a career in medicine in foreign lands. He got his wish when he arrived in Dejima.

Siebold established a medical school in Nagasaki, where he trained doctors and studied Japanese flora and fauna. The school trained as many as 50 students at a time, instructing them in the use of medical instruments and, when vaccines were successfully introduced to Japan in the 1840s, his students were the first to administer them.

"We have now to thank the Russians and not the Americans for the opening of Japan."
– Philipp Franz von Siebold

He lived with, but remained unwedded to due to Shogunate dictates, a Japanese woman, Kusumoto Otaki, and with her had a daughter, Ine, in 1827. In 1828, after completing his term at Dejima, his boat, bound for Batavia, was wrecked and washed ashore in the Ryuku islands during a typhoon. His belongings were searched, and it was revealed that a portrait of the Shogun and an official survey map of the entirety of Japan, recently completed for the government by Ino Tadataka, were in his possession. Foreigners were forbidden to have such items; Siebold was accused of being a Russian spy, and sentenced to house arrest. After one year of incarceration he was expelled from Japan and forbidden to return.

Back in The Netherlands he remarried and after donating his substantial botanical collection to the government, he was hired as an advisor to the King on Japanese matters. His banishment was ended in 1858 when The Netherlands and Japan signed the Treaty of Amity and Commerce ("The Harris Treaty"). He returned to Japan and was reunited with his Japanese wife and daughter.

His daughter Ine was now 32 and married with a child. She'd kept in touch with her father during his years in exile, while he'd sent her medical supplies, and his former students trained her in medicine. By the time her father returned, Ine was the first female doctor of Western medicine in Japan, specializing in gynecology.

Herman Melville and the whaling industry

On July 30, 1837, the SS *Morrison* dropped anchor at Uraga Bay, near Edo Bay, with the intention of returning seven Japanese castaways. Among her crew were Samuel Wells Williams, a linguist and missionary from upstate New York, based in Guangdong. The ship and her crew were fired upon with cannons, and aborted their attempt. The ship then sailed to Kagoshima, where they were also fired upon. Charles W. King, captain of the *Morrison*, returned to the United States in 1839 and wrote,"the next contact with Japan had better be left to the stronger and wiser action of the American Government."

"War should be carried on like a monsoon; one changeless determination of every particle towards the one unalterable aim."
– Herman Melville

It would be more than a decade before King's prophetic words came true, but in the meantime another activity was causing interaction between America and Japan. Beginning in the 1820s, American whaling ships became active in the Pacific Ocean between Japan and the Sandwich Islands (Hawaii). In 1842, Herman Melville journeyed through these waters during his four years on the whaling ship *Acushnet*. On his return to New York, he wrote two successful novels based on his experiences: *Typee* (1846) and *Omoo* (1847). He would return to his experiences in his novel *White-Jacket* (1850).

The following excerpt from *Typee* criticized the activities of missionaries in the Pacific, echoing many of the concerns the Shogunate had of the Portuguese missionaries:

> *"The naked wretch who shivers beneath the bleak skies, and starves among the inhospitable wilds of Tierra-del-Fuego, might indeed be made happier by civilization, for it would alleviate his physical wants. But the voluptuous India, with every desire supplied, whom Providence has bountifully provided with all the sources of pure and natural enjoyment, and from whom are removed so many of the ills and pains of life – what has he to desire at the hands of Civilization? She may 'cultivate his mind,' may 'elevate his thoughts,' – these I believe are the established phrases, but will he be happier? Let the once smiling and populous Hawaiian islands, with their now diseased,*

starving, and dying natives, answer that question. The missionaries may seek to disguise the matter as they will, but the facts are incontrovertible; and the devoutest Christians who visit the group with an unbiased mind, must go away mournfully asking – 'Are these, alas, the fruits of twenty-five years of enlightening?'"

White Jacket had graphic descriptions of flogging, and Melville's American publisher, Harper & Brothers, now HarperCollins, made sure every member of Congress got a copy: the book was instrumental in Congress banning flogging in the US Navy on September 28, 1850. Public interest in the issue had been piqued a decade earlier with another literary work, Richard Henry Dana's *Two Years Before the Mast*,

published in 1840. Melville would revisit the issue of flogging in Billy Budd, which was discovered in a lacquered ("japanned") tin box almost 30 years after his death in 1891.

Melville's novel *Moby Dick; or, The Whale*, published in 1851, is now considered one of the Great American novels. Among the many issues it comments on, the book argues for the importance of whale hunters – this was in the days when whale oil was one of the most valuable substances, used in oil lamps and in

"Human madness is oftentimes a cunning and most feline thing. When you think it fled, it may have but become transfigured into still subtler form." – Herman Melville

The cursed white whale, bane of Ahab, encircles his foe, before the final blow is struck.

manufacturing soap and margarine (manufacturers switched to petroleum a few years after *Moby Dick* was released, as a cheaper alternative to whale oil). Despite its importance, the crews of whaling ships were subject to harsh conditions and a worse reputation on shore. Melville made a strong case for the importance of the whaler in Chapter 24 of *Moby Dick*, which includes this line: "If that double-bolted land, Japan, is ever to become hospitable, it is the whale-ship alone to whom the credit will be due; for already she is on the threshold."

Before heading off to sea, the narrator Ishmael sees a memorial to Ezekiel Hardy, killed by a sperm whale off the coast of Japan. The boat he boards, the *Pequod*, lost its original masts in a typhoon near Japan during Captain Ahab's previous attempt to find the great white whale. As the *Pequod* approaches the whaling grounds near Japan in Chapter 119, Melville writes: "…in these resplendent Japanese seas the mariner encounters the direst of all storms, the Typhoon. It will sometimes burst from out that cloudless sky, like an exploding bomb upon a dazed and sleepy town."

Further rejection

In 1843, President John Tyler sent Caleb Cushing to Canton to open diplomatic relations with China, in the hope of ending British dominance in Chinese trade. The US and China signed the Treaty of Wanghia on July 3, 1844. Among its provisions, it gave American merchants immunity from local prosecution, and opened five ports to American ships, the largest being Shanghai. The easiest way to reach Shanghai was

by traveling from the Sandwich Islands through the Tsugaru Strait, which separates Honshu and Hokkaido.

In 1846, the SS *Columbus* and the SS *Vincennes*, under the command of Commodore James Biddle, anchored in Uraga Channel. Biddle requested that Japan open her ports for trade, citing the Treaty of Wanghia. The official response from the Shogunate was that trade was solely conducted with the Dutch at Nagasaki, and that Biddle should leave immediately.

"The winged words uttered in this House have gone forth to the world, on their mission of good or of evil."
– Caleb Cushing

The next American to reach Japan was a former bank clerk from the Oregon Territory named Ranald McDonald. He sailed to Japan aboard the SS *Plymouth*, and reached Rishiri Island, off Hokkaido, pretending to be shipwrecked. He was captured and sent to Nagasaki where he taught English to some of the local samurai, including Moriyama Einosuke – Moriyama would later become a translator for Matthew Perry (see next chapter).

McDonald was kept in Nagasaki, along with 18 other prisoners, sailors on the whaling ship *Lagoda* who had been captured off the coast of Japan in 1846. Lieutenant James Glynn learned of this situation whilst in Canton, and sent his ship the USS *Preble* to Nagasaki, where he demanded their release. All the prisoners were released and returned to the United States by 1849.

Japan's rejection of all attempts to open up trade with foreigners other than the Dutch continued with rigid intransigence. The English professor and writer Henry Morley, in his "Our Phantom Ship" collection of essays, serialized in *Household Words* (and edited by Charles Dickens), wrote the following excerpt about Japan, published on May 10, 1851:

> *"There is a mighty difference between this England, talking about liberty, or cherishing free trade, and that Dai Nippon, in which not a soul does as he pleases, and from which the commerce of the whole world is shut out. Dai (or great) Nippon is the name of the whole state, which the Chinese modify into Jihpun, and which we have further altered to Japan. On Kiusiu, a large southern island, Nagasaki is the only port into which, on any possible excuse, a foreign vessel is allowed to enter.*
>
> *This port we are now approaching; the dark rocks of the coastline are reflected from a brilliant sea; we pass a mountain island, cultivated to the very summit, terrace above terrace; green hills invite us to our haven, and blue mountains in the distance tempt us to an onward journey. There are white houses shining among cedars; there are pointed temple roofs; boats with their sails up make the water near us lively; surely we shall like Japan.*
>
> *We enter the bay now, and approach Nagasaki, between fruitful hills and temple groves, steeps clothed with evergreen oak, cedars, and laurels; picturesque rocks, attacked by man, and wheedled out of practicable ground for corn and cabbages. There is Nagasaki on a hillside, regularly built, every house peeping from its little nest of greens; and there is the Dutch factory, named Dezima. Zima in Japanese means "island," for this factory is built upon*

"I find the great thing in this world is not so much where we stand, as in what direction we are moving: To reach the port of heaven, we must sail sometimes with the wind and sometimes against it – but we must sail, and not drift, nor lie at anchor." – Oliver Wendell Holmes, Sr.

Aerial View of the Harbor of Nagasaki with the Dutch Frigate Cornelia *and* Henriette, painted by Kawahara Keiga.

an island. No Europeans but the Dutch; no Dutch except these managers of trade who are locked up in Dezima, may traffic with Japan; and these may traffic to the extent only of two ships yearly, subject to all manner of restrictions.

As for the resident Dutch, they are locked up in Dezima, which is an island made on purpose for them. As if three thousand, eight hundred and fifty were not enough, another little island, fan-shaped, was built up out of the sea a few yards from the shore of Nagasaki. There the Dutchmen live; a bridge connects their island with the mainland, but a high gate and a guard of soldiers prevent all unseasonable rambles.

In another part of the town there is a factory allowed to the Chinese. Other strangers entering this port are treated courteously, are supplied gratuitously with such necessaries as they want, but are on no account allowed to see the town, still less to penetrate into the country, and are required to be gone about their business as soon as possible. Strangers attempting entry at any other port belonging to Japan, are without ceremony fired upon as enemies.

The admitted Dutch traders are rigorously searched; everything betraying Christianity is locked up; money and arms are removed, and hostages are taken. Every man undergoes personal scrutiny. The Dutch are allowed no money. The Japanese authorities manage all sales for them; pay the minutest items of

"At his best, man is the noblest of all animals; separated from law and justice he is the worst." – Aristotle
The finely detailed engraving entitled *The accomplishments of the courts of Japan* was crafted by Jacques Nicolas Bellin, a famed French cartographer, hydrographer and traveler, during his journeys in the Orient.

expenditure, and charge it on the profits of their trade, which are then placed on the return vessel, not in money, but in goods. The Japanese deal justly, even generously, in their way; but it is their way to allow the foreigners no money power. They restrict their exports almost wholly to camphor and copper, and allow no native workmanship to go abroad. Yet among themselves, as between one island and another, commerce is encouraged to the utmost.

The Japanese territories range in the temperate zone through a good many degrees, and include all shades of climate between that of Liverpool and that of Constantinople. Between island and island, therefore, busy

*interchange takes place by means of junks, like these which now surround us
in the Nagasaki harbour.*

*You can observe how weak they look about the stems, with rudders
insecure. The law compels them to be so: for that is an acute device by which
they are prevented from travelling too far; they dare not trust themselves
too boldly to the mercy of the sea, and as it is, many wrecked men accuse
the prudence of their lawgivers. But life is cheap; the population of Japan is
probably near thirty million, and who should care for a few dozen mariners?"*

Japonism

International Exhibitions began with the Great Exhibition in London in 1851. At the
2nd London exhibition in 1862, British Consul General in Japan Rutherford Alcock
took Japanese items from his private collection and put them on display. Officially,
the first time Japan appeared at an exhibition was at the Vienna International
Exhibition in 1873, but it had another significant appearance a few years earlier.

In 1867, the Shogunate sent several objects to the International Exhibition in
Paris. The Parisian artists who attended were captivated by what they saw and
the artwork brought from Japan had a profound influence on their work, known as
"Japonism." Vincent Van Gogh and his brother Theo collected nearly 400 *ukiyo-e*
prints, and Vincent repainted some of them in his own style.

Édouard Manet's controversial painting *Olympia* featured a nude woman drawn
without depth, much like a Japanese print. Manet included a sketch of *Olympia*
within his painting of writer Emile Zola, which also has Japanese prints in the
background. Claude Monet had his wife pose in a Japanese kimono and painted her
in 1875. Giverny, where he lived, had a Japanese-style bridge which features in
some of his water lily paintings.

Artistic influence by Japan spread further than painting. While writing *The
Mikado*, W.S. Gilbert was struck by inspiration after a Japanese sword fell off the
wall in his study, and set the operetta in Japan. He also visited the Japanese village
exhibition in Knightsbridge while writing the work.

The first edition of Claude Debussy's orchestral work *La Mer* had "The Great
Wave off Kanagawa" on its front cover. Debussy had a copy of the world-famous
print in his office and some accounts claim that the print inspired the work itself.
Such was the interest in this mysterious island nation in the second half of the 19th
century – but we are getting ahead of ourselves: before the West could romanticize
Japan, it had to be forced to open its borders.

"I leave my brush in the East. And set forth on my journey. I shall see the famous places in the Western Land."
– Utagawa Hiroshige's Death Poem

Hiroshige's *Sudden Shower Over Shin-Ohashi Bridge and Atake,* painted in 1857. He never journeyed to the Occident, but his style influenced Cézanne, Monet, Van Gogh, and Whistler.

"All my work is based to some extent on Japanese art..." – Vincent Van Gogh

Van Gogh's *Bridge in the Rain,* an homage to Utagawa Hiroshige's own artful mastery.

"In the West what we admired most of all was this bold way of cropping images; these people taught us to compose differently." – Claude Monet

Monet's *La Japonaise* (*Camille Monet in Japanese costume*), painted in 1876.
Photograph © Museum of Fine Arts, Boston.

"Look, we love Japanese painting, we've experienced its influence – all the Impressionists have that in common." – Vincent Van Gogh

Van Gogh's *La Courtisane*, painted in 1887. His inspiration was drawn from the countless *ukiyo-e* purchased on the docks, particularly from his time in Antwerp.

Doors Open and a New Japan Emerges

Treaties, both fair and unfair

On July 8, 1853, four American ships, the *Mississippi*, *Plymouth*, *Saratoga*, and *Susquehanna* anchored in Uraga Bay. Between them, the *Mississippi* and *Susquehanna* were equipped with 16 Paixhans guns, also known as "canon-obusiers," which were nearly 10 feet (three meters) long and the first guns to fire explosive shells. Aboard the *Susquehanna* was Commodore Matthew Perry, a 44-year Navy veteran who had served in the War of 1812, the Mexican-American War, and the fight against the African Slave Trade.

"We know that the ancient laws of Your Imperial Majesty's government do not allow foreign trade except with the Dutch. But as the state of the world changes, and new governments are formed, it seems to be wise from time to time to make new laws." – Commodore Perry

Commodore Perry in conference with his Japanese counterparts.

In his hand, Perry had a letter from President Millard Fillmore asking Japan to open itself to trade with the United States. As before, he was told to go to Nagasaki, but he threatened to use force, and delegates of Shogun Ieyoshi ordered him to

"In conducting all my business with these very sagacious and deceitful people, I have found it profitable to bring to my aid the experience gained in former and by no means limited intercourse with the inhabitants of strange lands — civilized and barbarian — and this experience has admonished me that with people of forms it is necessary either to set all ceremony aside, or to out-Herod Herod in assumed personal consequence and ostentation." – Commodore Perry

Members of Matthew Perry's crew struggle to grasp Japanese culture, suffering at the hands of the martially virtuous society.

land at what is now Yokosuka, around the headland from Uraga, where they received President Fillmore's letter. Perry's fleet departed for China, promising to return with the expectation of a reply.

In fear of an American naval bombardment, the Japanese built fortifications around Edo. When Perry returned in 1854, this time with a fleet of eight ships, the Japanese had prepared a treaty that satisfied most of President Fillmore's requests. It was signed at Kanagawa on March 31, 1854. The door to Japan had finally been opened.

Perry returned to the United States, but made a stopover in Liverpool. There he met the American Consul and famous novelist Nathaniel Hawthorne, friend of Herman Melville and dedicatee of *Moby Dick*. Perry was looking for someone to turn his notes of the voyage into a literary epic. Hawthorne declined, but recommended Melville for the task. Perry rejected the offer; Hawthorne suspected that Perry knew *Moby Dick* was a financial disappointment, but the disinterest may have been due to the differences of opinion between Perry and Melville – Perry had not supported Congress's ban on flogging, which happened after the publication of *White Jacket*.

Perry was a devout Protestant, as was his eventual collaborator, Francis Hawks. His conservativeness is especially apparent in a passage of Perry's narrative, describing a bathhouse in Shimoda, on the Izu Peninsula, south of Mt Fuji:

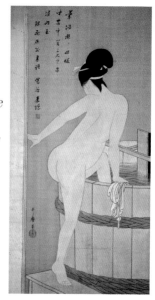

"A scene at one of the public baths, where the sexes mingled indiscriminately, unconscious of their nudity, was not calculated to impress the Americans with a very favorable opinion of the morals of the inhabitants. This may not be a universal practice throughout Japan, and indeed is said by the Japanese near us not to be; but the Japanese people of the inferior ranks are undoubtedly, notwithstanding their moral superiority to most oriental nations, a lewd people. Apart from the bathing scenes, there was enough in the popular literature, with its obscene pictorial illustrations, to prove a licentiousness of taste and practice among a certain class of the population, that was not only disgustingly intrusive, but disgracefully indicative of foul corruption."

Even before it opened up to the world, Japan had begun the process of industrializing to try and catch up with its Western peers. In 1852 the daimyo of Satsuma, Shimazu Nariakira, successfully petitioned the government to allow the construction of ocean-going vessels. A shipyard was built in his domain and in May 1853 it launched its first ship, the *Shohei Maru*, built using ship construction manuals obtained from the Dutch at Dejima.

Nariakira had long been interested in Western technology and studied it as a young man. In 1848 he obtained the first daguerreotype camera ever exported to Japan and ordered his retainers to study it. In 1857, his retainer Ichiki Shiro took a photograph of Nariakira, and the photograph is the oldest surviving photo taken by a Japanese photographer.

Above: *"A bath refreshes the body, tea refreshes the mind."* – Japanese Proverb
A Japanese lady elegantly sinks into a *furo*, a traditional wooden bath and key apparatus of the purifying bathing rituals characteristic of the nation.
Opposite: *"Gather information on all the events that happen along the coast of the Asian continent and near the coasts of our North-Western territories in America."* – Secret Instructions for Admiral Putiatin, from the Navy Ministry
Admiral Putiatin poses for the printmaker Yamatoya during his relatively brief diplomatic mission.

Meanwhile, at the same time as America's expedition, Russia sent a new ambassadorial expedition around the world, with a remit to establish relations with Japan. Aboard the *Pallada*, the expedition's lead vessel, novelist Ivan Gorachev worked as a secretary to the expedition leader Admiral Ephimy Putiatin. His book *The Frigate Pallada*, named for the ship, was published soon after they returned to St. Petersburg in 1855, and was very popular in its time.

Putiatin's expedition arrived in Nagasaki on August 21, 1853, six weeks after Matthew Perry had landed at Uraga. While there, following the example of his predecessor, he posed for a printmaker, but in December 1854 his ships were destroyed in the Ansei Tokai Earthquake and the ensuing tsunami. The Treaty of Shimoda, which established relations between Russia and Japan, was signed on February 7, 1855. On May 8, 1855, Putiatin returned to Russia aboard the schooner *Heda*, built by Russian and Japanese shipwrights.

When Commodore Perry returned to New York from negotiating the Treaty of Kanagawa, some critics thought the voyage had been a waste of time, as the treaty did not outline an agreement for bilateral trade. The criticism was squashed when the first American ambassador to Japan, Townsend Harris, negotiated a further treaty, which satisfied Perry's critics. The Harris Treaty (1858), the first in what Japan came to call the "Unequal Treaties" (*Fubyodo joyaku*), opened various ports to American traders.

Japan signed a total of five treaties in 1858, opening trade to five Western powers: the United States in July, The Netherlands, Russia, and Britain in August, and finally France in October. Jointly these were termed the Ansei Five-Power Treaties. Provisions in each ensured Western trading agents with immunity from prosecution, control of duties would be determined by each respective Western power, rather than by Japan, and in addition to Nagasaki, the ports of Edo (renamed Tokyo in 1868), Kobe, Niigata and Yokohama would become open for foreign trade.

"You have been more than a friend. You have been our benefactor and teacher. Your spirit and memory will live forever in the history of Japan." – Einosuke Moriyama, Japanese diplomat, in a letter to Consul General Harris The 1860 Japanese Mission to the United States, preserved in perpetuity by Matthew Brady.

The United States ratified the Treaty of Kanagawa in 1860. That same year, the Tairo (the Shogun's chief policy maker), Ii Naosuke, was assassinated outside Edo Castle. He had been one of the leading advocates of reopening the country to foreign trade, going as far as ordering the Ansei Purge in 1858, when the government forced out opponents of foreign trade. Naosuke's assassins carried a manifesto on them that read, in part:

> *"While fully aware of the necessity for some change in policy since the coming of the Americans to Uraga, it is entirely against the interest of the country and a stain on the national honor to open up commercial relations with foreigners, to admit foreigners into [Edo] Castle, to conclude treaties with them, to abolish the established practice of trampling on the picture of Christ, to permit foreigners to build places of worship for the evil religion, and to allow the three foreign Ministers to reside in the land. Under the excuse of keeping the peace, too much compromise has been made at the sacrifice of national honor; too much fear has been shown for foreigners' threats. Not only has the national custom been set aside and the national dignity impaired, but the policy followed by the Bakufu has no Imperial sanction... [Ii Naosuke] has proved himself to be an unpardonable national enemy... Our sense of patriotism could not brook this abuse of power at the hands of such a wicked rebel. Therefore we have consecrated ourselves to be the instruments of Heaven to punish this wicked man, and we have taken on ourselves the duty of ending a serious evil, by killing this atrocious aristocrat."*

The Ikokujin: foreign settlers

After the ratification of the unequal Ansei Treaties, Western firms began opening offices in Japan. Jardine Matheson was one of the first firms to arrive in each of the treaty ports, while the Hong Kong Shanghai Bank opened its first offices in Japan in 1866. Each of the five ports created foreign settlements specifically for alien traders. Nagasaki built its foreign settlement near the Oura Creek, ordering all foreign residents to move in once it was completed in 1862.

In 1859, a 21-year-old employee of Jardine Matheson transferred to Nagasaki. His name was Thomas Blake Glover; he would stay in Japan until his death, nearly 50 years later, and became one of the most well-known *gaijin* (outsiders) of his time. Glover was born in Aberdeenshire, and joined Jardine Matheson as soon as he finished school. He was sent to Shanghai, but a few years later was transferred to Nagasaki, where over the next decade he made a fortune selling ships to Japan and buying green tea from them, like his colleague William Alt (see below). By 1863, Glover & Company was the largest trading firm in Japan.

Glover also made a fortune selling arms to the daimyo of Choshu, who used those arms against the forces of the Shogun in the Boshin War. As a result, Glover was in the good graces of the Emperor Meiji when power was wrested from the Shogun in 1868.

Among the innovations Glover introduced to Japan were the railroad – the first track laid in Japan was an experimental track in Oura laid to demonstrate rail transport with the Iron Duke, brought over by Glover in 1868. The first passenger rail track, between Tokyo and Yokohama, was opened in 1872.

In 1870, Glover & Company went bankrupt and Glover moved to Osaka, where he worked in the management of the Tsukumo Trading Company,

"Glover was one of the few men who found admission to the inner shrine of Japanese life in days when the stranger from abroad rarely penetrated further than the genkan [doorway]."
– W.B. Mason, Japanese scholar and journalist
A portrait of Thomas Blake Glover in Nagasaki.

which changed its name to Mitsubishi in 1873. Among Glover's later achievements was being the first President of the Japan Brewing Company, now known as Kirin Brewing Company, one of the largest brewers in Japan.

Glover married Yamamura Tsuru and had two children with her. His house is now a museum and during the American occupation of Japan after World War II it was called the "Madame Butterfly House," giving rise to the misconception that he may have been the inspiration for Puccini's opera *Madame Butterfly*.

A contemporary of Glover's, and like him one of the most successful early foreign settlers in Japan, was William Alt, who arrived in Nagasaki in January 1860. He started as a commission agent for the British Consulate at the age of 19, attaining a role in governing the enclave, and soon gained prowess as a businessman, as he made a fortune buying Japanese green tea and selling British weapons and ships. He subsequently moved on to Osaka's newly opened foreign settlement in 1868, and to Yokohama 18 months later, before returning to England in 1871.

"Money... is none of the wheels of trade: it is the oil which renders the motion of the wheels more smooth and easy."
– David Hume, Scottish philosopher and diplomat

A street scene of the Oura area, site of the Oura Church and crucifixions of the 26 Japanese martyrs in 1597.

Another Westerner who settled in Nagasaki was Frederick Ringer, who started his career at Glover & Company selling Japanese tea. He quickly founded his own firm and was active in the political and social life of the city. He was among those who welcomed Ulysses S. Grant to Nagasaki in 1879, during the latter's world tour.

Studying the ways of the West

In 1863, with help from Glover & Company and William Matheson, five Japanese students were disguised as English sailors and sailed to London, where they studied at University College London. Known as the Choshu Five, they later returned and helped introduce many Western ideas to Japan, as well as making enormous contributions to its development. Endo Kinsuke helped create a unified national currency as head of the National Mint, while Inoue Masaru played a leading role in establishing railroads in Japan. Ito Hirobumi and Inoue Kaoru became the first

Prime Minister and first Foreign Minister of Japan respectively, when those positions were created in 1885. Ito also served as the first President of the House of Peers, which was modeled after the British House of Lords when the chamber was created in 1890. Yamao Yozo helped set up the Imperial College of Engineering (where he served as rector), the Department of Technology at Tokyo Imperial University, and was President of the Japan Engineering Society for 36 years. Mori Arinori, the first Japanese Minister of Education, followed the Choshu Five and studied at University College London in 1865. He served as Ambassador to the United States from 1871-1873.

In 1871, a group of Japanese officials led by Iwakura Tomomi set out on a mission to renegotiate the unequal treaties forced on Japan by the United States, Britain and other European powers. They were also tasked with investigating Western technology, government and culture. The mission was unsuccessful in repealing the treaties, but they brought back prolific notes on Western life. Ito Hirobumi joined a reception put on by the mission in Sacramento, saying, "We come to study your strength... that, by adopting wisely your better ways, we may hereafter be stronger ourselves."

The mission compiled notes on various systems of government, and noted how constitutions had limits placed on those in power and had an amendment process. Ideas from other constitutions gathered by the mission were incorporated into the Meiji Constitution. The mission also brought American David Murray to Japan. Dr. Murray was a professor of mathematics at Rutgers University, and under his advisory, public schools in Japan were created and modeled after their American counterparts.

"It is my opinion that there is no option but to use the barbarians' technology to hold the barbarians. If they have big battleships, we have to make big battleships too. If they have big canons, we have to make big canons, too." – Sakuma Shozan, an Edo Era politician, scholar and military scientist

The Choshu Five in London. Clockwise from left: Inoue Monta (seated), later Inoue Kaoru, the first Foreign Minister; Endo Kinsuke, director of the Mint Bureau; Nomura Yakichi (center), later Inoue Masaru, the "father of Japanese railways"; Ito Shunsuke, later Ito Hirobumi, the first Prime Minister; and Yamao Yozo, the "father of Japanese industrialization and engineering."

Xenophobia and the Battle of Shimonoseki Strait

However, as the unequal terms of the trade treaties came to light, a wave of xenophobia swept the land in the form of the Sonno Joi movement ("Revere the Emperor, Expel the Barbarians"). Emperor Komei, seeing an opportunity to garner and galvanize popular support, agreed with these sentiments and began playing a more active role in national affairs, in a bid to wrest the hereditary control of the state back from the Tokugawa Shogunate. On March 11, 1863, the Emperor issued the "Order to Expel Barbarians" (*Joi jikko no chokumei*).

Now with an Imperial seal of approval, attacks on foreigners increased, which infuriated the Western powers. When retainers of the daimyo of Satsuma killed a British trader, Charles Lenox Richardson, the Royal Navy bombarded Kagoshima in retaliation. The three-day conflict was known as the Anglo-Satsuma War.

In compliance with the Order to Expel Barbarians, in July forces loyal to Daimyo Mori Takachika of the Choshu Domain fired upon the US merchant ship *Pembroke* in the Straits of Shimonoseki. This bold if ultimately disastrous action was a clear expression of their loyalty to the revered Mikado (Emperor) of Japan, and ultra-nationalism. In response, perceiving the act as a harbinger of potential future dissent, the USS *Wyoming* arrived, under the auspices of the United States Minister in Japan, Robert H. Pruyn, and returned fire. The poorly manned Choshu fleet, despite assistance from land-based artillery, was decimated.

"Revere the emperor, expel the barbarians."
– Motto of the Sonno Joi movement

This 1861 poster expresses the anti-Western sentiments of Japan during the *Bakumatsu* ("End of Bakufu") period. The original concept derives from a contemporary of Confucius, who praised the original Chinese policy for preserving the nation's civilization.

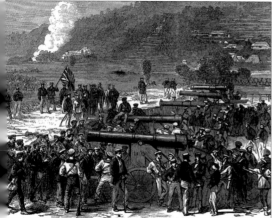

In a report to the Secretary of the Navy, Gideon Welles, the *Wyoming*'s commanding officer, Commander David McDougal, wrote:

"The Prince of Nagato [Daimyo Mori Takachika], it appears, has commenced this war on his own account, as he is one of the most powerful and influential of the princes of the Empire and bitterly opposed to foreigners, but the punishment inflicted and in store for him will, I trust, teach him a lesson that will not be soon forgotten."

On September 5, 1864, in response to further belligerent attacks on foreign traders, the British, French and Dutch navies launched a coordinated attack on the coast of Shimonoseki. The US Pacific Fleet had been withdrawn from Japan due to the ongoing Civil War, but sent the merchant ship *Ta-Kiang*, which had been chartered by the Navy the previous month, as a token show of support for the punitive action.

Oddly, the Satsuma and Choshu domains drew closer to Western powers during peace negotiations. The two domains had to pay reparations to the West, which they borrowed from the Shogunate and, because the Shogunate collapsed a few years later, never had to pay back.

"I passed into the fort and a distressing scene of carnage disclosed itself, frightful mutilations and groups of dead and dying meeting the eye in every direction. I walked around the ramparts on the west side. They were thickly strewed with dead – in the northwest angle thirteen were lying in one group around a gun. Signor Beato was here in great excitement, characterising the group as 'beautiful'."

Top: Smoke wafts over the Shimonoseki Straits, while the remnants of the Japanese batteries smolder in ruins.

Above: Featured in *The Illustrated London News* in 1564, this etching was based upon a photograph by renowned Italian-British Felice Beato.

The Boshin War and Meiji Restoration

By 1868 the Shogunate had weakened considerably. The Japanese people were furious that it had signed the unequal treaties and it had proved time and again that it was ineffective when it came to the basics of governing.

The samurai class, most of them loyal to the daimyo of Satsuma and Choshu, moved against the Tokugawa Shogunate, in what became known as the Boshin War. The daimyo of Choshu was a descendent of Mori Terumoto, who had been forced to give up his territory to Ieyasu 250 years earlier – it was time for revenge. Ironically, forces loyal to these daimyo were reacting to the Shogunate's failure to control foreign influence, and yet they were armed with weapons supplied by foreign traders.

"Though reproaches may be cast upon me, those who can fathom the depths of a warrior's heart will appreciate my motives." – Death poem written by one of the 11 Tosa samurai

Depiction of the Sakai Incident. On March 8, 1868, the French skiff *Dupleix* was attacked by samurai in the port of Sakai, near Osaka. Eleven French mariners were killed. Captain Dupetit Thouars demanded justice and 11 samurai who admitted to participating committed *seppuku*. Nine more samurai confessed and were banished.

The Tokugawa Shogunate – and thus the Edo Period – officially ended on November 19, 1867, when Shogun Yoshinobu resigned and transferred his powers to the 15-year-old Emperor Meiji, who had assumed the throne nine months earlier. The Emperor moved the Imperial headquarters to Edo, which was renamed Tokyo ("Eastern Capital").

"With our ample preparations we made short work of [the enemy], and this is an exceptional and extreme delight." – Saigo Takamori, *The Last Samurai*
Tokugawa samurai retainers, the elite *Shogitai*, defend the Kan'ei-ji Temple in which Shogun Yoshinobu hides. The Imperial forces from Choshu, under Saigo Takamori, are depicted breaking through the temple gates and furiously fighting in the courtyard.

Over the next four decades Japan transformed itself into a modern power, doing in 40 years what the Western powers had taken 100 years to do. Japanese delegations travelled the world and were inspired to remake their country based on what they saw.

Iwakura Tomomi led a delegation that spent two years traveling the globe. They stayed in the United States for almost half of that time, and many of the proposals they brought back to the Meiji government came from their sojourn in America, in particular their proposals related to education.

Many prominent political and military leaders came from Satsuma and Choshu, the provinces that had led the revolt against the Shogun. Samurai from these regions made up the foundation of the Imperial Japanese Army. In another ironic twist, French advisors oversaw the development of the army, even though France had initially supported the Shogunate during the Boshin War.

In 1871, the feudal system was abolished and prefectures replaced the various domains. Samurai swore their loyalty to the Emperor rather than to feudal lords, who were given peerage titles. The titles were modeled after Britain's nobility, and when Japan set up its government in the Meiji Constitution, it had an upper house for peers modeled after the House of Lords.

In the first years of the Meiji Restoration, the Emperor, as head of the Executive Branch, was responsible for all legislation and making sure laws were executed, as well as being head of state. There was, however, great concern that the Emperor could be found culpable if a piece of legislation was found unjust, so an arbitrary system was put in place to protect the Emperor from this accountability.

In 1881, Ito Hirobumi chaired a government bureau to study constitutions, and which system of government was best suited for Japan. Britain was rejected, because it gave too much power to parliament, and the US Constitution was rejected as too liberal. In the end, the Meiji Constitution was modeled after the Prussian system of government. The Constitution was adopted on February 11, 1889 – that date being symbolic as the day Emperor Jimmu had descended from heaven 2,500 years earlier. On April 1, 1889, 31 villages were upgraded to cities, giving them local autonomy. Among those villages were Hiroshima, Nagasaki, and Fukuoka (merging with Hakata). Tokyo was declared a city a month later.

Another important development sparked by Japan's open door policy was a change in fortunes for Christianity, which had been illegal in Japan since the beginnings of the Edo Period. That began to change when the foreign settlers in

"Whin we rapped on the dure, we didn't go in, they come out." – Mr. Dooley (Finley Peter Dunne)
An illustration of a main street in Tokyo's Ginza district circa 1873, by Utagawa Kuniteru II.

Nagasaki built a church at Oura. The Oura Cathedral was built in 1864 by two French missionaries and dedicated to the 26 Martyrs of Japan. In 1865, the priest found a group of Japanese citizens asking to come in and pray. It turned out they were from Urakami, underground Christians who had prayed in secret for two-and-a-half centuries. This discovery was hailed by the Pope as one of the great miracles of the century.

It was later discovered that nearly all villagers in Urakami were Christian. The Nagasaki magistrate decided to arrest the entire village, and a crackdown began on June 4, 1867, when 68 villagers were arrested and interrogated. Foreign powers protested and the Shogunate intervened and stopped it. In 1869, the Meiji government appointed Sawa Nobuyoshi as governor of Nagasaki. Nobuyoshi was a staunch nationalist and took the initiative to exile the entire village – 3,500 men, women and children were sent to various camps across Japan.

However, the Iwakura missions encountered constant questioning about the lack of freedom of worship in Japan as they traveled across the United States and Europe. When they arrived in France, the country's foreign minister gave them a petition for religious freedom signed by members of the Chamber of Deputies. Japan eventually granted religious freedom in 1873, by which time 650 Urakami Christians had died in exile.

Ulysses S. Grant's world tour

In 1865, Ulysses S. Grant was General of the Union Army and one of the most beloved figures in the United States. Townsend Harris, the first American ambassador to Japan, presented him with a samurai sword given to him by the Shogun when he retired from his post, saying to Grant, "It is my desire to transfer [the sword] to one of the bravest and worthiest of my countrymen, and the united voice of the whole world unmistakably points to you as the man I seek."

General Grant became President Grant in 1869, and would serve in that office for eight years. But when he left the White House in March 1877, his reputation at home was in ruins due to the scandals of his administration. Two months after leaving office, Grant and his wife Julia set out on a world tour that would last 32 months and take the Grants to Europe, the Holy Land, India, China, and finally to Japan.

Grant did not make his world tour in any official capacity, though he was treated as if he were a head of state everywhere he went; in America his reputation may have been tarnished, but for the rest of the world he was still the heroic army general who, along with Abraham Lincoln, had saved the Union.

In China, Grant met with Li-Hung Chang, who asked him to present China's colonial claims for the Ryuku Islands to the Japanese when he visited there. Journalist John Russell Young, who accompanied Grant and wrote *Around the World with General Grant*, wrote:

"We went to the viceregal palace in the Viceroy's yacht, and as we steamed up the river, every foot of ground, every spot on the junks, was covered with people. At the landing, troops were drawn up. A chair lined with yellow silk – such a chair as is only used by the Emperor – was awaiting the General. As far as the eye could reach the multitude stood expectant and gazing, and we went to the palace through a line of troops, who stood with arms at present. Amid the firing of guns, the beating of gongs, our procession slowly marched to the palace-door. The Viceroy, surrounded by his mandarins and attendants, welcomed the General. At the close of the interview, the General and the Viceroy sat for a photograph. This picture Li-Hung-Chang wished to preserve as a memento of the General's visit, and it was taken in one of the palace-rooms."

Grant arrived in Nagasaki on June 21, 1879 aboard the ship *Richmond*. Young's first sight of Japan elicited the following passage:

"Through green and smooth tranquil waters we steamed into the bay of Nagasaki, and had our first glimpse of Japan. Nagasaki is said to be among the most beautiful harbors in the world. But the beauty that welcomed us had the endearing quality that it reminded us of home. For so many weeks we had been in the land of the palm, and we were now again in the land of the pine. We had seen nature in luxuriant moods, running into riotous forms, strange and rank. We were weary of the cocoa-nut and the brown, parched soil, of the skies of fire and forests with wild and creeping things. It had become so oppressive that when over the course we turned toward the north there was great joy...

One never tires of a scene like Nagasaki, as you see it in evening more especially, the day ending and nature sheltering for repose in the embraces of night. Everything is so ripe and rich and old. Time has done so much for the venerable town, and you feel as the shadows fall that for generations, for centuries, they have fallen upon just such a scene as we look down upon from the brow of our hill. The eddies of a new civilization are rushing in upon Nagasaki, and there are many signs that you have no trouble in searching

The view over Nagasaki Harbor from J.R. Young's account *Around the World with General Grant.*

out. That Nagasaki has undergone a vast change since the day when Dutch
merchants were kept in a reservation more secluded than we have ever
kept our Indians, when Xavier and his disciples threaded over narrow
streets preaching the salvation that comes through the blood of Jesus, when
Christians were driven at the point of the spear to yon beetling cliff and
tumbled into the sea. These are momentous events in the history of Japan.
They were merely incidents in the history of Nagasaki."

Grant (and his wife Julia) planted two trees in Nagasaki Park, saying,"I hope that
both trees may prosper, grow large, live long, and in their growth, prosperity and
long life be emblematic of the future of Japan." At a dinner that evening, he spoke of
how:

"America has much to gain from the East… no nation has greater interests;
but America has nothing to gain except what comes from the cheerful
acquiescence of the Eastern people and insures them as much benefit as
it does us. I should be ashamed of my country if its relations with other

General Grant, and his wife Julia, meet Emperor Meiji and Empress Shoken on July 3, 1879.

countries, and especially with these ancient and most interesting empires in the East, were based upon any other idea… No nation needs from the outside powers justice and kindness than Japan, because the work that has made such marvelous progress in the past few years is a work in which we are deeply concerned, in the success of which we see a new era in civilization and which we should encourage."

– Grant (quoted in Young)

Grant met Emperor Meiji for the first time on July 4, 1879 – the Emperor's staff arranged it so the two would meet on America's Independence Day.

Young wrote of the meeting:

"His Imperial Majesty… advanced and shook hands with General Grant. This seems a trivial thing to write down, but such a thing was never before known in the history of Japanese majesty. Many of these details may appear small, but we are in the presence of an old and romantic civilization, slowly giving way to the fierce, feverish pressure of European ideas, and you can only note the change in those incidents which would be unnoticed in other lands."

Grant presented China's concerns about the Ryuku Islands and heard Japan's case. He was sympathetic to Japan's case and judged that their military was more powerful than China's. His world tour restored Grant's reputation in the United States to the point that the Republicans almost nominated him to run for a third term in 1880, but the up-and-coming James Garfield was chosen instead.

The Sino-Japanese War

Since Hideyoshi's time, Japanese with Imperial ambitions had seen Korea as the first stepping stone towards expansionism. When Japan opened up, it saw that the great powers were each expanding their empires and carving up Asia for their own purposes. Britain, France, Portugal, Spain and the Netherlands had all claimed land in Asia for their empires, and Japan wanted its own piece of the pie.

Germany had come to the Imperial land grab relatively late, owing to its disunity. That changed in 1871, when Otto Von Bismarck, the "Iron Chancellor," unified the fractious Teutonic states to create the German Empire. In the 1880s it began grabbing land in Africa and Asia, gaining the port of Tsingtao in 1898. That same year, Spain lost its colonies in Asia to the United States, another newcomer to Pacific colonization, as a result of the Spanish-American War.

War with Korea had been discussed within the Japanese government as early as 1873. Some members wanted to go to war with Korea because it refused to recognize the legitimacy of Emperor Meiji. Saigo Takamori, an

"Thus it is that in war the victorious strategist only seeks battle after the victory has been won, whereas he who is destined to defeat first fights and afterwards looks for victory." – Sun Tzu
Joseph Keppler Jr.'s cartoon depicting the European monarchs awaiting the outcome of the Eastern conflicts was featured in *Puck*.

Imperial commander of Satsuma troops during the Boshin War, even offered to go to Korea and act in such an insulting manner that the Koreans would be obliged to engage him in battle, likely killing him, but providing legitimate provocation for war. These plans were rejected by the Meiji government, and Takamori resigned his posts in government and returned to his hometown of Kagoshima.

In Kagoshima, a private military was established for ronin who also quit their positions in protest. Fearing a rebellion, the central government sent troops to Kagoshima, which provoked open conflict with the samurai. Saigo was persuaded to lead the rebels and ended up dying in what is now called the Satsuma Rebellion in 1877.

Tensions had been rising between China and Japan for many years, especially over Korea. On August 13, 1886, 500 Chinese soldiers disembarked from ships in Nagasaki and rioted. Nagasaki police pushed back, resulting in six deaths and hundreds of injuries on both sides. The Qing Dynasty refused to apologize for the incident and anti-Qing sentiment rose significantly in Japan.

In the summer of 1894, tensions were at breaking point. The assassination of Korean activist Kim Ok-gyun in Shanghai was taken by Japan as a further affront – Kim had been an advocate for bringing Western ideas into Korea by way of Japan, one of the rationales many Japanese had for invading Korea.

The final straw came when a peasant revolt forced Emperor Gwangmu of Korea to request Chinese assistance in the form of military reinforcements. Japan perceived this as an attempt to invade, and preemptively mounted an invasion force. By June 25, Japanese troops had captured Seoul, and the government was suffused with pro-Japanese rebels.

Members of the Fifth Imperial Army Division – based in Hiroshima – were among the first battalions to land in Korea (and also participated in the later capture of Liaodong Peninsula). The Imperial Japanese Navy, by this time, had four shipyards in operation, including the Kure shipyards (near Hiroshima) and the Sasebo shipyards (near Nagasaki).

During the first Sino-Japanese War, Hiroshima became the center of national administration. Emperor Meiji proclaimed that the move from Tokyo was motivated by the desire to reassure the fighting men that he was with them, whilst the Diet [the legislative assembly] was transferred at the insistence of Interior Minister Inoue Karoue, to ensure that the Emperor could read his rescript, on the opening session of the Diet, in person.

In Emperor Meiji's address, he pronounced that China had forgotten its mandate to maintain peace in the Orient, and that Japan would not stop fighting until peace was achieved. The reality was that the Emperor had little interest in the conflict, and busied himself with leisurely pursuits – kickball, archery, painting, and writing poetry. Among his verses, the most famous was set to music and performed during the victory celebrations:

Our dauntless warriors
Stepping over the corpses of friend and foe,
Advance, their spirits high.

On October 24, 1894, Japanese troops crossed the Yalu River and entered Qing China. They headed south and by the following month they had taken the Liaodong Peninsula and captured the strategic port city of Dalian (Port Arthur). The Qing army was poorly equipped, having failed to modernize as Japan had, and after a series of humiliating defeats the Chinese sued for peace.

The Sino-Japanese War ended with the Treaty of Shimonoseki, signed on April 17, 1895. Among its provisions, China was forced to recognize the independence of Korea, removing the peninsula from its sphere of influence. The treaty further humiliated China by ceding territory to Japan, notably the Liaodong Peninsula and Formosa (modern-day Taiwan). Adding insult to injury, China was strong-armed into repaying Japan's wartime expenses.

The precedent for demanding and receiving reparations from their vanquished foes had been established in 1874, when in May of that year a punitive expedition force of 3,600 Japanese soldiers landed on Formosa, charged with punishing the indigenous Paiwan for the massacre of 54 shipwrecked Ryukuan sailors three years previously. The mission was largely an embarrassing failure; the Japanese troops, led by Saigo Judo, younger brother of Saigo Takamori (leader of the Satsuma Rebellion), killed only 30 locals, while during the Battle of Stone Gate six Japanese soldiers were killed and 30 were wounded. In addition, during their six-month occupation one out of seven Japanese soldiers were lost to various tropical diseases. The expedition left the island only when the Qing government intervened, making reparations of 500,000 Kuping taels, equal to 18.7 metric tons of silver. Sir Harry Parkes, the British Minister to Japan at the time, stated that the interaction demonstrated "China's willingness to pay to be invaded."

Immediately after the treaty became public, Russia expressed concern. It had its own designs on a sphere of influence in the East, as well as a desire to have a

"From the point of view of the nation's power, it was obvious that while we were fighting the Sino-Japanese war, every effort was to be made to avoid adding to our enemies and opening additional fronts." – General Tojo Hideki, speaking about the Second Sino-Japanese War

A battle in 1894 on the Liaodong Peninsula, during the First Sino-Japanese War. Painted by Toyohara Kuniteru III.

year-round port on the Pacific – its port at Vladivostok was only open in the summer. Russia demanded that Japan cede the Liaodong Peninsula to them. France had cordial relations with Japan, but was in an alliance with Russia and seconded this demand. Germany, new to the table, also joined the negotiations, seeing an opening for their own colonial ambitions.

Five days after signing the Treaty of Shimonoseki, Japan signed a treaty with Russia in which it relinquished its claim to the Liaodong Peninsula, withdrawing all of its troops.

Opposite: "'Black Octopus' is a name newly given to Russia by certain prominent Englishmen. For the black octopus is so avaricious, that he stretches out his eight arms in all directions, and seizes up everything that comes within his reach. But as it sometimes happens he gets wounded seriously even by a small fish, owing to his too much covetousness. Indeed, a Japanese proverb says: 'Great avarice is like unselfishness.' We Japanese need not to say much on the cause of the present war. Suffice it to say, that the further existence of the Black Octopus will depend entirely on how he comes out of this war. The Japanese fleet has already practically annihilated Russia's naval power in the Orient. The Japanese army is about to win a signal victory over Russia in Corea and Manchuria. And then... St. Petersburg! Wait and see! The ugly Black Octopus! Hurrah! Hurrah! for Japan." – Kisaburo Ohara, March 1904

RUSSIA, THE "YELLOW PERIL" AND WARRING NATIONS

Throughout the second half of the 19th century Russia had been aggressively expanding its territory in the East, acquiring Outer Manchuria and Sakhalin from China in the 1860 Treaty of Peking, as well as constructing its Pacific Naval Base at Vladivostok (which translates as "Ruler of the East"). In 1871, a telegraph line was established between the Russian port and Nagasaki, and by the 1890s the Imperial Russian Navy had a significant presence in the coastal Japanese city.

Tsar Nicholas II arrived there on April 27, 1891 on a far-reaching tour, and noted how many Japanese were versed in Russian. He had been reading the book *Madame Chrysanthème*, written by a French lieutenant named Julien Viaud, and in imitation

of a character from the book Nicholas decided to have a tattoo (officially tattooing had been outlawed by Emperor Meiji, but was still widely practiced). It took the artist seven hours to ink a dragon onto Nicholas' right arm. The Tsar also survived an assassination attempt whilst in Japan, which left a gash on his forehead.

(Viaud's book *Madame Chrysanthème* subsequently influenced a short story by American John Luther Long titled *Madame Butterfly*. This was adapted into a one-act play by David Belasco, which was seen by the Italian composer Giacomo Puccini in London in 1900. The similarly titled opera that resulted was initially poorly received, but after considerable revisions it eventually became a huge global success, and has stood the test of time as one of the most popular Italian operas.)

Russia's designs in Asia were connected to a broader political stage encompassing the machinations of the European powers. The term "Yellow Peril" is generally attributed to Kaiser Wilhelm II of Germany, who first used it in a letter to Tsar Nicholas II (his first cousin) on September 26, 1895. He included a drawing illustrating his idea of the yellow peril, which showed the European powers called by the Archangel Michael against the "inroad of Buddhism, heathenism and barbarism for the Defense of the Cross."

The Yellow Peril by Herman Knackfuss, after a sketch by Wilhelm II. *Harper's Weekly* reprinted it in their January 22, 1898 issue with a full-page critique by French realist painter Jean-Francois Raffaelli. In the magazine it is captioned "Nations of Europe! Join in the defense of your faith and your homes!" A note from the editors preceded the review: "There was a time when the world watched the multifarious activities of Emperor William of Germany with considerable apprehension. But repeated shocks to the nervous system deaden the the susceptibilities, and accordingly, when the telegraph flashed the news that the emperor had given the historical painter Hermann Knackfuss a sketch and instructions to work it up into a historical picture, the world for the most part smiled."

On January 4, 1898, Wilhelm sent Nicholas another drawing, which showed Russia and Germany as "sentinels at the Yellow Sea for the proclaiming of the Gospel of Light and Truth in the East." According to Wilhelm biographer Alan Palmer, the Kaiser was so convinced his sketch would create a good impression that he showed it to the then Chancellor of Germany, Chlodwig, Prince of Hohenlohe-Schillingsfürst. The Chancellor was not interested in "dynastic diplomacy by visual aid," but told a diplomat, "I did not risk attempting to dissuade him." In a letter to the Kaiser, he told him that, "The great task of the future for Russia [is] to cultivate the Asian continent and to defend Europe from the inroads of the Great Yellow Race. In this you will always find me on your side."

Wilhelm had ulterior motives for voicing these fears to Nicholas, and later to his uncle, King Edward VII of Britain. He wanted Germany to dominate Europe and sought to undermine alliances that would prevent that from happening, especially the Franco-Russian alliance, or as he called it, "the hideous pincers of Gallo-Russia." He therefore needed the Imperial Russian Army to be preoccupied by conflicts on its eastern front, so that it would be less inclined to encroach on its western borders, which included Germany and Triple Entente member Austria-Hungary.

Wilhelm expressed his sentiments to his ministers, saying succinctly, "We must try to tie Russia down in East Asia so that she pays less attention to Europe and the Near East." His thoughts clearly echoed those of his father's Chancellor, Otto von Bismarck, who had said, "Russia has nothing to do in the West. There she can only catch Nihilism and other diseases. Her mission is in Asia, where she represents civilization."

Wilhelm also told Britain's King Edward VII that Asians (particularly Japanese) were "the greatest peril menacing Christendom and European civilization. If the Russians went on giving ground, the yellow race would, in 20 years time, be in Moscow and Posen." The Anglo-Japanese Alliance had been fostered under his reign, and as such Edward rebuked his nephew, saying, "the Japanese are an intelligent, brave and chivalrous nation, quite as civilized as Europeans, from whom they only differ by the pigmentation of their skin."

"To try and avoid such a calamity as a European war I beg you in the name of our old friendship to do what you can to stop your allies from going too far." – Tsar Nicholas II to Kaiser Wilhelm II
Cousins Kaiser Wilhelm II of Germany and Tsar Nicholas II of Russia, each wearing the other's national uniform.

Drawing the battle lines

As soon as Japan had reluctantly ceded the Liaodong Peninsula to Russia in 1895 (see end of last chapter), Russian contingents poured into the city of Dalian, and set to work heavily fortifying Port Arthur (now Lüshun Port). Meanwhile, their Pacific Fleet migrated from Vladivostok to the warm-water port. China leased the waters off the peninsula to the Russian Navy in 1898.

"What this country needs is a short, victorious war to stem the tide of revolution." – Vyacheslav von Plehve, director of the Russian Imperial police and Minister of the Interior

A German cartoon created at the start of the Russo-Japanese War, alluding to the interferences of the Western Empires – England backing the Japanese, bolstering their navy, the French siding with the Russians.

The agreement also guaranteed the construction of a branch of the Chinese Eastern Railway from Port Arthur to Harbin in the north. The railway was attacked during an anti-foreigner uprising in 1900 that became known as the Boxer Rebellion – the "boxers" being members of a secret society called The Righteous and Harmonious Fists. In retaliation, the Russian Empire invaded Manchuria. After signing the Boxer Protocol of 1901 in Beijing, Russia promised to withdraw from Manchuria, but by 1903 the Empire still hadn't made a timetable for withdrawal, and even made proposals to Japan to make Korea north of the 39th parallel (Pyongyang) a neutral buffer between Japan-administered southern Korea and Manchuria.

The Russo-Japanese War began on February 8, 1904, when Japan fired on Russian warships near Port Arthur. No ships were sunk, but Russian firepower forced the Japanese ships to retreat. The Russians sustained 150 casualties to 90 Japanese and the battle was initially considered a Russian victory. A formal declaration of war was issued by Japan on February 10.

In April, American banker Jacob Schiff of Kuhn, Loeb & Co., the principal rival of J.P. Morgan & Co., extended loans to Japan worth US$30 million (US$774 million today). This cash infusion financed half of Japan's war effort. It is believed that Schiff made these loans in order to punish Russia for its anti-Semitic pogroms.

Schiff financed efforts to incite a revolution in Russia that would see that Jews got equal rights. *Outlook* magazine correspondent and explorer George Kennan, with Schiff's support, visited Japanese POW camps and distributed revolutionary materials to the Russians held there. When Prime Minister of Russia Sergei Witte visited Portsmouth, he met with Schiff, who demanded that Jews be given equal rights.

From July 30, 1904 to January 2, 1905, Japan laid siege to Port Arthur on both land and sea. The Russian Empire's Pacific Fleet was decimated, and the morale of the troops on the ground was gravely depleted. Much of their army had been transported from Moscow on the newly opened Trans-Siberian Railway, a journey that took two months – the soldiers were under equipped and undernourished by the time they arrived.

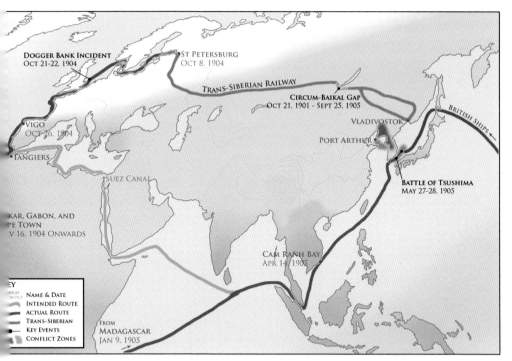

"The battle of Tsushima is by far the greatest and the most important naval event since Trafalgar."
– Sir George Sydenham Clarke

There were three viable routes by which Russian forces could be deployed near Japan: first, infantry, cavalry and artillery could make assaults on land bases, after arriving on the Trans-Siberian railroad; second, ships could sail via the Suez Canal. The last resort, which crushed the morale, strength and stealth of the Tsushima mission, was the rerouting of the Second Pacific Squadron around the Cape of Good Hope.

Britain, meanwhile, had not joined Russia, France and Germany in objecting to Japan's occupation of the Liaodong Peninsula in 1895, and it retained good relations with Japan. During the following decade it cemented their alliance, with *The Times'* Tokyo correspondent Francis Brinkley and Orientalist Edwin Arnold arguing for an Anglo-Japanese Alliance (*Nichi-Ei Domei*) to counterbalance the Franco-Russian Alliance. An Anglo-Japanese Alliance was signed on January 30, 1902. In response, France and Russia reaffirmed their alliance on March 16.

A disastrous event that occurred on the other side of the world had serious consequences for Russia in the Far East. The Russian Empire's Baltic Fleet left port on October 15, 1904, departing with freshly recruited crewmen following alarming reports that Japanese submarines may have reached the North Sea. On their sixth night out of St. Petersburg, the highly strung, inexperienced seamen fired upon a British trawler, mistaking it for a Holland-class Japanese submarine, in Dogger Bank area. Three British fishermen were killed. The British Royal Navy, outraged by the unprovoked attacked prepared for war, but before the situation could escalate further, the two nations met and negotiated a peace. The Russian Empire was commanded, by the International Committee of Inquiry at The Hague to pay £65,000 in damages.

As a consequence of the incident, the Baltic Fleet was also barred by the British from using the Suez Canal, which would have halved their journey time to the Pacific. The fleet finally arrived at Tsushima seven months later, on May 27, 1905 having traveled 20,000 miles, only to be annihilated by the Japanese Imperial Fleet, under Admiral Togo Heihachiro, within 45 minutes. The battle cost the Russians 4,830 lives and six of eight battleships. On the Japanese side, 110 were killed and three of its 89 ships were sunk. This complete humiliation sent shockwaves throughout the world. Belief in the superiority of Western firepower was shaken, and Japanese confidence in its military might soared.

The war correspondents

Foreign correspondents for Western newspapers had been around since the Crimean War of 1853, a showdown between a Franco-Anglo-Ottoman coalition and the Russian Empire. American newspapers, especially those owned by William Randolph Hearst and Joseph Pulitzer, were engaged in a fierce rivalry for subscriptions. The American Civil War created such a demand for newspapers that they started printing special Sunday editions, and the Spanish-American War of 1898 dramatically increased the number of American newspaper readers. This was also one of the first times American journalists were sent abroad as war correspondents. Hearst's *New York*

War correspondents aboard a ship in 1904, en route to Japan. From left to right: James H. Hare, Collier's; Robert L. Dunn, Collier's; J. Sheldon Williams; Captain Lionel James, *London Times*; Jack London, *San Francisco Examiner*; Frederick Palmer, Collier's; Percival Phillips; O.K. Davis, *New York Herald*.

Journal, and Pulitzer's *New York World* sent their star reporters into the field – Richard Harding Davis and Stephen Crane, respectively – to provide colorful reports of bravery.

Spurred on by the successes of Davis, Crane and many others, the American media craved equal success when they sent reporters to Japan to cover the Russo-Japanese War. Several veteran reporters of the Spanish-American War went along. Davis traveled to Japan as the managing editor of *Harpers Weekly*. Pulitzer sent Joseph Creelman, who had covered the first Sino-Japanese War as well as the Spanish-American War, while Hearst sent novelist Jack London to report for his newspapers, which included London's hometown paper, *The San Francisco Examiner*. London had become world famous for his novel *Call of the Wild* published in 1903.

This was not London's first time in Japan. In 1893 at the age of 17 he had hopped aboard a sealing ship, the *Sophia Sutherland*, bound for Yokohama. After seven months, he returned to San Francisco and the first thing he ever published was an article in the *San Francisco Morning Call* entitled "Story of a Typhoon off the Coast of Japan." The following is from that article:

> *"To reef the mainsail we were forced to run off before the gale under the single reefed jib. By the time we had finished the wind had forced up such a tremendous sea that it was impossible to heave her to. Away we flew on*

"The huge, violent waves are taller than a house, Black smoke from the ship rises and spreads into the night sky, I see the moon above the vast ocean, And looking behind me, I desire to see the skies over Japan."
– Nakai Jiromu, Japanese poet and Anglo-Japanese mediator

'The Distress'd Situation of the ship Eliza in a Typhoon in the Gulph of Japan', painted by the Chinese painter Guan Zuolin, better known in the West as Spoilum.

the wings of the storm through the muck and flying spray. A wind sheer to starboard, then another to port as the enormous seas struck the schooner astern and nearly broached her to. As day broke we took in the jib, leaving not a sail unfurled. Since we had begun scudding she had ceased to take the seas over her bow, but amidships they broke fast and furious. It was a dry storm in the matter of rain, but the force of the wind filled the air with fine spray, which flew as high as the crosstrees and cut the face like a knife, making it impossible to see over a hundred yards ahead. The sea was a dark lead color as with long, slow, majestic roll it was heaped up by the wind into liquid mountains of foam. The wild antics of the schooner were sickening as she forged along. She would almost stop, as though climbing a mountain, then rapidly rolling to right and left as she gained the summit of a huge sea, she steadied herself and paused for a moment as though affrighted at the yawning precipice before her. Like an avalanche, she shot forward and down as the sea astern struck her with the force of a thousand battering rams, burying her bow to the catheads in the milky foam at the bottom that came on deck in all directions – forward, astern, to right and left, through the hawse-pipes and over the rail."

In early February 1904 London arrived at Moji, a staging area for the Japanese Imperial Army on the northernmost peninsula of Kyushu, across from Shimonoseki. In an article titled "The Yellow Peril," London wrote:

"The Japanese are a race of mastery and power, a fighting race through all its history, a race that has always despised commerce and exalted fighting. Today, equipped with the finest machines and systems of destruction the Caucasian mind has devised, handling machines and systems with remarkable and deadly accuracy, this rejuvenescent Japanese race has embarked on a course of conquest the goal of which no man knows. The head men of Japan are dreaming ambitiously, and the people are dreaming blindly, a Napoleonic dream. And to this dream the Japanese clings and will cling with bull-dog tenacity.

The Japanese is not an individualist. He has developed national consciousness instead of moral consciousness. He is not interested in his own moral welfare except in so far as it is the welfare of the State. The honor of the individual, per se, does not exist. Only exists the honor of the State, which is his honor. He does not look upon himself as a free agent, working out his own personal salvation. Spiritual agonizing is unknown to him. He has a 'sense of calm trust in fate, a quiet submission to the inevitable, a stoic composure in slight of danger or calamity, a disdain of life and friendliness with death.' He relates himself to the State as, amongst bees, the worker is related to the hive; himself nothing, the State everything; his reasons for existence the exaltation and glorification of the State.

The most admired quality today of the Japanese is his patriotism. The Western world is in rhapsodies over it, unwittingly measuring the Japanese patriotism by his own conceptions of patriotism. 'For God, my country, and the Czar!' cries the Russian patriot, but in the Japanese mind there is no differentiation between the three. The Emperor is the Emperor, and God and country as well. The patriotism of the Japanese is blind and unswerving loyalty to what is practically an absolutism."

While taking pictures in Moji, the Japanese authorities arrested London, and his camera was confiscated as a "weapon." James Ricalton, a correspondent for *Traveler's Magazine* was similarly arrested when he tried taking photos of Japanese soldiers. London was released after the intervention of the American ambassador, Lloyd Grissom. Ricalton was released with the intervention of Admiral Nogi.

"Oh, why can't the men and women of this world learn that playing the game in the small way is the losing way? They are always doomed to failure when they play against the one who plays in the large way."
– Jack London

Jack London stands amid a group of Koreans. They wear *jeongjagwan*, traditional formal headwear, made from horse hair, worn by the ruling class during the Joseon period.

London got a ferry from Moji to Busan, and then privately chartered a fishing boat from Mokpo to Chemulo (Incheon). He then hired a horse, whom he named "Belle," and headed north to Ping Yang (now Pyongyang), which the Russians had captured, and continued north before being turned back to Seoul. He asked Hearst if he could be transferred to the Imperial Russian Army, but before this could happen he was arrested again, this time for assaulting a Japanese stable hand. Richard Harding Davis cabled his friend President Roosevelt asking for his help in releasing London. With the help of the US Ministry in Tokyo, London was released and sent home.

The Portsmouth Treaty

As early as July 1904 Japan sought a means to conclude its war with Russia via an intermediary. Its chosen arbiter was America's President Theodore Roosevelt. This was largely due to the efforts of Kaneko Kentaro, Prime Minister Ito Hirobumi's personal secretary. Kaneko had gone to the United States as a member of the Iwakura Mission in 1871 and was a classmate of Roosevelt at Harvard University. While Roosevelt had a mixed opinion of both countries, he admired Japan for its ability to stand against Russian expansionism, saying, "Japan, shaking off the lethargy of centuries, has taken her rank among the civilized modern powers." Roosevelt hoped the end result of the peace negotiations would leave both Russia and Japan

"Far better is it to dare mighty things, to win glorious triumphs, even though checkered by failure... than to rank with those poor spirits who neither enjoy nor suffer much, because they live in a gray twilight that knows not victory nor defeat."
– President Roosevelt

Russian and Japanese ambassadors meet aboard President Roosevelt's yacht at Oyster Bay on Long Island.

Left to right: Sergei Witte, Prime Minister of Russia, Roman Rosen, Russian Ambassador to the United States, Theodore Roosevelt, President of the United States, Komura Jutaro, Foreign Minister of Japan, and Takahira Kogoro, Japan's ambassador to the United States.

weakened, but wrote to his Secretary of State John Hay, "The Russians think only with half a mind... I think that the Japanese will whip them handsomely."

Russia initially refused to come to the table, believing it would be victorious. However, after its defeat at the Battle of Tsushima, it was ready to negotiate. Roosevelt hosted the peace conference on neutral ground, in Portsmouth, New Hampshire, which had a cooler climate than Washington D.C. During the negotiations, Japan asked for the southern half of Sakhalin Island, which it received after Japanese negotiators dropped demands for financial reparations from Russia. However, when this was reported in the Tokyo newspapers its citizens were incensed. In what is known as the Hibiya Incident, angry mobs rampaged through the city, destroying 350 buildings and killing 17

"It was most certainly the first time they had seen a strong, sharp sword of Japan"
– Nakai Jiromu, Japanese poet and Anglo-Japanese mediator

A French cartoon presenting the bloody outcome of the Russo-Japanese War, both carry banners with the slogans "Russian State Fund" and "Japanese State Debt." The Englishman's ship droops underarm as he looks forlornly over his shoulder, as the French protagonist, akin to Joan of Arc, assists the battered bear from the battleground. Vultures swoop upon the bloody masses left in their wake.

people. Prime Minister Katsura Taro, a veteran general of the Boshin War and a pivotal member in the Meiji Restoration, resigned in January 1906 as a result of public disaffection.

Japan's claims in Korea were recognized, while Russia returned Port Arthur and Dalian to China. Russia also had to turn over the Southern Manchuria Railway and its mining concessions in the region to Japan, but was allowed to keep the Chinese Eastern Railway in northern Manchuria. The Treaty of Portsmouth was signed on September 5, 1905, with Japan ratifying it on October 10 and Russia on October 14.

President Roosevelt received the 1906 Nobel Peace Prize for his efforts. Roosevelt was a robust character who championed the benefits of "the strenuous life." He took up boxing as a child to deal with bullies, and expanded into wrestling as an older man. In 1904, he took up Judo after being introduced to it by art collector William Sturgis Bigelow. He received further training from Yahashita Yoshitsugu, a former *kohai* (protégé) of Sensei Jigoro Kano, the founder of Judo.

Yahashita taught Judo at the US Naval Academy for two years after meeting Roosevelt, who set up training mats in the White House basement and practiced with anyone willing to fight three afternoons a week in March and April 1904. Roosevelt would eventually attain a brown belt in Judo – the first American to earn one – and wrote, "The art of *jiu-jitsu* is worth more in every way than all of our athletics combined."

Despite its seeming good relations with the US, Japan was concerned about the treatment of its citizens in America. In 1907, the San Francisco Public School Board decided to send Chinese and Japanese students to schools separate from (mostly white) American citizens. Japan sent letters of concern to President Roosevelt, and a "Gentleman's Agreement" was reached, whereby the United States would accept citizens of Japan already residing there, but Japan would not issue passports to its citizens for the United States.

However, this agreement included two loopholes: Japan could still issue passports for citizens to emigrate to Canada and Mexico. Once there, they could continue to the continental US with few restrictions. The agreement also allowed family members and spouses of Japanese-Americans to emigrate to the United States and the "picture bride" industry took off thanks to this loophole. Japanese (male) laborers in the US would send a photo to a matchmaker, who would match them with a Japanese wife. The Japanese government then allowed her to move to the US with her new husband.

World War I and its effect on Asia

As the European powers bickered, and America and Japan modernized, China was swiftly being left behind with its head in the sand. The colonial empires chipped away at China's territory, the resulting anti-foreigner Boxer Rebellion weakened the Qing Dynasty to the point of collapse, and when the Republic of China was born, its first president, Sun Yat-sen, gave this appraisal of his nation's state during his Lectures on the Three Principles:

> "What is the standing of our nation [China] in the world? In comparison
> with other nations we have the greatest population and the oldest culture,
> of 4,000 years' duration. We ought to be advancing in line with the nations
> of Europe and America. But the Chinese people have only family and clan
> groups; there is no national spirit. Consequently, in spite of 400 million
> people gathered together in one China, we are in fact but a sheet of loose
> sand. We are the poorest and weakest state in the world, occupying the
> lowest portion in international affairs; the rest of mankind is the carving
> knife and the serving dish, while we are the fish and meat. Our position is
> now extremely perilous; if we do not earnestly promote nationalism and weld
> together our 400 million into a strong nation, we face a tragedy – the loss of
> our country and the destruction of our race. To ward off this danger, we must
> espouse nationalism and employ the national spirit to save the country."

Japan entered World War I on the side of Britain on August 7, 1914, three days after Britain declared war on Germany. Under the terms of their bilateral treaty (the Anglo-Japanese Alliance), Britain requested Japanese assistance against German forces in Asia, specifically the Far East Squadron of the Reichsmarineamt, stationed at Tsingtao (now Qingdao). A week before it officially declared war with Germany, the Japanese gave the forces at Tsingtao an ultimatum, demanding they remove all German men-o-war from Japanese and Chinese waters, and surrender Tsingtao to Japanese control. The first air-to-sea battle in history took place during the Siege of Tsingtao, when a seaplane from the Japanese transport ship *Wakamiya* attacked the German ships *Kaiserin Elisabeth* and *Jaguar*. Neither ship was hit.

Tsingtao was captured on November 7, 1914. The Japanese took 4,700 Germans back to Japan as prisoners of war. Some of them had worked at the Germania Brewery (now the Tsingtao Brewery, the second largest brewery in China) and these were transferred to Osaka to work in the Dai-Nippon Brewery (now the Asahi and Sapporo breweries, the top two beers in Japan). Many of the German POWs found

menial jobs during their captivity
and when the war ended, 170 of
them chose to remain in Japan.
The pastry company Juchheim
(based in Kobe) and the processed
food company Lohmeyer (based
in Nasushiobara) were founded by
German POWs who chose to stay
in Japan.

"To affirm that the aeroplane is going to 'revolutionize' naval warfare of the future is to be guilty of the wildest exaggeration." – an ironic quote from Scientific American, July 16, 1910
Two Maurice-Farman seaplanes owned by the Imperial Japanese Navy, stationed on land near Tsingtao, 1914.

Four months after the Siege of Tsingtao, on January 18, 1915 the Empire
of Japan, under Prime Minister Okuma Shigenobu, sent China the "Twenty-One
Demands" (*Taika Nijuikkajo Yokyu*), in which China was forced to acknowledge
the legitimacy of Japan's claim to Chinese territories, strengthening its hold on
Manchuria. Eight of the demands were later dropped, as they would have given
Japan substantial control over the Chinese economy, something the Western powers
would not accept, maintaining that China should remain open to trade with all

"It would shame me more to surrender Tsingtao to the Japanese than Berlin to the Russians." – Kaiser Wilhelm II
General Kamio Mitsuomi leading Allied forces into Tsingtao, November 1914. He latterly assumed the
role of Governor of Tsingtao, and was honored with the Order of the Rising Sun, as well as the Order of St
Michael and St George.

countries on an equal footing, known as the Open Door Policy. The British Foreign Office and American Secretary of State William Jennings Bryan issued concerns that the demands were violations of that policy. They opposed the remaining demands that Japan placed on China, arguing that they were violations of Chinese sovereignty.

At the end of World War I, the allied powers gathered at Versailles, outside Paris, and negotiated what should be done in the wake of one of the worst conflicts in modern history. At the negotiations, China's representative, Wellington Koo, under popular pressure, demanded the return of the territories in Shandong that they had leased to Germany in 1897 and had subsequently been seized by Japan. Japan refused to comply and the other powers paid little attention to China's demands. As the refutation became public, on May 4, 1919 Chinese students rioted, starting the May Fourth Movement. Many of the initiators of the student-led dissent founded the Chinese Communist Party in 1921. The refutation to return the Shandong Peninsula was a point of considerable contention, and resulted in China's refusal to sign the Treaty of Versailles.

"Don't talk to me about atrocities in war; all war is an atrocity." – Lord Kitchener
Representatives of the Allied nations discussing WWI. This conference at Versailles took place on March 27-28, 1916, with the image featuring in *The Mirror*. The Japanese ambassador, Matsui Keishiro, is seated at top right, opposite Lord Kitchener (centre, with back to camera).

Unassimilable and undesirable

In 1922, Takao Ozawa petitioned the federal government for the right to become a US citizen, asking to be classified as "white." Ozawa was born in Japan, but graduated from the University of California. He'd converted to Christianity, married and had three children, all born in the United States. At the time of the case he lived in Honolulu and worked as a salesman. Ozawa's case went before the US Supreme Court, which said in a unanimous opinion that Japanese were ineligible for citizenship (it is often reported that the court said Japanese were of an "unassimilable" race, but the word does not appear in the ruling).

Restrictions on who could become a US citizen had been mired in xenophobia and racism since the 1790 Naturalization Act, which extended naturalization only to those who were "white, free and of good character." In 1870, naturalization was extended to include those of African descent, but not Asians. In 1875, the Page Act was the first US law to target immigrants from Asia. It prohibited the immigration of "undesirables," applying to Asian men who might work as forced laborers and Asian women who would engage in prostitution.

In 1913, California passed the Alien Land Law, which prohibited "aliens ineligible for citizenship" (ie immigrants from Asia) from owning land. Japan, through its Ministry of Foreign Affairs, sent a letter to the State Department saying the law was "unfair and inconsistent... with the sentiments of amity and good neighborhood which have presided over the two countries," but it was passed anyway. The US Supreme Court upheld the constitutionality of the law in 1923. (In 1952 the California Supreme Court decided the laws were unconstitutional.)

Due to xenophobia, the first "Red Scare," and other racial tensions in the wake of World War I, Congress passed the Immigration Act of 1924, which severely restricted immigration from all nations and completely forbade it from countries in Asia. Such harsh policies ramped up tensions within Japan, leading to attitudes such as those expressed by Lt. Colonel Hashimoto Kingoro in the document "Addresses to Young Men" at the International Military Tribunal for the Far East:

"There are only three ways left for Japan to escape from the pressures of surplus population... emigration, advance into world markets, and expansion of territory. The first door, emigration, has been barred to us by anti-Japanese immigration policies in other countries. The second door... is being pushed shut by tariff barriers and the abrogation of commercial treaties. What should Japan do when two of the three doors have been closed against her?"

A New Martial Agenda

As World War I ended and the major powers jostled to find their place in the modern world, the Japanese remained very concerned about the unequal Ansei Treaties of the 1850s. In 1919 they proposed an amendment to the Covenant of the League of Nations, the Racial Equality Proposal, which would have barred discrimination based on race or nationality in member nations. American President Woodrow Wilson, who needed pro-segregationist Democrats to ratify the treaty back home, dismissed the proposal, and was quickly backed by Australian Prime Minister Billy Hughes and British delegate Robert Cecil. Wilson put the proposal to a vote, requiring it to pass unanimously. Eleven of the 17 delegates – a majority – voted in favor, but it failed to find acceptance. The Imperial Japanese representative, Makino Nobuaki, was affronted by this injustice, and at a press conference stated: "We are not too proud

"There is nothing so cooling to a hot temper as a piece of cool steel." – Curtis D. Wilbur, Secretary of the Navy
The Conference on Limitation of Armaments, held in Washington in the early 1920s. Japanese delegates can be seen in the bottom left.

to fight but we are too proud to accept a place of admitted inferiority in dealing with one or more of the associated nations. We want nothing but simple justice."

In 1922, the Washington Naval Conference added to Japan's feeling of injustice, mandating that Tsingtao and other Japanese-claimed territories captured in their World War I campaign should be returned to China. Japanese delegates came to the conference with the express remit to retain control of their spoils, as they were concerned about the expansion of the British and American Pacific Fleets. However, the Western powers, united with China by a common goal, now wanted Japan to renounce its territorial claims and reduce its armed presence on a number of strategic islands, including Formosa, the Bonin Islands and the Ryuku Islands.

The Washington Naval Treaty, drafted by Secretary of State Charles Evans Hughes, saw Japan agree to return Shandong to China. In return, one of the outcomes of the discourse was a restriction on the number and size of naval vessels each nation could build. The American negotiation was aided by cryptographers, who intercepted messages from Japan to its delegation, revealing the lowest requirements they would accept. The cryptographers were working for the Cipher Bureau, also known as the Black Chamber, which was closed down in 1929 by Secretary of State Henry Stimson, who said, "gentlemen do not read each other's mail."

Hard times

Due to the restrictions placed on its navy by the Washington Naval Treaty, Japan's economy began to falter. The most powerful forces in the economy were an oligarchical quadrumvirate, the *zaibatsu*, literally translating as the "financial clique." This "Big Four" were Sumitomo, Mitsui, Mitsubishi, and Yasuda, who could trace their founding back to the Meiji Restoration, if not the Edo Period. Their most lucrative ventures were shipbuilding and military equipment, but while profits now faltered, they were spared total bankruptcy because of their diverse portfolios, which included banking, mining, fishing, and real estate.

The Great Depression hit everyone hard, and Japan was no exception. Remarkably, though, it recovered much faster than everyone else, in part due to the actions of the Bank of Japan and the Ministry of Finance, both of which had close relationships with the major corporations. Since the Russo-Japanese War, major businessmen had become enmeshed in national politics, each striving to foist his own ideas into economic policy. Due to their considerable influence, the zaibatsu conglomerates received favorable concessions, and the Japanese government gave them almost complete control over heavy industry. By 1930, the two major political parties had two zaibatsus as their principle financial backers: Mitsubishi backed The Rikken Minseito and Mutsui backed the Rikken Seiyukai. Members of the Diet were mostly businessmen.

Finance Minister Takahashi Korekiyo is largely credited with helping Japan out of the depression, bringing the yen off the gold standard in 1931 and dramatically increasing domestic spending. He is sometimes called the "Japanese Keynes," since his policies mirrored those advocated by John Maynard Keynes in his book *The General Theory of Employment, Interest and Money*, which came out five years after Takahashi had already deployed them in Japan.

"Economic development should raise standards of living, not just make the state rich and powerful."
–Finance Minister Korekiyo

Takahashi had been a key player in Japan for decades. He had negotiated with Jacob Schiff, who financed half of the Russo-Japanese War, was the 20th Prime Minister, a member of the Diet, Governor of the Bank of Japan, and President of Yokohama Specie Bank (now the Bank of Tokyo). Unfortunately, despite his laudable service to his country, when a coup d'état was attempted on February 26, 1936 by the radical and disgruntled Kodo-ha military faction, Takahashi was assassinated (the rebels were subsequently routed and surrendered to the main Imperial Army).

Military ascendancy

Another famous victim of assassination was Prime Minister Tsuyoshi Inukai, the 16th to hold the title, who had been elected for his support of offensive action in Manchuria, and his objections to the London Naval Treaty, which sought to restrict submarine warfare and naval shipbuilding. However, in 1932 he was being criticized for trying to negotiate with the Chinese and attempting to limit troop deployments in Manchuria. He had been a war correspondent for *Yubin Hochi Shimbun*, and had been embedded with the Imperial forces during the Satsuma Rebellion of 1887-88.

On May 15, 1932, 11 junior naval officers shot Tsuyoshi to death. Their original plan was to assassinate the prime minister the day before, during his reception for the film star Charlie Chaplin, who arrived on May 14. Chaplin may have been among the targets, but was spared, as at the time of the assassination, he was watching a sumo wrestling match with the Tsuyoshi's son Takeru and was unharmed.

"If I could speak, you would understand." – Tsuyoshi Inukai's last words
Prime Minister Tsuyoshi Inukai, accompanied by Korekiyo Takahashi, Takaaki Kato, and Yukio
Ozaki, in a *chashitsu* (tea room).

After returning to the United States, Chaplin wrote a book about his travels, *A Comedian Sees The World*, in which he wrote about the assassination:

> *"The tragedy is well-known –how the murderers, dressed as soldiers, shot and killed several guards, then broke into the prime minister's sitting room and with the points of their guns confronted the old gentleman and his family; how he led them to another room, remarking that if they intended to kill him to spare his wife and children the scene of such violence. The heroic courage of the Prime Minister was worthy of his exalted position. Not one word passed the assassins' lips as they were led by the august gentlemen down a long corridor into the little room where he calmly told them to state their grievances. Without a word, however, these murderers cruelly poured fire into their defenseless victim and left."*

Throughout the 1930s, the Japanese government strove to remain outside the control of the military. However, the Imperial Army began operating without government sanctions as early as 1931, when it invaded Manchuria, and in 1936 the attempted coup allowed the military to wrest political control and influence from the establishment.

One of the rationales the Japanese had for imperial expansion was the so-called "East Asian Co-Prosperity Sphere." It justified the invasion of many countries in Asia

"The sight of numerous brightly colored kimonos against the background of smoke-stacks and the drab, grey docks was paradoxically beautiful." – Charlie Chaplin

Charles and Sydney Chaplin, Kono, Mrs Haruko Mogi and Shioyoshi, captain of the *Suwamuru*, wearing *kimonos* during dinner.

in order to "liberate" them from Western colonialism – namely the Dutch East Indies, American Philippines and Mariana Islands, French Indochina and British Hong Kong, Singapore, Burma and Malaya.

Prime Minister Fumimaro Konoe first articulated this idea in 1940, while Foreign Minister Hachiro Arita deployed it. When US Secretary of State Cordell Hull opposed Japan's territorial expansion, Japanese intellectuals countered that the Co-Prosperity Sphere was comparable to America's Monroe Doctrine which, as spelled out by namesake President James Monroe in 1823, asserted American policy to oppose European colonization in the Americas. In 1904, Theodore Roosevelt had added "The Roosevelt Corollary," which asserted the right of the United States to intervene in affairs of countries of the Americas. This corollary had been used to justify occupying the Dominican Republic in 1905, depose the government of Nicaragua in 1909, and occupy Haiti in 1915 and Nicaragua in 1923.

In 1934 Franklin Roosevelt, Theodore's fifth cousin and now President, renounced the corollary and declared a "Good Neighbor" policy, reminiscent of von Bismarck's *Realpolitik*, which favored economic ties rather than military intervention with Latin America. But Japan was not to be put off its desire to conquer new territory.

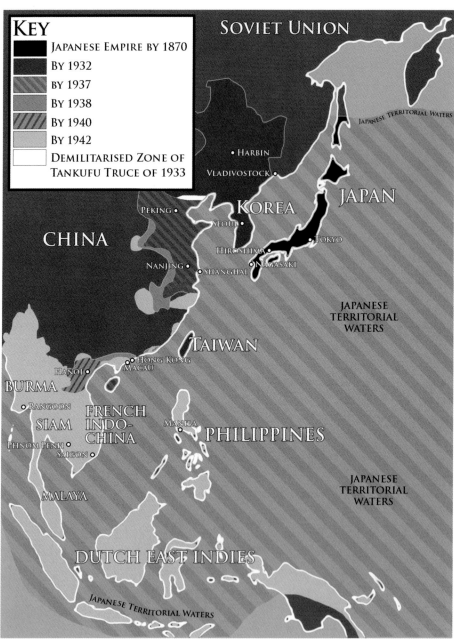

KEY

■	JAPANESE EMPIRE BY 1870
■	BY 1932
▨	BY 1937
▨	BY 1938
▨	BY 1940
▨	BY 1942
□	DEMILITARISED ZONE OF TANKUFU TRUCE OF 1933

SOVIET UNION

JAPANESE TERRITORIAL WATERS

• HARBIN

VLADIVOSTOCK •

JAPAN

PEKING •

KOREA

SEOUL •

CHINA

HIROSHIMA • • TOKYO

NANJING • • SHANGHAI • NAGASAKI

JAPANESE TERRITORIAL WATERS

TAIWAN

HONG KONG
MACAU

HANOI •

BURMA

• RANGOON

FRENCH INDO-CHINA

SIAM

MANILA •

PHILIPPINES

PHNOM PENH •
SAIGON •

JAPANESE TERRITORIAL WATERS

MALAYA

DUTCH EAST INDIES

JAPANESE TERRITORIAL WATERS

"While the history begins with good because of being the divine work, that of freedom begins with evil because of being the human work." – Kiyoshi Miki, a Japanese philosopher whose idea for the Co-Prosperity Sphere was bastardised by the Imperial Japanese Army

The territorial expansion of the East Asian Co-Prosperity Sphere from 1932–1942.

Japan's manifest destiny

"I am convinced that a war with Japan is about as likely as a war with Mars."
– Senator Thomas J. Walsh

Georges Bigot's *The Asian Empire,* conquered at the point of a blade, by Japan.

"...Japanese writers pointed to the spacious territories of other countries, complaining about the injustice of it all, especially since these other countries were not making the most of their land by achieving the high per-acre yields that Japanese farmers obtained. They looked enviously upon not only China's vast land resources but those of Western countries. Why, the military propagandist Sadao Araki asked, should Japan remain content with 142,270 square miles, much of it barren, to feed 60 million mouths, while countries like Australia and Canada had more than three million square miles to feed 6.5 million people each? These discrepancies were unfair. To the ultra nationalists, the United States enjoyed some of the greatest advantages of all: Sadao Araki pointed out that the United States possessed not only three million square miles of home territory but 700,000 square miles of colonies.

If expansion westward to the Pacific Ocean was the manifest destiny of the nineteenth-century United States, then China was twentieth-century Japan's manifest destiny. It was almost inevitable that this homogenous people of high personal esteem would see the socially fragmented and loosely governed expanse of China as having been put there for their use and exploitation.

Nor were Japan's covetous intentions limited only to Asia. In 1925, just a short three years after Japan entered into a capital ship limitation treaty with the United States, Great Britain, France, and Italy that afforded it a distinctive role as the world's third largest naval power, Okawa Shumei, a member of the army general staff, wrote a book that insisted not only on Japan's destiny to "free" Asia but also on the inevitability of world war between Japan and the United States. In the concluding chapter of his book, he was more prophetic than he realized when he predicted a divine – almost apocalyptic – struggle

*between the two powers: 'Before a new world appears, there must be a
deadly fight between the powers of the West and the East. This theory is
realized in the American challenge to Japan. The strongest country in Asia is
Japan and the strongest country that represents Europe is America. These
two countries are destined to fight. Only God knows when it will be.'"*

Iris Chang, The Rape of Nanking

The Second Sino-Japanese War

On September 18, 1931, a minor incident near Mukden (now Shenyang, Liaoning
Province) was used as a pretext for Japan to invade Manchuria, establish the
puppet state Manchukuo and install the deposed Qing Emperor Pu Yi as its head.
The Western powers strongly condemned this move, but the League of Nations
revealed an inherent fallibility when it was unable to punish Japan. A token
effort was made by US Secretary of State Henry Stimson by refusing to recognize
Manchukuo as a Japanese territory.

The League formed a commission to investigate the incident, led by the Earl of
Lytton. The subsequent report refuted Japan's justifications:

*"While Japanese officers in Manchuria on the night of September 18, 1931,
might have believed that they were acting in legitimate defence, the Japanese
military operations at Mukden and other places cannot be regarded as being
in self-defence, anymore than Japan's subsequent military measure, which,
inspired by political considerations, acquired control of all the important
towns."*

When the resolution condemning Japan was proposed in 1933, Japan withdrew from
the League of Nations. Over the next few years China, weakened by internal strife,
was forced to sign away more of its territory to Japan, namely Inner Mongolia in
1935. Japan saw Manchuria and Inner Mongolia as buffer states against the Soviet
Union, with whom it had a series of border conflicts from 1931 until April 13, 1941
(see "The Battle of Halhgol"), when the two nations signed the Soviet-Japanese
Neutrality Pact.

In 1936, Emperor Hirohito approved the creation of a unit within the Kwantung
Army that would research chemical and biological weapons. This project, overseen
by Surgeon Colonel Ishii Shiro, was to be known as Unit 731. It is comparable to
the Nazi human experiments done in the concentration camps, but the scientists
involved were interested in new kinds of weapons and their effects on humans.

"I do not think there is the slightest prospect of any war." – Viscount Robert Cecil

Bernard Partridge's interwar cartoon, depicting the Japanese stranglehold on the proverbial "Chinese Dragon", its tail, Manchukuo, already hacked off. The *mon*, or family emblems, of the Yamanouchi and Ouchi appear upon the samurai's *shitagi* (jacket). Doves of peace fly towards Mount Fuji in the background.

S. O. S.

CHINESE DRAGON. "I SAY, DO BE CAREFUL WITH THAT SWORD! IF YOU TRY TO CUT OFF MY HEAD I SHALL REALLY HAVE TO APPEAL TO THE LEAGUE AGAIN."

Prisoners were injected with syphilis, Bubonic plague, botulism, smallpox and other diseases for study. Others were vivisected without anesthetics and new weapons like flamethrowers were tested on prisoners. In all, tens of thousands of men, women and children (most of them Chinese and Russian) were killed during the experiments.

The experiments were discussed at the War Crimes tribunals in Tokyo, but no charges were brought due to insufficient evidence. American microbiologists described the research as "invaluable" and Douglas MacArthur arranged that the documents would be turned over to the Americans and no one else. In return, Surgeon General Ishii and other participants were made immune to prosecution. Some of these documents found their way into the hands of the Russians, who opened a chemical research facility in Sverdlovsk (now Yekaterinburg). In 1949, the Soviet Union prosecuted 12 Japanese officers and doctors for war crimes related to the experiments. All 12 were found guilty and sentenced to up to 25 years in labor camps. The United States dismissed the trials as "Communist propaganda."

Unit 731, like other contemporary incidents, is a contentious historical issue in contemporary Japan and a source of tension with China, which occasionally expresses anger that Japan has not adequately apologized for it.

The Rape of Nanking

On July 8, 1937, the Sino-Japanese conflict took an egregious turn, as Japanese troops crossed into Greater China, first laying siege to Shanghai and then the temporary capital of Nanking. When Nanking finally fell, hundreds of thousands of civilians were murdered, maimed, sexually assaulted and tortured in what has been called the "Rape of Nanking."

This horrific historic event was to determine to a large extent global opinion of the Japanese for decades to come. As an old Japanese proverb says: "The reputation of a thousand years is determined by the conduct of one hour."

In her book *The Rape of Nanking*, Iris Chang posits one possible reason for the atrocities that occurred in the city:

"In the 1930s, Japanese military leaders had boasted – and seriously believed – that Japan could conquer all of mainland China within three months. But when a battle in a single Chinese city [Shanghai] alone dragged from summer to fall, and then from fall to winter, it shattered Japanese fantasies of an easy victory. Here, this primitive people, illiterate in military

science and poorly trained, had managed to fight the superior Japanese to a standstill. When Shanghai finally fell in November, the mood of the imperial troops had turned ugly, and many, it was said, lusted for revenge as they marched toward Nanking."

During the Nanking massacre, a horrified *Nichi Mainichi Shimbun* reporter watched Japanese line up Chinese prisoners on top of the wall near Chungshan Gate and charge them with bayonets fixed on rifles. He wrote:

"One by one prisoners fell down to the outside of the wall. Blood spattered everywhere. The chilling atmosphere made one's hair stand on end and the limbs tremble with fear. I stood there at a total loss and did not know what to do."

He was not alone in his reaction. Many other reporters – even seasoned war correspondents – recoiled at the orgy of violence, and their shocked reports found their way into print. Yukio Omata, a Japanese military correspondent at Hsiakwan wharf, wrote:

"Those in the first row were beheaded, those in the second row were forced to dump the severed bodies into the the river before they themselves were beheaded. The killing went on non-stop from morning until night, but they were only able to kill 2,000 persons in this way. The next day, tired of killing in this fashion, they set up machine guns. Two of them raked a cross-fire at the lined-up prisoners. Rat-tat-tat. Triggers were pulled. The prisoners fled into the water, but no one was able to make it to the other shore."

Imai Masatake, another Japanese military correspondent, had this to say:

"On Hsiakwan wharves, there was a dark silhouette of a mountain made of dead bodies. About fifty to one hundred people were toiling there, dragging bodies from the mountain of corpses and throwing them into the Yangtze River. The bodies dripped blood, some of them still alive and moaning weakly, their limbs twitching. The laborers were busy working in total silence as in a pantomime. In the dark one could see the opposite bank of the river. On the pier was a field of glistening mud under the moon's dim light. Wow! That's all blood!

After a while the coolies had done their job of dragging corpses and the soldiers lined them up along the river; rat-tat-tat machine gun fire could be heard. The coolies fell backward into the river and were swallowed by the

Bodies of the victims of the Nanking Massacre piled along the Qinhuai River outside the West Gate.

raging currents. The pantomime was over. A Japanese officer at the scene estimated that 20,000 persons had been executed."

In Chang's *The Rape of Nanking*, she quotes General Matsui Iwane, the commander of the Imperial Japanese Army in Nanking, as saying:

"The struggle between Japan and China was always a fight between brothers within the 'Asian Family'... It has been my belief during all these days that we must regard this struggle as a method of making the Chinese undergo self reflection.

We do not do this because we hate them, but, on the contrary because we love them too much. It is just the same as in a family when an elder brother has taken all that he can stand from his ill-behaved younger and has to chastise him in order to make him behave properly."

This euphemistic analogy stands in stark contrast to the reality, as reported time and again from multiple sources. In *The Japan Advertiser* on December 7, 1937, the following "contest" was cheerfully detailed:

"Sub-Lieutenant Mukai Toshiaki and Sub Lieutenant Noda Takeshi, both of the Katagiri unit at Kayung, in a friendly contest to see which of them will first fell 100 Chinese in individual sword combat before the Japanese forces completely occupy Nanking, are well in the final phase of their race, running almost neck to neck. On Sunday (December 5)... the 'score' according to the Asahi was: Sub-Lieutenant Mukai, 89, and Sub-Lieutenant Noda, 78."

Sub-Lieutenants Tsuyoshi Noda and Toshiaki Mukai sit amidst the ruins of Nanking.

The killing and raping subsided when General Matsui entered the city on the morning of December 17 for a ceremonial parade (a bout of tuberculosis meant he had not been present at the start of the atrocities). Astride a chestnut horse, he faced the direction of the Imperial Palace in Tokyo and, according to Chang in *The Rape of Nanking* again, led a triple *banzai* for the Emperor for Japan's national radio broadcasting company:

"'Great Field Marshall on the steps of Heaven – banzai – ten thousand years of life!'

He rode down a boulevard that was carefully cleared of dead bodies and flanked by tens of thousands of cheering soldiers and arrived at the Metropolitan Hotel in the northern part of town, which held a banquet for Matsui that evening. It was sometime during this banquet, the record suggests, that Matsui suspected that something had gone terribly amiss at Nanking.

That evening he called a staff conference and ordered all unnecessary troops out of the city. The next day the Western news media reported that the Japanese army was engaged in a giant conspiracy of silence against Matsui to prevent him from knowing the full truth of the Nanking atrocities. When Matsui began to comprehend the full extent of the rape, murder and looting, he showed every sign of dismay. On December 18th, 1937 he told one of his civilian aides:'I now realize that we have unknowingly wrought a most grievous

"The struggle between Japan and China was always a fight between brothers within the 'Asian Family'...
It had been my belief during all these days that we must regard this struggle as a method of making the
Chinese undergo self-reflection. We do not do this because we hate them, but on the contrary because we
love them too much. It is just the same as in a family when an elder brother has taken all that he can stand
from his ill-behaved younger and has to chastise him in order to make him behave properly."
– General Matsui

General Matsui Iwane and Prince Asaka Yasuhiko parade through Nanking in December 1937.

effect on this city. When I think of the feelings and sentiments of my Chinese
friends who have fled from Nanking and of the future of the two countries, I
cannot but feel depressed. I am very lonely and can never get in a mood to
rejoice about this victory.'

Later that day when the Japanese command held a burial service for
the Japanese soldiers who died during the invasion, Matsui rebuked the
three hundred officers, regimental commanders, and others on the grounds
for the orgy of violence in the city: 'Never before,' Matsumoto, a Japanese
correspondent wrote, 'had a superior officer given his officers such a scathing
reprimand. The Military was incredulous at Matsui's behavior because one of
the officers present was a prince of imperial descent.'

By Sunday, December 19th, Matsui was moved to Asaka's headquarters
outside the city and put on a destroyer the following day to be sent back to
Shanghai. But once there he made an even more shocking move, one perhaps
driven by desperation: he confided his worries to the New York Times and
even told an American correspondent that 'the Japanese army is probably
the most undisciplined in the world today.' That month he also sent a bold
message to Prince Asaka's chief of staff. 'It is rumored that unlawful acts
continue,' he wrote, 'especially because Prince Asaka is our commander,

military discipline and morals must be that much more strictly maintained. Anyone who misconducts himself must be severely punished.'

On New Year's Day Matsui was still upset about the Japanese soldiers' behavior at Nanking. Over a toast he confided to a Japanese diplomat: 'My men have done something very wrong and extremely regrettable.'

But the raping went on, and the killing went on. Matsui seemed incapable of stopping it. If one can believe the story Matsui told years later his brief visit to Nanking even reduced him to tears in front of his colleagues: 'Immediately after the memorial services, I assembled the higher officers and wept tears of anger before them,' Matsui told his buddhist confessor before his hanging in 1948. 'Both Prince Asaka and and Lieutenant General Yanagawa… were there. I told them everything had been lost in one moment through the brutalities of the soldiers. And can you imagine it, even after that, those soldiers laughed at me.'"

General Matsui was found guilty of war crimes relating to the Nanjing Massacre and sentenced to death by the International Military Tribunal for the Far East. He was executed on December 23, 1948.

The Battle of Halhgol

The little-known Battle of Halhgol (also called the Battle of Khalkhin Gol, or to the Japanese the Nomonhan Incident after a village in the vicinity) was the largest modern-style battle before World War II and saw the first massed use of infantry, artillery, armor and air power. (In fact, some historians claim the battle featured the largest aerial battle in history, with hundreds of aircraft on both sides taking part.)

The year was 1939, and the Japanese occupied Manchuria and Inner Mongolia, from where they cast a covetous eye on resource-rich eastern Siberia. Believing the Soviet military to be weakened by the Stalinist purges – and Mongolia too going through a similar upheaval – the Japanese were, at the least, testing Moscow's response when they claimed the Halh River (in Russia-controlled Mongolia) as the western boundary of their puppet state of Manchukuo. Anticipating the threat ahead, thousands of Soviet troops and equipment had already been brought in, and a railroad had been constructed down to Choibalsan.

The battle began simply enough on May 11, 1939 when Mongolian cavalry crossed over to the eastern side of the Halh River. Chased away by local Manchukuo troops, the Mongolians soon returned in greater force and reoccupied their land. Japanese troops then intervened but were badly beaten and retaliated with a

Manchukuoan cavalrymen march across the Mongolian steppes under the banner of the Rising Sun.

damaging air strike against a Soviet airbase farther west on the Great Eastern Steppe. Then-Lieutenant-General Georgy Zhukov arrived in early June to beef up the Soviet-Mongolian forces as skirmishes continued.

Using an estimated 30,000 infantry backed by tanks, artillery and aircraft, the Japanese launched a massive two-pronged offensive at the end of June. The northern task force broke across the river and occupied Bayantsaagan Hill. They were turning south to link up with the second force crossing the river when Zhukov sprang his trap. Using 450 fast-moving tanks and armored cars but no infantry units, the Soviets virtually encircled the Japanese, forcing their withdrawal back across the river. The second crossing over Kawatama Bridge also failed, and when the Japanese massed their troops and artillery for another attempt at the end of

July, they were again defeated with heavy casualties.

Although the Japanese had suffered some 5,000 casualties, they reinforced themselves with up to 75,000 troops backed by armored vehicles and hundreds of aircraft, and planned a

Some of the more than 500 planes deployed at Halgol, thought to represent the first major air battle in history.

third offensive. Despite the appearance of a battlefield stalemate, Zhukov was busy building up a massive 50,000-man force of tanks, mechanized infantry, artillery and aircraft that included running scores of truck convoys from the Choibalsan railhead 250 miles (400km) away. On August 28, 1939, in a brilliant tactical maneuver that would become his trademark in World War II, Zhukov pinned down the center of the Japanese line and then flanked them on both sides with the massive use of armored units, completely encircling them. When the Japanese refused to surrender, Zhukov ordered massive air and artillery strikes. The battle ended on August 31, 1939, the day before Hitler invaded Poland, touching off World War II. The Soviets and Japanese signed a ceasefire two weeks later.

Casualties were heavy on both sides. The official figures from the Japanese were 8,440 killed and 8,766 wounded, while the Soviets claimed a much higher 60,000 Japanese killed and wounded, and 3,000 taken prisoner. Archival work in post-Communist Russia puts Soviet casualties at 7,974 and 15,251 wounded. In strategic terms, the Battle of Halhgol spelled an end to any Japanese thoughts of pushing west. Instead, they now turned their eyes to the resources of Southeast Asia and began planning their surprise attack on the Americans at Pearl Harbor in 1941.

"One man's death: that is a tragedy. A hundred thousand dead: that is a statistic."
– Kurt Tucholsky, German-Jewish writer
Imperial Japanese soldiers pose prior to battle, demonstrating their equipment's readiness.

WORLD WAR II AND THE TERRIBLE POWER OF THE ATOM

Death from above

By the 1930s, the practice of aerial bombing had been in place for almost a century. The first recorded use of an aerially deployed explosive was in the subduing of the Republic of San Marco, during the First Italian War of Independence, when a number of unmanned balloons, fitted with shrapnel shells, were released above Venice on August 20, 1849. The devices, designed by Austrian Imperialist Franz von Uchatius, were intended to incite "extreme terror" and affect the morale of the inhabitants, and are the first expressed usage of aerial missiles to directly kill, maim, and demoralize a civilian population.

"Air power may either end war or end civilization." – Winston Churchill
The first demonstration of a hot-air balloon in Umegasaki, Japan in 1805 by Swiss physicist Johann Caspar Horner. This prototype was made from *washi* paper.

Rapid innovations in air and explosive technology, driven by the military industrial complex, made it the most destructive tool in every nation's arsenal. Companies like Boeing (US), Heinkel (Germany), and Aichi (Japan) made aircraft for their respective militaries that specialized in dropping bombs.

In 1923, The Hague's Rules for Air Warfare spelled out how nations could drop bombs from the air, but it was never adopted. It specifically banned terror bombing (article 22) and said aerial bombardment could only happen against military targets (article 23-24), and states who bombed illegitimate targets would be liable to pay restitution (article 24). Western powers agreed that aerial bombing civilian targets should be illegal at the 1932 World Disarmament Conference in Geneva, but the colonial powers wanted to reserve the right to bomb what the British delegation called "outlying places." Frances Stevenson, the wife of former British Prime Minister David Lloyd George wrote in her diary, "At Geneva other countries would have agreed not to use aeroplanes for bombing purposes, but we insisted on reserving the right, as [George] puts it, to bomb niggers."

At the same conference, Japan proposed banning the production of aircraft carriers, even though the Imperial Japanese Navy had one of the first aircraft carriers, *Hosho* and a few years later would convert their ship *Akagi* to an aircraft carrier. The conference failed, and shortly afterwards, British Lord President Stanley Baldwin told Parliament:

> *"There is no power on earth that can protect him from being bombed. Whatever people may tell him, the bomber will always get through; the only defense is in offense, which means that you have to kill more women and children more quickly than the enemy if you want to save yourselves."*

Japan first dropped bombs on China during the January 28th incident in 1932, when Japanese carrier aircraft bombarded Shanghai in response to anti-Japan protests spurred by the occupation of Manchuria.

During the second Sino-Japanese War, a Chinese torpedo boat attacked the flagship of the IJN's Third Fleet, *Izumo*, on August 14, 1937. *Izumo* survived the attack and responded by sending aerial bombers to Shanghai. The Navy sent more bombers to Shanghai on August 28, which destroyed the Shanghai South Railway Station. Amid the wreckage of the station, Hearst newspaper photograph H.S. Wong took the famous "Bloody Saturday" photograph. The image was widely printed across the world and caused shock and outrage. Senator George W. Norris of Nebraska saw the photo and condemned the Japanese as "disgraceful, ignoble, barbarous, and cruel, even beyond the power of language to describe."

"I see your American newspapers have nicknamed me the Babykiller." – Admiral Koichi Shiozawa of the Imperial Japanese Navy, speaking to *The New York Times*

H.S. "Newsreel" Wong's infamous photo *Bloody Saturday*, depicting a baby alone, sitting amongst the smoldering ruins of a Shanghai railway station.

While reporting on the bombing of civilians decreased as the war went on, even leaders at the top recognized the futility of bombing civilians. Near the end of World War II Winston Churchill was disturbed by the bombing of Dresden and told General Hastings Ismay, his chief military advisor, that bombing civilians "simply for the sake of increasing the terror should be reviewed. Otherwise we shall come into control of an utterly ruined land."

The vast majority of the 60 million who died during World War II were civilians, and in 1949, the 4th Geneva Convention stipulated that, in war, military forces would not target civilians in any way.

On September 27, 1940, Japan signed the Tripartite Treaty, aligning itself with Germany and Italy, a triumvirate of Axis powers, acknowledging each other's spheres of influence and promising to assist each other in times of need. With this treaty Japan set its course, bringing it into direct confrontation with the as yet unformed but potentially overpowering forces of the United States of America.

"Tomorrow, the Tripartite Pact will become an instrument of just peace between the peoples. Italians! Once more arise and be worthy of this historical hour! We shall win." – Prime Minister Benito Mussolini

Bernard Partridge's satirical primate trio — Hirohito, Hitler and Mussolini — hearing, seeing and speaking "no good!", whilst supported by the "Totalitarian Axis."

TRIPARTITE PACT

"Hear no good!"   "See no good!"   "Speak no good!"

The Fugu Plan

In the late 1930s tens of thousands of Jews fled Nazi-occupied areas of Europe and headed for Asia, including China and Japan. Due to the Unequal Treaties signed by China after the Opium Wars, Jews could enter the country with no passport or visa. In 1938, Japan decided not to expel them from either their own shores or occupied territories. In fact, the Japanese, much to the chagrin of the Nazis, encouraged the influx of Jews. The 1904 bankrolling of the Russo-Japanese war by Jewish financier Jacob Schiff had deeply endeared the group to the Japanese authorities. Their evident business acumen, which had ignited Russian and German hatred, was seen as highly desirable in the East, and in 1939 the Imperial government sought to incentivize collaboration with Asia-based Jews, especially within the Greater East Asia Co-Prosperity Sphere, through the "Fugu Plan."

Fugu (a Japanese pufferfish) is a notorious Japanese delicacy, made infamous by the inherent danger of being fatally poisoned or paralyzed by the fish's tetrodotoxin, which must be carefully extracted from the whole. The name was no doubt inspired by the risk for Japan of fraternizing with – in fact harboring – a people whom their allies were so diligently attempting to exterminate. In fact, the Fugu Plan came to fruition mere months after Adolf Hitler's Reichstag speech, where he alluded to the *Endlösung*, the Final Solution to the Jewish Question, on January 30, 1939:

> *"We must finally break away from the notion that a certain percentage of the Jewish people are intended, by our dear God, to be the parasitic beneficiary of the body, and of the productive work, of other peoples.*
>
> *If the international finance-Jewry inside and outside Europe should succeed in plunging the nations into a world war yet again, then the outcome will not be the victory of Jewry, but rather the annihilation of the Jewish race in Europe!"*

The Japanese Empire was clearly aware of Hitler's anti-Semitism, and yet perceived the potential benefits to outweigh any costs. German representatives proposed building a concentration camp in the Far East for Jewish refugees, but Japan refused. It did, however, construct a Jewish ghetto in the Hongkou district of Shanghai, which Jews could only leave with special permission. Two thousand Jews died in the ghetto over the course of the war.

Meanwhile in Europe: A World War II timeline (1938–1941)

Nazi troops parade through the streets of Tirol, Austria, in the wake of *"Anschluss,"* Germany's absorption of Austria in March 1938.

1938

March 12/13: Germany announces *"Anschluss"* (union) with Austria.

August 12: German mobilizes its military.

September 30: British Prime Minister Chamberlain appeases Hitler at Munich.

November 9/10: *Kristallnacht* – The Night of Broken Glass.

1939

March 15/16: Nazis take Czechoslovakia.

May 22: Nazis sign "Pact of Steel" with Italy.

August 25: Britain and Poland sign a Mutual Assistance Treaty.

September 1: Nazis invade Poland.

September 3: Britain, France, Australia and New Zealand declare war on Germany.

September 5: United States proclaims its neutrality.

September 29: Nazis and Soviets divide up Poland.

December 14: Soviet Union expelled from the League of Nations.

1940

May 10: Nazis invade France, Belgium, Luxembourg and the Netherlands; Winston Churchill becomes British Prime Minister.

May 26: Evacuation of Allied troops from Dunkirk begins.

June 10: Italy declares war on Britain and France.

June 14: Germans enter Paris.

June 18: Soviets begin occupation of the Baltic States.

June 22: France signs an armistice with Nazi Germany.

July 10: Battle of Britain begins; air battles and daylight raids over Britain.

September 3: Hitler plans Operation Sea Lion (the invasion of Britain).

September 7: German Blitz against Britain begins.

Top: A lady walks past broken windows in the aftermath of *Kristallnacht* on November 10, 1938 in Germany. Bottom: German soldiers at the beginning of Operation Barbarossa, June 22, 1941.

September 16: United States military conscription bill passed.

September 22: Japanese forces seize Haiphong and cut the railway line to Kunming.

September 27: Tripartite (Axis) Pact signed by Germany, Italy, and Japan.

November 5: Roosevelt re-elected as US president.

1941

March 11: President Roosevelt signs the Lend-Lease Act.

April 6: Nazis invade Greece and Yugoslavia.

May 10/11: Heavy German bombing of London; British bomb Hamburg.

May 27: Sinking of the *Bismarck* by the British Navy.

June 14: United States freezes German and Italian assets in America.

June 22: Germany attacks Soviet Union as Operation Barbarossa begins.

July 3: Stalin calls for a scorched earth policy.

July 12: Britain and Soviet Russia agree a Mutual Assistance Pact.

July 26: Roosevelt freezes Japanese assets in United States and suspends relations.

July 31: Göring prepares for the Final Solution (extermination of the Jews).

August 1: United States announces an oil embargo against aggressor states.

August 14: Roosevelt and Churchill announce the Atlantic Charter.

August 20: Nazi siege of Leningrad begins.

September 3: First experimental use of gas chambers at Auschwitz.

September 19: Nazis take Kiev (subsequently 33,771 Jews are murdered there).

October 2: Operation Typhoon begins (German advance on Moscow).

December 6: Soviet Army launches a major counter-offensive around Moscow.

December 7: Japanese bomb Pearl Harbor; Hitler issues the Night and Fog decree.

December 8: United States and Britain declare war on Japan.

Top: Survivors of the Dachau concentration camp demonstrate the operation of the crematorium between April 29 and May 10, 1945. The image was doctored by the USSR propaganda department to grotesquely show the corpse of a Jew being loaded into the oven. Colorization was added by a netizen.

Pearl Harbor

On December 7, 1941, at 7.48am (Hawaiian Time), Japan attacked the US Naval fleet stationed at Pearl Harbor, on the island of Oahu. Simultaneously, forces were unleashed upon Singapore, Hong Kong, Thailand, the Philippines, and British Malaya.

The next day, at 12.30pm (Eastern Time), President Franklin D. Roosevelt addressed a joint session of Congress, calling the previous day, "A day that will live in infamy." A few hours later, the United States declared war on Japan and the Axis Powers.

Japan, of course, had a different view of that fateful historic moment:

Remember the 8th of December
When world history changed.
When Anglo-Saxon supremacy
Was refused by the land and the sea of East Asia
It was Japan that refused white supremacy.
A little country in the Eastern sea
Country of the gods
Reigned over by Emperor Showa
The power of America and Britain,
Monopolists of the world's wealth,
Was refused here in our country.
To refuse is our justice.
We demand that East Asia be returned to the East Asians,
Our neighbors have all been sapped of strength by their exploitation.
It is we who will break the grip of their nails and fangs
We who will rise up, gather our strength
Old and young, men and women
Every one a soldier
We'll fight till our mighty opponents admit they were wrong
Remember December 8th,
The day world history was broken in two.

– Kotaro Takamura (Translated by Kawasaki Takeshi)

"Before a new world appears, there must be a deadly fight between the powers of the West and the East. This theory is realized in the American challenge to Japan. The strongest country in Asia is Japan and the strongest country that represents Europe is America... these two countries are destined to fight. Only God knows when it will be." – Okawa Shumei, Imperial General Staff

The USS *Arizona*, a Pennsylvania-class 'super-dreadnought', lists into the ocean in the aftermath of the Pearl Harbor attack. Onboard, 1,177 officers and crew were killed, and she remains submerged, a memorial to the dead.

"It's the right idea, but not the right time." – John Dalton

The history and science of the atomic bomb

We must now briefly step back in time in order to chart the process that culminated in the momentous events of August 6 and August 9, 1945. Atomic theory dates back to 1808, when John Dalton, a secretary at the Manchester Literary and Philosophical Society, proposed the atom as the smallest unit of matter. A few years later Amedeo Avogadro, a math and physics teacher in Vercelli in the Kingdom of Sardinia (now Italy), built on Dalton's research to define molecules as clusters of atoms.

But by the turn of the 20th century physicists' understanding of atoms and subatomic particles was still negligible. The French engineer Henri Becquerel discovered radioactivity in March 1896:

> *"I kept the apparatuses prepared and returned the cases to the darkness of a bureau drawer, leaving in place the crusts of the uranium salt. Since the sun did not come out in the following days, I developed the photographic plates on the 1st of March, expecting to find the images very weak. Instead the silhouettes appeared with great intensity... One hypothesis which presents itself to the mind naturally enough would be to suppose that these rays, whose effects have a great similarity to the effects produced by the rays studied by M. Lenard and M. Röntgen, are invisible rays emitted by phosphorescence and persisting infinitely longer than the duration of the luminous rays emitted by these bodies."*

Building on Becquerel's research, in 1898 Gerhard Schmidt of the University of Erlangen discovered that thorium is radioactive while Pierre and Marie Curie at the University of Paris discovered radioactive elements radium and polonium. The Curies and Becquerel shared the 1903 Nobel Prize in Physics for their discoveries.

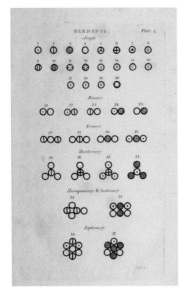

"Matter, though divisible in an extreme degree, is nevertheless not infinitely divisible. That is, there must be some point beyond which we cannot go in the division of matter... I have chosen the word 'atom' to signify these ultimate particles." – John Dalton

The first page of John Dalton's *A New System of Chemical Philosophy*, published in 1808. The first element in the top left represents hydrogen; the third is carbon. Number 37 demonstrates the molecular structure of sugar.

Over the next few decades, physicists at the Cavendish Laboratory at Cambridge University discovered subatomic particles: first J.J. Thomson discovered the electron, then Ernest Rutherford revealed the atomic nucleus, and later the proton when he demonstrated that hydrogen's most common isotope (H1) is a single proton.

Rutherford's colleague Frederick Soddy discovered that radiation occurs as a result of an element decaying into another isotope, specifically that thorium decayed into radium. Soddy named this process "nuclear transmutation," despite the protestations of Rutherford, who said, "Don't call it transmutation. They'll have our heads off as alchemists."

Among the many readers of Soddy and Rutherford's work was the British author and political activist H.G. Wells. In 1914 he published his book *The World Set Free*, dedicated to Soddy. In it, Wells described a bomb that had "Carolinum" as the source of its power, rather than more conventional explosives like the nitroglycerine used in dynamite. Wells' radioactive substance would start a continuous explosion that would burn for the length of Carolinum's half-life, which Wells put at 17 days.

In the late 1920s Robert Atkison and Fritz Houtermans first outlined nuclear fusion, and in 1932 James Chadwick discovered the neutron. Leo Szilard, a Hungarian physicist living in London, read Wells' book in 1932. Szilard, following up on the idea that elements that underwent nuclear fusion could create a chain reaction – which is what Wells had speculated earlier – found that the energy released came in the form of free neutrons that would cause more atoms to fuse and release more free neutrons. He patented the idea of a neutron chain reaction in 1934 (British Patent No. 630,726 "Improvements in or Relating to the Transformation of Chemical Elements").

In 1938 Szilard was offered a post at Columbia University and moved to New York. Soon after, the university hired Italian physicist Enrico Fermi, who had fled Italy due to Mussolini's racial laws that affected his Jewish wife, Laura. That same year, German scientist Otto Hahn, and his assistant Fritz Strassmann, discovered nuclear fission. In fission, free neutrons are absorbed by an atom, excite it and cause it to split into smaller elements, expelling more free neutrons. In 1939, after several unsuccessful tests, Szilard and Fermi discovered that uranium-235 (the number at the end is the number of protons and neutrons in the nucleus) could undergo a chain reaction using this process.

There are two natural isotopes of uranium. Uranium-238 (U-238) is by far the most common. It is not fissile, meaning it cannot undergo fission, but uranium-235 (U-235), which accounts for 0.7 percent of naturally occurring uranium, can. Japanese physicist Arakatsu Bunsaku, a former student of Albert Einstein, performed the first atomic nucleus collision experiments in Asia in 1934 and discovered that each nuclear fission of U-235 atoms yields on average 2.6 free neutrons.

In 1941, Dr. Glen Seaborg, of the University of California discovered that uranium-238 atoms would absorb free neutrons when bombarded and become plutonium-239 (Pl-239). Plutonium-239 proved to be much easier to undergo fission than uranium-235. Both elements were shown to undergo spontaneous nuclear fission when a sufficiently large quantity was assembled (called "critical mass"). Uranium-235 underwent fission with 50kg (110lbs) but plutonium-239 achieved critical mass with only 10kg (22lbs).

Nuclear fusion was proved by arguably the most famous equation in physics, $E=mc^2$, the formula Albert Einstein used to show the relationship between the mass of an object and energy. Einstein proposed it in the fourth of his *annus mirabilis* ("Extraordinary Year") papers, published in 1905 by Annalen der Physik and titled "Does the Inertia of a Body Depend Upon Its Energy Content?" Later experiments confirmed the relationship between energy and mass.

The equation showed that during nuclear reactions, the energy released would be vastly greater than the mass. (At Hiroshima, "Little Boy" carried 64kg (141lbs) of uranium-235 and less than 1kg – 1.38 percent of the mass – underwent fission, but the energy released (yield) was the equivalent of 13,000 tons of TNT. At Nagasaki, "Fat Man" carried 6.19kg (13.6lbs) of plutonium-239 and about 1kg (2.2lbs) underwent fission, with a yield of 20,000 tons of TNT.)

Research into nuclear weaponry

On August 2, 1939, President Franklin Roosevelt received a letter, written by Leo Szilard and signed by Albert Einstein, warning that the Germans were developing an atomic bomb.

Germany officially started an atomic bomb development program – its *Uranprojekt*, known informally as the *Uranverein* (Nuclear Society) – in 1939, but ended it around the time it invaded Poland and many of the scientists were drafted into the *Wehrmacht*. A second program was initiated two weeks after the invasion, but by 1943, research had slowed and most of the energies of the scientists went into nuclear power. In 1942 scientists at Leipzig built a nuclear reactor, but it caught fire during a test and set the

"I know not with what weapons World War III will be fought, but World War IV will be fought with sticks and stones." – Albert Einstein, photo by Lucien Chavan

building ablaze. Many of the key scientists in the project abandoned it and most of the buildings were destroyed by British and American air raids in 1942 and 1943.

The first industrial uranium mine in the world, in Jachymov, Czechoslovakia was under the control of the Nazis by 1938. British spies monitored the mine throughout the war for signs of any large-scale activity, but no plans came to fruition at the site. The largest uranium mines were in the Belgian Congo (now the Democratic Republic of Congo), and Belgium was vulnerable to a German invasion. In 1940, the Union Minière du Haut Katanga (UMHK) had a near monopoly on the world's uranium trade. Engineers from the company discovered uranium ore (known as Uraninite) at the Shinkolobwe mine in 1915 and began extracting it in 1921.

When Leo Szilard wrote the famous letter to President Roosevelt in 1939, one of his concerns was about Shinkolobwe falling into German hands. However, when Germany occupied Belgium in May 1940, the Belgian Congo remained loyal to the Allies and the Belgian government-in-exile, based in London, ensured that their colony was defended. Germany was hampered in Africa by the loss of its colonial possessions after World War I. German East Africa, which bordered the Belgian Congo, was now a League of Nations Mandate under the control of Britain (present-day Tanzania) and Belgium (present-day Rwanda and Burundi).

Edgar Sengier, Director of UMHK, learned about the possibilities of weapons-grade uranium from British scientists, and was warned about allowing the Congo to fall into enemy hands. In 1939 Sengier arranged for 1,000 tons of uranium ore from the Shinkolobwe mine to be secretly shipped to New York, and stored in a Staten Island warehouse. Almost all of the uranium was sold to the Manhattan Project in 1942.

"The United States has only very poor ores of uranium in moderate quantities. There is some good ore in Canada and the former Czechoslovakia, while the most important source of uranium is the Belgian Congo." – Albert Einstein, in his 1939 letter to President Roosevelt

A photograph of the UMHK ore processing plant in Élisabethville (modern-day Lubumbashi), in the south of the former Belgian Congo.

Roosevelt responded to Szilard and Einstein's letter by convening an advisory committee charged with investigating the possibility of a nuclear bomb. He charged Lyman Briggs, Director of the National Bureau of Standards, to establish and coordinate the "Briggs Advisory Committee on Uranium" to investigate the feasibility of creating an atomic bomb.

Meanwhile, across the Pacific the Japanese were also investigating nuclear weapons. The head of nuclear research at the RIKEN Institute (a Tokyo-based scientific research institute) was a former student of Niels Bohr named Nishina Yoshino. Nishina proposed nuclear weapons research to the Imperial Japanese Navy in 1939, fearing the United States would soon develop one. The Navy created a committee to investigate such weapons, but in 1943 it concluded that it would be "difficult even for the United States to realize the application of atomic power during the war," and the Navy lost interest.

The Imperial Japanese Army, however, maintained an interest in nuclear weapons, and with the RIKEN Institute set up the Ni-Go project, which attempted to separate U-235 by thermal diffusion. The project was unsuccessful and the firebombing of Tokyo destroyed the building housing the laboratory.

The Manhattan Project – "destroyer of worlds"

As the war progressed, in England two German scientists exiled in Birmingham, Otto Frisch and Rudolf Peierls, demonstrated how fissile uranium-235 was (its capability of sustaining a nuclear fission chain reaction), and calculated that a bomb carrying merely 1kg of the element would still be devastating. In a note to one of their colleagues, they called it a "radioactive super-bomb." The note, and their findings, were passed to Henry Tizard, the chair of the Committee on the Scientific Survey of Air Defence. At his request, six physicists (four of them Nobel Prize winners) convened under the Military Application of Uranium Detonation (MAUD) Committee in the United Kingdom.

The MAUD Committee issued its final report on the feasibility of a nuclear bomb in July 1941 and sent it to, among others, Vannevar Bush (co-founder of defense contractor and manufacturing giant Raytheon) at the National Defense Research Committee (NDRC). The MAUD Committee was especially anxious to develop a bomb, since Britain was already embroiled in war, whilst the US at that time maintained its neutrality. Australian physicist Marcus Oliphant, one of MAUD's project leaders, traveled to Washington in August 1941, and asked Lyman Briggs why no action had been taken based upon the report's findings. He discovered that Briggs had put the report in his safe, and never disclosed MAUD's conclusions to his fellow Uranium Committee members.

"It was essential to do this job, hateful though it was, because we knew the Germans were hot on the trail." – Marcus Oliphant
Courtesy of the University of Adelaide Archives.

In Oliphant's subsequent meeting with the Uranium Committee, he said an atomic bomb was not only inevitable, but that it was vital in the fight against Germany. Oliphant said it would cost US$25 million to produce the weapon, money that Britain was unable to allocate.

The Uranium Committee was replaced by the S-1 Uranium Committee, which first met on December 18, 1941. By now Britain was already developing nuclear weapons, under the codenamed program "Tube Alloys." President Roosevelt approved the American atomic weapons program on October 9, 1941, to be overseen by a top council comprising the President himself (though he never attended any council meetings); Vice-President Henry Wallace; Secretary of War Henry Stimson; Army Chief of Staff General George Marshall; Dr. James Conant, President of Harvard University, and Dr. Vannevar Bush, Head of the Office of Scientific Research and Development (OSRD)

The Army commandeered the project and, on August 16, 1942 it established the Manhattan Engineer District (MED), with Colonel Leslie Groves heading the program. The headquarters was on the 18th floor of 270 Broadway in Manhattan, and thus the program became known as the Manhattan Project.

Groves was a difficult man – he was rude, stubborn and paranoid. This led to a long list of complaints throughout his career as well as while overseeing the Manhattan Project. His superiors let this slide during the war because he delivered results. As Groves himself put it, "who cares whether they liked you or not? That wasn't the objective; it was to have things running well." In 1948, General Dwight Eisenhower recounted to Groves a long list of complaints, and made it clear he would never be Chief of the Corps of Engineers. Groves retired, but not before being promoted to Lieutenant General. He died in 1970, and is buried at Arlington National Cemetery.

When Groves took charge of the Manhattan Project, he prevented the sharing of information with the British, whom he did not trust. However, in 1943 Britain and America agreed to share their nuclear development research and the Tube Alloys program was integrated into the Manhattan Project. Churchill and Roosevelt further agreed that this cooperation should be perpetuated, even in the aftermath of the war.

In 1943 the Army Corps of Engineers began building a facility near Oak Ridge, Tennessee, called the Y-12 National Security Complex, to enrich uranium. They did this using gaseous diffusion, a process developed in part by Chinese-American Wu Chien-shiung, a professor of chemistry at Columbia University. The uranium came from mines in the Belgian Congo and the Southwest United States.

Top right:
Question: *"Is there such a thing being planned as a super bomb?"*
Groves: *"No, I don't think so. They talk about airplanes that will go around the world, etcetera. This thing has just started and no one knows just what will develop."*
– Transcript from the Oak Ridge Press Conference, September 29, 1945.

Bottom right:
"We can train you how to do what is needed, but cannot tell you what you are doing. I can only tell you that if our enemies beat us to it, God have mercy on us!"
– Unnamed manager of "Calutron girl" Gladys Owens
Calutron operators at their panels in the Y-12 plant at Oak Ridge, Tennessee.

A second remote site, at Hanford, Washington, produced plutonium. The Manhattan Project employed up to 129,000 people – most of them construction workers who worked on building the laboratories. The program ended up costing around US$2 billion (US$26 billion at 2014 values), considerably more than the US$25 million James Oliphant had originally speculated. When Harry Truman announced the bombing of Hiroshima, he mentioned this fact as part of his justification for using it.

The most important man on the Manhattan Project was its Director, J. Robert Oppenheimer. He is credited with "achieving the implementation of atomic energy for military purposes," and is considered to be one of, if not *the* "Father of the Atomic Bomb." However, he is well-known for his utterance of the famous phrase from the Bhagavad Gita,"Now I am become Death, the destroyer of worlds," upon witnessing the Trinity test.

Dr. Oppenheimer started his career under J.J. Thomson at Cambridge University, and then studied theoretical physics under Max Born, one of the pioneer researchers into

"The optimist thinks this is the best of all possible worlds. The pessimist fears it is true." – J. Robert Oppenheimer

quantum mechanics. He returned to the United States and became a professor at the University of California at Berkeley. Oppenheimer was often ill, and would spend time in New Mexico recovering. He fell in love with the American Southwest and it was at his recommendation that the Manhattan Project set up its secret laboratory at Los Alamos, not far from his ranch.

Oppenheimer and his team first experimented with a gun-type bomb, initially called "Thin Man," later "Little Boy." They discovered that the very low critical mass of plutonium-239 prevented detonation in the gun-type bomb. The team subsequently designed the implosion-type bomb that was eventually deployed at Trinity and in the "Fat Man" bomb dropped on Nagasaki.

While Oppenheimer was relieved when Trinity was shown to be a phenomenal success, the bombing of Nagasaki disturbed him and his fellow scientists. Almost immediately afterwards, he began pleading with the Truman Administration to ban nuclear weapons. During a meeting with President Truman in October 1945, Oppenheimer said he felt he had "blood on his hands," and Truman ended the meeting. Truman later said, "I don't want to see that son-of-a-bitch in this office ever again."

After the war, Oppenheimer became director of the Institute for Advanced Study in Princeton, New Jersey, where he invited top intellectuals to solve the most important questions of the day. He also served as an advisor to the Atomic Energy Commission, and used that position to advocate against nuclear proliferation and the arms race with the Soviet Union.

Oppenheimer's reputation was ruined by the House of Un-American Activities (HUAC) hearings in which colleagues revealed him as a supporter of the Communist Party in the 1930s. He lost his government positions and his security clearance, and stayed out of the public eye for years. He still opposed nuclear weapons, but was not present at major protests against them in the 1950s because of his tarnished reputation. As a sign of reconciliation, the US Government gave him the Enrico Fermi Award in 1963 in recognition of his scientific achievements.

"In accordance with my verbal directive of July 15, it is desired that clearance be issued to Julius Robert Oppenheimer without delay irrespective of the info which you have concerning Mr Oppenheimer. He is absolutely essential to the project." – Colonel Leslie Groves, July 20, 1943

J. Robert Oppenheimer and Colonel Leslie Groves at the Trinity Site.

THE BOMBS THAT CHANGED THE WORLD

The "greater good"

On February 19, 1942, President Roosevelt issued Executive Order 9066, which allowed the US Army to designate swathes of land as "military zones," and displace inhabitants when deemed necessary. This power was used to detain over 100,000

A soldier posts notifications of Japanese relocation under Civilian Exclusion Order 1 on Bainbridge Island, Washington.

Japanese-American men, women and children living on the west coast of America in a series of camps. Sixty-two percent of those interned were American citizens. In Hawaii, where Japanese-Americans comprised 35 percent of the population, internment was limited to a few thousand.

General John L. DeWitt, during the government's defense of Executive Order 9066 before the Supreme Court in 1942, offered the following absurd reasoning:

"The Japanese race is an enemy race and while many second- and third-generation Japanese born on United States soil possessed of US citizenship have become "Americanized", the racial strains are undiluted. It then follows that along the vital Pacific Coast over 112,000 potential enemies, of Japanese extraction, are at large today. There are indications that these were organized and ready for concerted action at a favorable opportunity. The very fact that no sabotage has taken place to date is a disturbing and confirming indication that such action will be taken..."

On April 23, 1943, First Lady Eleanor Roosevelt visited the Gila River internment center in Arizona, after which she wrote an essay for Collier's on her visit:

"To undo a mistake is always harder than not to create one originally but we seldom have the foresight. Therefore we have no choice but to try to correct our past mistakes and I hope that the recommendations of the staff of the War Relocation Authority, who have come to know individually most of the Japanese Americans in these various camps, will be accepted. Little by little as they are checked, Japanese Americans are being allowed on request to

leave the camps and start independent and productive lives again. Whether you are a taxpayer in California or in Maine, it is to your advantage, if you find one or two Japanese American families settled in your neighborhood, to try to regard them as individuals and not to condemn them before they are given a fair chance to prove themselves in the community.

'A Japanese is always a Japanese' is an easily accepted phrase and it has taken hold quite naturally on the West Coast because of fear, but it leads nowhere and solves nothing. A Japanese American may be no more Japanese than a German-American is German, or an Italian-American is Italian, or of any other national background. All of these people, including the Japanese

"He found the situation that he was facing most difficult, with the antagonisms on the part of much of the American public against the Japanese because we were at war with Japan and many people did not differentiate between the Japanese Americans and the Japanese with whom we were at war." – Dillon Myer on Milton, younger brother to President Eisenhower, who resigned from the WRA after three months. Eleanor Roosevelt, accompanied by Dillon Myer, Director of the War Relocation Authority (WRA) and Commissioner of the Bureau of Indian Affairs, visits the Gila River War Relocation Center, an Indian Reservation in Arizona. More than 13,000 individuals with Japanese ancestry were interned at Gila.

Americans, have men who are fighting today for the preservation of the democratic way of life and the ideas around which our nation was built.

We have no common race in this country, but we have an ideal to which all of us are loyal: we cannot progress if we look down upon any group of people amongst us because of race or religion. Every citizen in this country has a right to our basic freedoms, to justice and to equality of opportunity. We retain the right to lead our individual lives as we please, but we can only do so if we grant to others the freedoms that we wish for ourselves."

– Eleanor Roosevelt, *Collier's Magazine*, October 10, 1943

The mistreatment of Americans of Japanese descent during World War II was not properly acknowledged by the government until 1988, when the US officially apologized for the internment and paid compensation to the victims totaling US$1.2 billion.

The Pacific campaign

Fifteen miles east of Hiroshima stood the Kure Naval Arsenal, which constructed some of the Imperial Japanese Navy's largest vessels – two of the aircraft carriers used at Pearl Harbor – *Soryu* and the flagship *Akagi* (meaning "Blue Dragon" and "Red Castle" respectively) – were built there. Admiral Yamamoto Isoroku, who had directed the Battle of Pearl Harbor, commanded at the Battle of Midway from the battleship *Yamato*, also constructed at Kure.

At Pearl Harbor, Japanese naval aircraft bombarded the American ships with

Type-91 torpedoes, which were used by all air forces under the command of the Imperial Japanese Navy. The first Type-91 torpedoes were made at the Mitsubishi Heavy Industries factory in Nagasaki – it was subsequently destroyed by the atomic bomb.

"Japan will eventually be a nation without cities – a nomadic people." – Arthur Radford, commander in the US Third Fleet

Leaflet #2093 depicting American GIs island-hopping through the nations cleared of Japanese occupiers, while the Air Force drones overhead. The Japanese islands of Honshu, Shikoku, and Kyushu are all that remain unconquered by the Allies.

The Battle of Midway came only six months after the Pearl Harbor attack, but it was a pivotal moment in the conflict between the US and Japan. Admiral Yamamoto believed that his superior naval force could defeat the US Navy and in one blow take control of the Pacific, but when the two sides met near Midway Island to the west of Hawaii, it was the US forces who triumphed, sinking four Japanese aircraft carriers (including the *Soryu* and *Akagi*). Without these vessels, and lacking the resources to build replacements and man them with skilled crews fast enough, Japan's power in the Pacific was irrevocably diminished, and from that moment on it waged a defensive war as the United States Armed Forces slowly but surely took over islands in Micronesia and the South Pacific, advancing across the Pacific territories towards Japan.

> KILL THE BASTARDS!
> DOWN THIS ROAD MARCHED ONE OF THE REGIMENTS OF THE UNITED STATES ARMY
> KNIGHTS SERVING THE QUEEN OF BATTLES
> TWENTY OF THEIR WOUNDED IN LITTERS WERE BAYONETED, SHOT AND CLUBBED BY THE YELLOW BELLIES
> KILL THE BASTARDS!

"When a Japanese soldier was 'flushed' from his hiding place... the unit... was resting and joking. But they seized their rifles and began using him as a live target while he dashed frantically around the clearing in search of safety. The soldiers found his movements uproariously funny. Finally... they succeeded in killing him... The veteran emphasized the similarity of the enemy soldier to an animal. None of the American soldiers apparently ever considered that he may have had human feelings of fear and the wish to be spared." – Jesse Glenn Gray, American philosopher drafted in 1941

A propaganda poster created by the US Army.

Meanwhile, as the Manhattan Project made progress towards cataclysmic success and the creation of the ultimate weapon, President Roosevelt decided that an air raid against Japan would boost morale and serve as payback for Pearl Harbor. The first raid occurred on April 18, 1942, when Tokyo, Yokohama, Nagoya, Osaka, and Kobe were all bombed by American B-25 bombers under the command of Lieutenant Colonel James "Jimmy" H. Doolittle.

The Army Air Force (AAF) had been planning to firebomb Japan as early as November 1943. However, Brigadier General Haywood "Possum" Hansell, who commanded the XXI Bomber Command, opposed the tactic as "morally repugnant," and accordingly the division engaged in precision bombing. In the European Theater the AAF relied on precision bombing, but the B-17 had to fly low to hit its target.

"Allied air power was decisive in the war in Western Europe. Hindsight inevitably suggests that it might have been employed differently or better in some respects. Nevertheless, it was decisive." – United States Strategic Bombing Survey, September 30, 1945 Brigadier General Haywood Hansell points to Tokyo Bay during a briefing at XXI Bomber Command, November 1944.

But strong crosswinds and cloud cover complicated precision bombing over Japan; a precision bombing campaign against the Iwate Steelworks in Fukuoka in 1944 resulted in only a single bomb out of 376 hitting the intended target.

In mid-1944, America took control of the Mariana Islands, notably Guam and Saipan, and the XXI Bomber Command launched a series of campaigns against Japan using the newly introduced B-29 Superfortress plane, which flew higher, but was less accurate.

In January 1945, Hansell was replaced by Lieutenant Colonel Curtis "Bombs Away" LeMay. AAF Captain Robert McNamara (who would later become Secretary of Defense) described LeMay as, "the finest combat commander of any service I came across in war. But he was extraordinarily belligerent, many thought brutal."

LeMay had no issues with firebombing, and more than 100 B-29 bombers were loaded with explosives, reminiscent of the weapons H.G. Wells had described in *The World Set Free* a generation earlier. Area bombs were loaded with magnesium, white phosphorus and napalm. Their explosions would be relatively small, but the cocktail of chemical compounds ensured that they were highly combustible and near inextinguishable. The fact that most buildings in Japan were made of wood did not help their situation. Throughout the remainder of the war, the AAF bombed 67 cities in Japan in this manner.

The most devastating firebomb raids were in Tokyo on March 9-10, 1945 when a firebombing campaign destroyed 16 square miles of the city. Flying at 7,000 feet, 334 B-29s dropped 1,665 tons of incendiaries on the conurbation in the space of six hours. At least 100,000 people were killed (some analysts put the death toll as high as 200,000). The beleaguered Tokyo Fire Department lost 88 firemen and 96 fire engines. A *Time Magazine* article on March 19, 1945 stated: "Properly kindled, Japanese cities will burn like autumn leaves."

"It was an ocean of fire. My mother held my hand as we entered the chaotic stream of refugees and headed for the Arakawa embankment. This painting is of something I saw on the way and have never been able to forget. A pregnant woman was standing there like a ghost; at her feet was a child of perhaps three or four years. The child wasn't moving at all. The way they were lit up by the flames around them – it was a sight I saw at 12 [years old] that was so horrifying I'll never be able to forget it."
– Miyamoto Kenzo, survivor of the Tokyo firebombing

Main picture: An aerial image of Tokyo ablaze, taken from a B-29.

Top right: Three of the 517 B-29 Superfortresses that bombed Yokohama on May 29, 1945, and subsequently took part in the firebombing of Tokyo.

Left, top to bottom: *Umaya Bridge in Flames*, a painting by Fukushima Yasusuke, six years old.
The City Burned Long Ago – As If We Were Vermin, by Kawai Mitsuru, 12 years old.
My Child, by Miyamoto Kenzo, 12 years old.

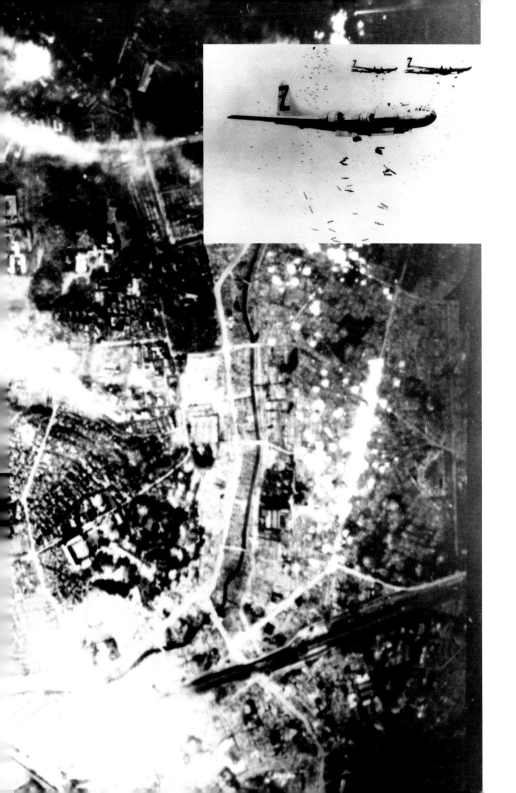

"These are the eggs which will make an omelet of the Jap capital."

"Just a few of the thousands of heavy bombs which Superfortresses will shuttle from Saipan to Tokyo are shown in this picture of ordnance men loading a train of trailers with cargo for Saipan B-29s." – Original caption accompanying declassified image #A38758

Pathfinder planes that went ahead of the bombers marked the targets with a large flaming X, which was centered on the densely populated Chuo and Koto wards, where the population density was an average of 103,000 inhabitants per square mile. Eighty-seven percent of the target zone was residential. The number of casualties likely exceeded the Great Kanto Earthquake that had struck Tokyo in 1923.

"It might have been better for me to die quickly than to see such a terrible thing. If the people up there in the B-29s were really human beings like us, I'd have liked to drag them out of their planes and make them witness it too. But there was nothing I could do for those poor people. I just gave a bow in their direction and walked away." – Shizuo Tsuzuki

Bodies in Ishihara-cho, Honjo ward, a photograph by police officer Koyo Ishikawa, one of possibly five individuals with a camera on that day.

On December 17, 1944, the AAF created the 509 Composite Group, a flying squadron with the specific purpose of dropping the atomic bombs. Captain Paul Tibbets was assigned to head the mission due to his experience in the field as well as being a test pilot for the B-29. Tibbets was promoted to Colonel in January 1945, and was the pilot of the *Enola Gay* (named for his mother) when it dropped the atomic bomb on Hiroshima.

Plans of attack, and a new president

The Allies were planning to invade Japan if it did not surrender by November 1, 1945. They had suffered 50,000 casualties in taking Okinawa alone and military leaders estimated as many as 800,000 American fatalities if they invaded Japan. For comparison, the US had 405,399 fatalities in all of World War II and 750,000 in its deadliest conflict, the Civil War.

The plan was determined by Japan's geography. The US controlled Okinawa, and would work its way up the Ryuku Islands to Kyushu, then proceed to Honshu. Realizing this, the Japanese government fortified Kyushu and southern Honshu. In February 1944, Prime Minister and Minister of War Tojo Hideki issued an emergency proclamation calling for "100 million honorable deaths." The General Army Headquarters was split in two, with half remaining in Tokyo and the other migrating to Hiroshima.

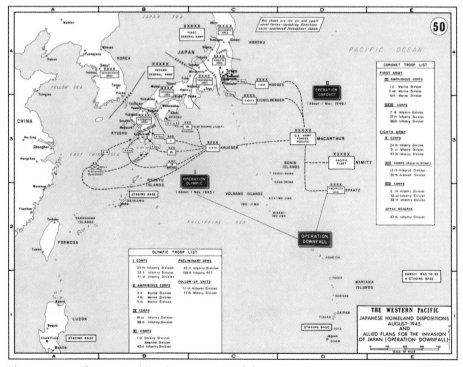

"The supreme art of war is to subdue the enemy without fighting." – Sun Tzu

A map of the movements of American Armed Forces in the execution of Operation Downfall, comprised of a two-pronged attack – Operation Coronet and Operation Olympic – on the Japanese mainland, on Kyushu and Honshu.

A declassified memo details a meeting in which Leslie Groves thought the atomic bomb should be dropped on the Truk Lagoon, where the Imperial Japanese Navy was harbored at the time. The reasoning was that if the bomb failed, it would land in deep water where it would be difficult to get hold of, and even if Japan managed to salvage it, they would have a harder time reverse engineering the device and creating their own atomic bomb. The minutes of a Military Policy Meeting on May 5, 1943 show the American fear of this new atomic technology being used against them: "The Japanese were selected as they would not be so apt to secure knowledge from it as would the Germans."

Leo Szilard recognized the dangers of a nuclear arms race early, and using another letter from Albert Einstein, asked for a meeting with Roosevelt to discuss it. First Lady Eleanor Roosevelt scheduled such a meeting for May 8, 1945, but it never took place. Roosevelt died of a cerebral hemorrhage on April 12, and Vice-President Harry Truman became President.

Speaking to reporters following his swearing in as the 33rd President of the United States of America, President Truman said:

"Boys, if you ever pray, pray for me now. I don't know if you fellas ever had a load of hay fall on you, but when they told me what happened yesterday, I felt like the moon, the stars, and all the planets had fallen on me."

Truman's emergence as President was something of a shock to everyone, because there were two other candidates who might easily have been in his place. Henry Wallace had been Roosevelt's Vice-President during his third term, but Wallace was a liberal from Iowa who campaigned against racial discrimination and poverty. Democratic party bosses therefore wanted him removed from the 1944 Presidential ticket, and Postmaster General and Democratic National Committee chair Robert Hannegan organized a campaign where Roosevelt met a series of politicians who opposed Wallace's renomination while Wallace was on a goodwill mission to China and the Soviet Union. By the time Wallace returned in July 1944, he had lost favor and political ground.

Roosevelt's next choice for Vice-President was James F. Byrnes, a conservative from South Carolina, former Supreme Court Justice and Director of the Office of War Mobilization. However, big city bosses opposed his nomination because they reasoned his status as an ex-Catholic would offend Roman Catholics, who were part of the New Deal Coalition. Others opposed him due to his defense of lynching and opposition to racial integration, fearing that Byrnes on the ticket would alienate

"Power intoxicates men. It is never voluntarily surrendered. It must be taken from them." – James F. Byrnes, former Secretary of State, Supreme Justice and Governor of South Carolina

Secretary of State James F. Byrnes, President Harry S. Truman and Secretary of Commerce Henry A. Wallace at the funeral of Franklin D. Roosevelt, April 14, 1945.

African-American voters. Labor unions also opposed his nomination due to his opposition to a minimum wage.

Byrnes' nomination was eventually dropped, and in what was later called "the second Missouri Compromise," Roosevelt and the Democrats agreed to have Senator Harry Truman assume the Vice-Presidency to satisfy everyone in the coalition. Thus the heavy burden of momentous decisions was laid on the shoulders of an unlikely and relatively unprepared individual.

On May 7, 1945, one day before Szilard's scheduled meeting, Germany surrendered. Three days later, the Targeting Committee met, in Los Alamos, New Mexico to decide where the atomic bomb should be dropped. Dr. Joyce Stearns, the director of the Metallurgical Lab at the University of Chicago, made a list of five potential targets:

• Kyoto, the former capital. In the committee minutes, it is justified thus: "From a psychological point of view there is the advantage that Kyoto is an intellectual center for Japan and the people there are more apt to appreciate the significance of such a weapon."

• Hiroshima, an army depot and shipyard.

• Yokohama, an urban industrial area where many industries moved after the destruction in Tokyo.

• Kokura, due to its heavy industry.

• Niigata, due to its growing importance as other port cities were bombed.

None of the viable target cities had been firebombed; this ensured that they were clean targets. On June 1, Secretary of War Henry Stimson removed Kyoto from the target list, owing to its cultural importance and his belief that bombing it would anger Japan and prolong the war.

In his diary on July 25, 1945, Truman wrote: "Even if the Japs are savages, ruthless, merciless and fanatic, we as the leader of the world for the common welfare cannot drop this terrible bomb on the old capital or the new." Kyoto's spot in the list was replaced by Nagasaki.

The first atomic explosion took place at 5.29am on July 16, 1945 in the New Mexico desert. A plutonium bomb, codenamed Trinity, it created an explosion with the equivalent power of 18,000 tons of TNT. The US finally had "the bomb."

The bomb drops

By this time, President Truman was heading to Potsdam, to decide, with the Allied powers, the terms under which Japan should surrender. Japan was attempting to broker peace through the Soviet Union, through which it had a non-aggression pact. Japan's Imperial War Cabinet had discussions about surrender in May, and on June 22 the Emperor told the cabinet he desired a swift end to the war.

"Our people have not forgotten that the Japanese struck us the first blow in this war without the slightest warning. They believe that we should continue to strike the Japanese until they are brought groveling to their knees. We should cease our appeals to Japan to sue for peace. The next plea for peace should come from an utterly destroyed Tokyo." – Senator Richard Russell, August 7, 1945, in a telegram to President Truman

A map of the main Japanese islands indicating the five sites targeted by the 1945 Committee.

Opposite: An enlarged section of the July 17, 1945 Petition to President Roosevelt by Dr Leo Szilard and his fellow scientists from the atomic project.

A PETITION TO THE PRESIDENT OF THE UNITED STATES

ies of which the people of the United States are not awa
s nation in the near future. The liberation of atomic p
es atomic bombs in the hands of the Army. It places in
, the fateful decision whether or not to sanction the us
se of the war against Japan.

undersigned scientists, have been working in the field o
have had to fear that the United States might be attacke
d that her only defense might lie in a counterattack by
feat of Germany, this danger is averted and we feel impe

nas to be brought speedily to a successful conclusion and
ery well be an effective method of warfare. We feel, hov
ould not be justified, at least not unless the terms whic
on Japan were made public in detail and Japan were give

ublic announcement gave assurance to the Japanese that
evoted to peaceful pursuits in their homeland and if Jap
our nation might then, in certain circumstances, find it
f atomic bombs. Such a step, however, ought not to be r
onsidering the moral responsibilities which are involved

opment of atomic power will provide the nations with nev
tomic bombs at our disposal represent only the first ste
e is almost no limit to the destructive power which will
of their future development. Thus a nation which sets t
y liberated forces of nature for purposes of destruction
lity of opening the door to an era of devastation on an

his war a situation is allowed to develop in the world
in uncontrolled possession of these new means of destruc
s as well as the cities of other nations will be in cont
All the resources of the United States, moral and mat
revent the advent of such a world situation. Its preve
esponsibility of the United St es—singled out by

One of the points of contention at Potsdam was whether to compromise, and permit Japan to retain its Emperor. Byrnes, now Secretary of State, opposed making this promise, telling Truman he would be "crucified" by Republicans for making a deal with the Japanese, comparing it to making a deal with Hitler or Mussolini to remain in power.

Leo Szilard had petitioned the president, along with 69 co-signers (the actual number of signatories is disputed), to give a formal demonstration of the atomic bomb to Japan before using it. It was still a highly classified secret, yet Szilard hoped a demonstration might cow the Japanese generals. Not even the engineers at the Tennessee or Washington plants knew what they were making. However, the Targeting Committee, who believed the psychological shock of the destruction would force Japan to surrender, ultimately rejected the petition.

On July 25, 1945, Truman signed the order authorizing the atomic bombs to be dropped. The next day, the Potsdam Proclamation was issued, with no mention of the Emperor or the bomb. The proclamation became known in Japan through radio broadcasts sent by the Office of War Information and through leaflets dropped on major cities. It was never submitted through official diplomatic channels.

As the proclamation was announced, Truman promised Japan "prompt and utter destruction" if they did not sign it. Prime Minister Suzuki Kantaro publicly rejected the declaration, saying Japan would fight to the bitter end.

Atomic Bomb Blues
It was early one morning when all the good work was done
It was early one morning when all the good work was done
And that big bird was loaded, with that awful atomic bomb

Wrote my baby, I was behind the risin' sun
Wrote my baby, I was behind the risin' sun
I told her don't be uneasy, because I'm behind the atomic bomb

Nation after nation, was near and far away
Nation after nation, was near and far away
Well, they soon got the news, and there where they would stay

Over in East Japan, you know, they let down and cried
Over in East Japan, you know, they let down and cried
And poor Tojo, had to find a place to hide

– lyrics by Homer Harris, recorded by Muddy Waters in 1946

"Formosa is in flames and Iwo Jima has fallen to the Americans. Tokyo, Nagoya and Kobe have been intensely bombed. A great American army has landed on Okinawa. The tide of battle has passed beyond you. The Gumbatsu have left you to rot."

"Your greatest duty now, and most important, is to live; to be ready for the reconstruction of your beloved homeland."
– Words accompanying Leaflet 101-J-1

This air-dropped leaflet depicts the impending attack on the main Japanese islands, as Allied (US) naval and aerial forces close in. Bombs fall, foreshadowing the imminent final solution.

In the early morning of August 6, 1945 the B-29 bomber *Enola Gay* took off from Tinian, one of the Mariana Islands, carrying a 4.8-ton bomb nicknamed Little Boy. A scout plane ahead of it triggered air-raid sirens in Hiroshima, but when it seemed no Superfortresses were coming, the all-clear was sounded at 7.31am.

At 8.15am a group of six bombers came into view. The *Enola Gay* released Little Boy, intending to hit the T-shaped Aioi Bridge, due to its distinctiveness from the air. Just 44 seconds after release, Little Boy detonated. The bomb contained

"The 509 Composite Group, 20th Air Force will deliver its first special bomb as soon as weather will permit visual bombing after about August 3, 1945 on one of the targets: Hiroshima, Kokura, Niigata, and Nagasaki." – Thomas T. Handy, Acting Chief of Staff on July 25, 1945

Hiroshima before and after the deployment of "Little Boy." The Aioi Bridge can be seen intersecting with the first of the concentric 1,000ft rings radiating from the true point of impact.

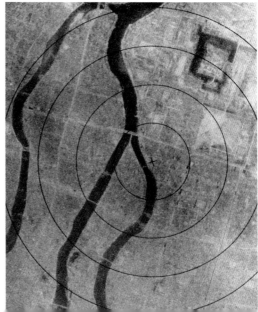

64kg of uranium-235, and less than 1kg underwent fission. The remainder was scattered by the explosion, floating through the atmosphere, and came down as black rain.

At an altitude of 1,900 feet above the Shima Surgical Clinic, its trajectory altered by strong crosswinds, Little Boy unleashed its payload. The energy of 15,000 tons of TNT erupted over Hiroshima. The blast was directed downwards and destroyed nearly every building within a two mile radius. The shipyards and army depots at Ujina Harbor – the alleged targets – were barely affected by the blast.

"A bright light filled the plane. The first shockwave hit us. We were eleven and a half miles slant range from the atomic explosion but the whole airplane cracked and crinkled from the blast... We turned back to look at Hiroshima. The city was hidden by that awful cloud... mushrooming, terrible and incredibly tall."

– Colonel Paul Tibbets

The flight and ground crew of the *Enola Gay*. Paul Tibbets, captain of the flight, stands in the center with a pipe in his mouth; to the left, looking downwards, stands navigator Theodore Van Kirk.

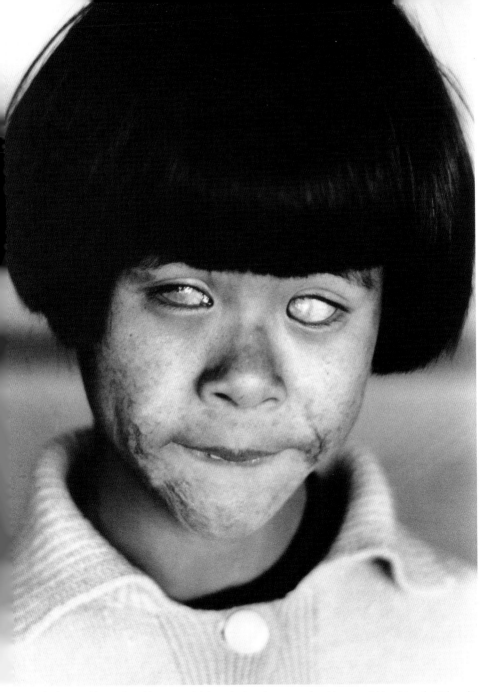

"I had no problem with it. I knew we did the right thing because when I knew we'd be doing that I thought, yes, we're going to kill a lot of people, but by God we're going to save a lot of lives. We won't have to invade." – Paul Tibbets

Witness to atomic destruction: A portrait of a girl blinded by the bright light emitted as "Little Boy" exploded over Hiroshima, photo by Christer Strömholm.

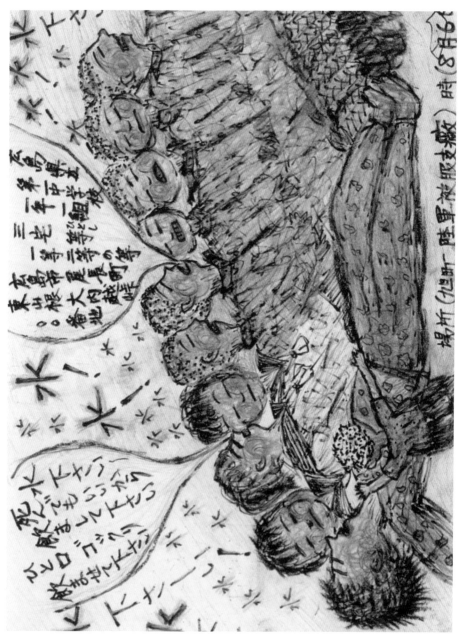

"Water, water, water! Water please!" Voices reverberated through the brick building. The faces of the junior boys and girls lined up on the floor looked the same. They were blown up like balloons, their eyes narrowed to slits." – A Zuroku A-bomb drawing by a survivor, Hiroshima Peace Museum.

Their Faces Upturned

The morning, again, was hot. Father Kleinsorge went to fetch water for the wounded in a bottle and a teapot he had borrowed. He had heard that it was possible to get fresh tap water outside Asano Park... There were many dead in the garden. At a beautiful moon bridge, he passed a naked, living woman who seemed to have been burned from head to toe and was red all over. Near the entrance to the park, an Army doctor was working but the only medicine he had was iodine, which he painted over cuts, bruises, slimy burns, everything – and by now everything he had painted had puss on it.

Outside the gate of the park Father Kleinsorge found a faucet that still worked – part of the plumbing of a vanished house – and he filled his vessels and returned. When he had given the wounded water he made a second trip. This time the woman on the bridge was dead. On his way back with the water he got lost on a detour around a fallen tree and as he looked for his way through the woods, he heard a voice ask from the underbrush, "Have you anything to drink?" He saw a uniform. Thinking there was just one soldier, he approached with the water. When he penetrated the bushes, he saw that there were about twenty men, and they were all in the same nightmarish state: their faces wholly burned, their eyesockets were hollow, the fluid from their melted eyes had run down their cheeks. (They must have had their faces upturned when the bomb went off; perhaps they were anti-aircraft personnel.) Their mouths were merely swollen, puss-covered wounds, which they could not bear to stretch enough to admit the spout of the teapot. So Father Kleinsorge got a large piece of grass and drew out the stem to make a straw and gave them all a drink of water that way.

One of the soldiers said, "I can't see anything." Father Kleinsorge answered, as cheerfully as he could, "There's a doctor at the entrance to the park, he is busy now, but he'll come soon and fix your eyes, I hope."

Father Kleinsorge filled the containers a third time and went back to the riverbank. There amidst the dead and dying, he saw a young woman with a needle and thread mending her kimono. Father Kleinsoge joshed her. "My, but you're a dandy!" he said. She laughed.

(John Hersey, *Hiroshima*)

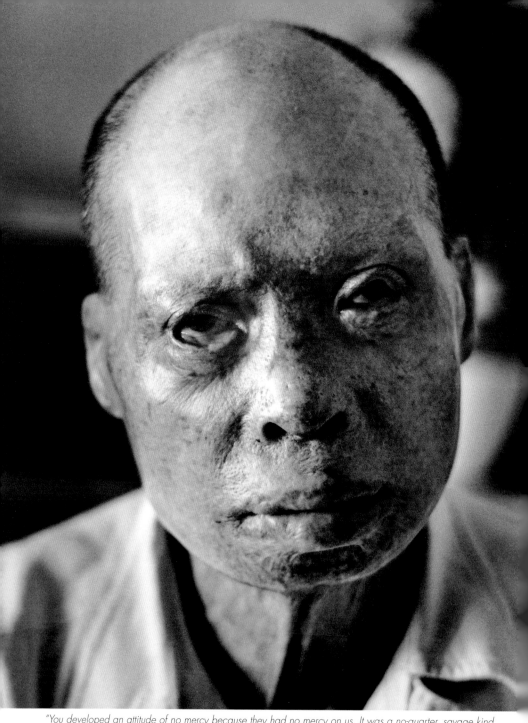

"You developed an attitude of no mercy because they had no mercy on us. It was a no-quarter, savage kind of thing." – Eugene B. Sledge, US Marine and university professor

A victim of the Hiroshima bombing, his suffering captured in this poignant portrait by Christer Strömholm.

"The mushroom cloud was really shaped more like a jellyfish than a mushroom. Yet it seemed to have a more animal vitality than any jellyfish, with its leg that quivered and its head that changed color as it sprawled out slowly toward the southeast, writhing and raging as though it might hurl itself on our heads at any moment. It was an envoy of the devil himself, I decided: who else in the whole wide universe would have presumed to summon forth such a monstrosity? Should I ever get away alive? Would my family survive? Was I, indeed, on my way home to rescue them? Or was I seeking refuge for myself alone?"

– from *Black Rain*, by Masuji Ibuse

The next three days

In announcing the atomic bombing of Hiroshima on August 6, 1945, President Truman said: "If they do not now accept our terms they may expect a rain of ruin from the air, the like of which has never been seen on this earth."

"I took no pride or pleasure then, nor do I take any now, in the brutality of war, whether suffered by my people or those of another nation. Every life is precious. But I felt no remorse or guilt that I had bombed the city where I stood." – Charles Sweeney

Charles W. Sweeney stands, hands on hips, wearing his captain's cap. Remnants of the 1945 crew stand with him upon its delivery to Wright-Patterson Air Force Base, Ohio.

The first sign in Tokyo that Hiroshima had been decimated came when an operator at Radio Tokyo noticed the Hiroshima station had gone offline. He tried to contact the station without success, and the Japanese military immediately sent planes to survey the damage, believing nothing serious had taken place. The pilots circled the destroyed city, incapable of comprehending the enormity of the catastrophe. They reported what they saw to Tokyo and landed. The Army Marine Headquarters at Ujina Harbor, mildly damaged by the bomb, immediately began mobilizing relief efforts.

The day after the bombing, the New York newspaper *PM* devoted its entire issue to the atomic bomb, discussing the science behind it and some of the lead-up to what had happened the day before, using now public information. The issue started with an editorial by Irving Brant, in which he wrote,"There is no escape. The split atom may shatter humanity, but not before then will it retreat into the physical void from which it came. The dust of creation is in our hands. We must master it."

Toward the end of the issue there are graphics and articles speculating what would happen if an atomic bomb were dropped on New York.

"The city, for the first time in its long history, is destructible. A single flight of planes no bigger than a wedge of geese can quickly end this island fantasy, burn the towers, crumble the bridges, turn the underground passages into lethal chambers, cremate the millions. The intimation of mortality is part of New York now in the sounds of jets overhead, in the black headlines of the latest editions.

All dwellers in cities must live with the stubborn fact of annihilation; in New York the fact is somewhat more concentrated because of the concentration of the city itself, and because, of all targets, New York has a certain clear priority. In the mind of whatever perverted dreamer might loose the lightning, New York must hold a steady, irresistible charm."

– *"Here is New York,"* by E.B. White,
first published in *Holiday* magazine, April 1949

During the following days, millions of leaflets were dropped on Japan, warning Japanese that a second bomb would be dropped unless the government surrendered. In Washington DC on August 6, President Truman issued the following statement:

"Sixteen hours ago, an American airplane dropped one bomb on Hiroshima, an important Japanese army base. That bomb had more power than 20,000 tons of TNT. It had more than 2,000 times the blast power of the 11-ton British 'Grand

"We Japanese, a vanquished people, must now walk along a path that is full of pain and suffering." – Dr. Nagai
Doctor Nagai Takashi amidst the ruins of the Nagasaki Medical College.

Slam,' which is the largest bomb ever yet used in the history of warfare.

It is an atomic bomb. It is a harnessing of the basic power of the universe. The force from which the sun draws its power has been loosed against those who brought war to the Far East.

We are now prepared to obliterate more rapidly and completely every productive enterprise the Japanese have above ground in any city. We shall destroy their docks, their factories, and their communications. Let there be no mistake; we shall completely destroy Japan's power to make war."

Immediately after the bombing of Hiroshima, Minister of War General Anami Korechika said, "I am convinced that the Americans had only one bomb, after all." He was sadly mistaken.

On August 8, the B-29 bomber *Bockscar* was loaded with the second atomic bomb, nicknamed Fat Man, due to its large spherical shell-casing. Major General Thomas Farrell, the Field Operations Manager for the Manhattan Project, autographed the bomb "To Hirohito, with love and kisses, T.F. Farrell."

The casing was the same as the pumpkin bombs that the AAF had dropped on Japan earlier in the year. But inside Fat Man was 6.2kg of plutonium, and its detonation mechanism was the same as the one exploded in New Mexico less than a month earlier.

The bombing of Nagasaki

The initial target of the second atomic bomb was the steelworks at Kokura. *Bockscar* and a fleet of five other B-29s took off from Tinian at 3.49am on August 9th. The *Enola Gay* conducted weather reconnaissance for Kokura, and determined that the visibility over the city was obscuring the designated target. *Bockscar* made three runs over the city before heading for its secondary target, Nagasaki, around 10.30am.

Just as in Hiroshima, the air-raid sirens were sounded, but the all-clear was sounded a few minutes later and when the six bombers approached, the watchers on the ground assumed they were reconnaissance planes and didn't sound the alarm. Nagasaki also had cloud cover, and the crew of the *Bockscar* debated what to do. Lacking sufficient fuel to return to Iwo Jima, as originally intended, they considered landing at Okinawa with the bomb, or dropping it in the ocean. However, at 11.01am the clouds over Nagasaki parted briefly, and Fat Man was released.

Forty-seven seconds later the plutonium in Fat Man reached critical mass 1,650 feet above a tennis court in Urakami. The blast yielded the equivalent of 21,000 tons of TNT. Because of the city's valleys the blast was contained, and the casualty estimates were about half of those for Hiroshima, but that can be of little consolation to those who suffered through the nightmare of destruction and its aftermath.

"As I watched, two things that looked like great big hideous lizards crawled in slowly making croaking, groaning sounds. Others followed. I was paralyzed with horror for minutes. Then the light got a little stronger and I could see they were human beings –skinned alive by fire or heat, their bodies all smashed where they had been thrown against something hard.

After a few minutes I saw something coming up the road along the river that looked like a parade of roast chickens. Some of them kept asking for 'Water! Water!'

They were all naked and they were skinned. The skin of their hands had been torn away at the wrists. It was hanging from their fingertips just behind the nails, turned inside-out like a glove. In the dim light I thought I saw many other children lying all about the yard."

– Nagai Takashi (from *We of Nagasaki*)

Opposite: A mother and young child, dazed in the aftermath, stand holding *onigiri* (rice balls).
Yamahata Yosuke captured this iconic image in Nagasaki.

LEADERS AND THEIR LEGACIES

The Imperial Cabinet

As the Emperor issued the official surrender of Japan during his "Jewel Voice Broadcast" (*Gyokuon-hoso*), the Imperial War Council governed the country. The Council had been formed in the Meiji Era, but it was reorganized in 1944 as the Supreme Council for the Direction of the War (also known as the "Big Six") by Prime Minister Koiso Kuniaki. In the 1930s Koiso had been a member of the *Sakurakai* ("Cherry Blossom Society"), who tried twice to overthrow the government and establish a military dictatorship with the Emperor as its head.

Koiso resigned on April 7, 1945, the same day the Battleship *Yamato* was sunk, and the next council was in power from that day until August 15, 1945. All of its members signed the Potsdam Declaration and resigned from their posts shortly afterwards, except the Emperor Showa, who remained in power until his death in January 1989.

Emperor Showa (Hirohito)

The head of state since 1926, Emperor Hirohito's reign had been chaotic from the beginning. The Great Depression hit three years after his ascendance, and the invasion of Manchuria came shortly afterwards. He was the target of at least two assassination attempts, the 1923 Toranomon Incident, and the 1932 Sakuradamon Incident. From the beginning he sought to boost morale among troops, but after the American victories on Iwo Jima and Okinawa, he began urging his ministers to negotiate for peace.

At a meeting of the Supreme War Council on June 22, 1945, he said:

"We have heard enough of this determination of yours to fight to the last soldier. We wish that you, leaders of Japan, will strive now to study the ways and the means to conclude the war. In doing so, try not to be bound by the decisions you have made in the past."

The Emperor's role in the war has been controversial to this day, with no historical consensus on just how great a part he played in Japanese decision-making.

Admiral Suzuki Kantaro, Prime Minister

Suzuki was a navy veteran of the First Sino-Japanese War and the Russo-Japanese War. In the latter conflict he participated in the Battle of Tsushima. Suzuki opposed war with the United States and spent much of the war in retirement.

On his appointment as Prime Minister in 1945, he called two Imperial conferences on the Potsdam Declaration to negotiate between the military officers (who opposed surrender) and the Emperor, who agreed to accept the declaration on August 14.

Togo Shigenori, Foreign Minister

Togo was a career diplomat from Kagoshima who served in the Japanese missions to Switzerland in 1916 and the United States in 1926. In the late 1930s, he served as Japanese Ambassador to Germany, and in the same role to the Soviet Union in 1938. He opposed going to war with the United States, and attempted to arrange negotiations with Franklin Roosevelt to avoid the conflict. He was appointed Foreign Minister in October 1941, and resigned in 1942 in protest of the creation of a special ministry for occupied territories.

When he returned to the post in 1945, Togo was supportive of accepting the Potsdam Declaration. In light of his historic dealings, he hoped for more favorable terms from the Soviet Union, with whom Japanese diplomats were furiously negotiating. These efforts were unsuccessful, as the Soviet Union declared war on Japan on August 9, 1945. Togo resigned, along with the rest of the cabinet, after signing the Potsdam Declaration and his successor, Shigemitsu Mamoru, signed the instruments of surrender that officially ended the war.

After the war he was arrested and tried for war crimes during the Tokyo Tribunal. He was found guilty and sentenced to 20 years in prison, where he died in 1950.

General Anami Korechika, Minister of War

General Anami's military career was not primarily in combat roles, but in administrative positions. He served as an aide-de-camp to the Emperor for a year, and at the beginning of the Second Sino-Japanese War he commanded forces in China. During the war he was occasionally recalled to Japan to oversee military administration there.

In December 1944, Anami was recalled to Japan to serve in the Supreme Council for the Direction of the War, and as chief of the Army Aeronautical Department. He was promoted to Minister of War in April 1945. Anami opposed surrender and was ready to fight the allies if they ever invaded Japan.

However, superseding his dogmatism was his loyalty to the Emperor. When army officers (including War Ministry staff) tried to overthrow the Emperor after his acceptance of the Potsdam Declaration, Anami refused to participate due to his loyalty.

He eventually gave in to the Emperor's desires and signed the Potsdam Declaration on August 14, 1945, committing seppuku the following day, though he was initially unsuccessful and his brother-in-law finished the act. His sword and

blood-drenched uniform are on display at the Yushukan Museum in Tokyo, within the grounds of the Yasukuni Shrine. His suicide note reads, "I – with my death – humbly apologize to the Emperor for the great crime."

Admiral Yonai Mitsumasa, Minister of the Navy

Admiral Yonai entered service at the end of the Russo-Japanese War. After a distinguished career, he became Minister of the Navy in 1937 and served as Prime Minister for six months in 1940. He opposed the growing tensions with Britain and the United States and also opposed the Tripartite Pact with Germany and Italy, signed two months after he resigned as Prime Minister. Despite his desire to ease tensions with the Allies, he supported the building of *Yamato*-class battleships in violation of the Washington Naval Treaty.

In 1944 he returned to politics as Deputy Prime Minister and Minister of the Navy under Prime Minister Koiso Kuniaki. He maintained the position of Navy Minister during Suzuki's premiership, and urged the council to sign the Potsdam Declaration. Unlike the rest of the council, he did not resign after signing the Declaration and oversaw the dissolution of the Imperial Japanese Navy.

General Umezu Yoshijiro, Chief of the Army General Staff

For most of the war, General "Stoneman" Umezu was the Governor-General of Kwantung and commander of the Kwantung Army. It was under his leadership that Unit 731 of the Kwantung Army carried out its experiments, though he (and no one else) was charged for its activities. Umezu wanted the Potsdam Declaration modified to guarantee protection of the Emperor.

Umezu was the senior representative of the Imperial Japanese Army who signed the Instrument of Surrender. He was arrested and charged with war crimes. At the Tokyo Tribunals he was found guilty and sentenced to life in prison. He converted to Christianity during his incarceration, and died in 1949.

Admiral Toyoda Soemu, Chief of the Navy General Staff

Toyoda was promoted to full admiral two months before Pearl Harbor. He opposed attacking the United States, seeing such a conflict as "unwinnable." He later said that Japan "could have avoided the [Pacific] war if it had tried hard enough."

In 1942 Admiral Toyoda joined the Supreme War Council and lobbied for greater air power in Japan's navy, mostly unsuccessfully. As Commander in Chief of the Combined Fleet, Toyoda drafted and approved many of the more infamous operations of the fleet, including Operation Ten-Go, which sent the *Yamato* to Okinawa, where it was defeated by a combination of aerial bombardment and torpedoing.

Toyoda wanted the Potsdam Declaration to be changed to more favorable terms, but after the atomic bombings, he believed Japan should fight to the last man. He was tried for war crimes in Tokyo, but acquitted and released in 1949. In an interview with the United States Strategic Bombing Survey, Toyoda said:

> *"I do not think it would be accurate to look upon use of the Atomic Bomb and the entry and participation of Soviet Russia into the war as direct cause of termination of the war, but I think that those two factors did enable us to bring the war to a termination without creating too great chaos in Japan."*

US presidents and their stance on nuclear weapons

Every living president since August 1945 has had to grapple with the reality of nuclear weapons and their consequences, both immediate and long term.

Herbert Hoover (1929)

In August 1945, Hoover was the only living former president. He was also a Quaker, which reflected in many of his opinions regarding foreign policy. Two days

after Hiroshima was bombed, Hoover wrote to his friend Colonel John Callan O'Laughlin, saying, "The use of the atomic bomb, with its indiscriminate killing of women and children, revolts my soul." According to biographer Richard Norton Smith, Hoover said the bomb should have been described in graphic detail to the Japanese before being used. Hoover never wavered from his strong opposition to nuclear weapons, but in 1964, months before his death at the age of 90, he endorsed Barry Goldwater for president despite Goldwater's willingness to use them.

Harry S. Truman (1945)

Publicly, Truman promised Japan "prompt and utter destruction" both before and immediately after using the atomic bomb. In his letters he was more careful not to completely demonize the Japanese. When Senator Richard Russell of Georgia asked Truman in an August 7 telegram that the United States "carry the war to them until they beg us to accept unconditional surrender," Truman replied:

"I know that Japan is a terribly cruel and uncivilized nation in warfare but I can't bring myself to believe that, because they are beasts, we should ourselves act in the same manner...

My object is to save as many American lives as possible but I also have a humane feeling for the women and children in Japan."

On August 10, Japan offered to accept unconditional surrender. Truman discussed the proposal with his cabinet, which included Commerce Secretary Henry Wallace. In Wallace's diary for that day, he notes that Truman received the first reports and photos of Hiroshima's destruction and upon seeing them ordered a halt to atomic bombs. From the diary: "[Truman] said the thought of wiping out another 100,000 people was too horrible. He didn't like the idea of killing, as he said, 'all those kids'." Despite this entry, Truman always publicly maintained using the atomic bombs was correct and he never lost sleep over his decision to use them. In a 1959 retrospective on his presidency, and in a 1963 letter to *Chicago Sun-Times* columnist Irv Kupcinet, Truman said he never regretted using the bomb, arguing it saved millions of American and Japanese lives by making an invasion of Japan unnecessary.

Dwight D. Eisenhower (1953)

The Supreme Commander of the Allies in Europe, Eisenhower came into office promising to end the war in Korea. In April 1953, Eisenhower delivered the "Chance for Peace" speech, in which he said, "Every gun that is made, every warship launched, every rocket fired signifies, in the final sense, a theft from those who hunger and are not fed, those who are cold and are not cold."

Behind the scenes, in meetings with the Joint Chiefs of Staff, Eisenhower agreed that the threat of nuclear weapons would drive back the Chinese from Korea. This threat was given to the Chinese and armistice negotiations intensified. All sides signed a ceasefire in July of that year.

In 1954 during the Straits of Taiwan crisis, Eisenhower and his Secretary of State John Foster Dulles considered using nuclear weapons in order to prevent an invasion of Taiwan by the PRC. Dulles said as much publicly in February 1955, and the crisis ended in May. During Eisenhower's administration, nuclear weapons became more sophisticated and testing increased. His Democratic opponent, Adlai Stevenson, proposed a ban on atmospheric testing of nuclear weapons in 1956, which at the time was a fringe position. As his term was ending, Eisenhower called for Americans to be vigilant of the "military-industrial complex" and in 1963 he told *Newsweek* that Japan had been ready to surrender, and "it was not necessary to hit them with that awful thing."

John F. Kennedy (1961)

On January 23, 1961, three days after Kennedy was inaugurated, a B-52 carrying two 2.5-megaton bombs broke apart near Goldsboro, North Carolina. The arming switches on both bombs were activated as a result of the crash, but neither detonated because one switch on each of them was in the safe position. Each individual bomb had a payload 125 times greater than Fat Man.

Kennedy's Defense Secretary, Robert McNamara, originated the idea of "Mutually Assured Destruction," that a large enough nuclear arsenal would deter any attacks by other nuclear powers (namely the Soviet Union). This theory was put to the test during the Cuban Missile Crisis in October 1962, when missile sites capable of launching nuclear warheads were discovered in Cuba. After a tense 13-day standoff, the Soviet Union withdrew the sites and Kennedy stepped up rhetoric in favor of nuclear disarmament.

In July 1963, five months before Kennedy's assassination, the US signed the Partial Nuclear Test Ban Treaty, which banned atmospheric testing.

Lyndon B. Johnson (1963)

In keeping with his 1964 campaign slogan ("Let Us Continue"), Johnson continued Kennedy's ideas, succeeding domestically where Kennedy had not, in passing the Civil Rights Act and the Great Society programs. Johnson said very little on nuclear weapons, but during the 1964 election, his Republican opponent, Senator Barry Goldwater, said he'd be willing to use nuclear weapons to defend America if necessary. Johnson's campaign portrayed Goldwater as crazy and trigger-happy (culminating in the infamous "daisy ad"). Johnson signed the Non-Proliferation Treaty in 1968, something he and Kennedy had wanted for years.

Richard Nixon (1969)

Nixon came into office promising an end to the war in Vietnam, though his foreign policy strategy frequently sabotaged the Paris Peace Talks. While Nixon signed important treaties like the Anti-Ballistic Missile treaty and the SALT treaty, both of which limited nuclear-capable warhead production, Nixon's foreign policy team portrayed him as a volatile madman who might do something crazy like use nuclear weapons, in the hope of spooking other countries (namely North Vietnam) into doing what they wanted.

Recently unearthed documents show that Nixon ordered bombers armed with thermonuclear weapons to fly close to the Soviet Union in October 1969 in order to intimidate them into ending the Vietnam War. Nixon aides also portrayed the 1970 bombing of Cambodia as "the madman is on the loose." While much of this was exaggerated, Nixon was not above this kind of hyperbole, even with his own inner circle. In 1972 he proposed using nuclear weapons in Vietnam to Secretary of State Henry Kissinger, and when Kissinger advised against it, Nixon exclaimed, "I just want you to think big Henry, for Chrissakes!"

Gerald Ford (1974)

Ford was thrust into the Vice-Presidency when Spiro Agnew resigned due to corruption, and became President when Richard Nixon also resigned due to corruption. He would be in the Oval Office for 2.5 years, but in that time he became the first sitting president to visit Japan. A 2009 investigation by Japanese newspaper *Asahi Shimbun* revealed that it was suggested he visit Hiroshima, but he ultimately did not. On that same trip, he visited the Soviet Union and signed a tentative agreement with Soviet General Secretary Leonid Brezhnev to limit the production of nuclear weapons.

Jimmy Carter (1977)

The historical consensus has been that Jimmy Carter was a better man than he was a president, and accomplished more after leaving the White House than when he was there. Since leaving office, his work at the Carter Center has included work to try and draw down nuclear stockpiles and urging nuclear powers to give up these weapons. Work like this earned him the 2002 Nobel Peace Prize. As president, Carter opposed nuclear weapons, but in 1980 he signed the Nuclear Weapons Employment Policy, which gave the president more flexibility in the planning and execution of nuclear war. Carter visited the Hiroshima Peace Museum in 1984,

three years after leaving office, making him the first US president to visit the city.

Ronald Reagan (1981)

Especially in his first term, Ronald Reagan's rhetoric against the Soviet Union was strong and his military programs like the Strategic Defense Initiative ("Star Wars") rattled the public. His critics gave him the derisive nickname "Ronnie Raygun" for this reason. Despite this, Reagan deeply opposed nuclear weapons and especially the idea of mutually assured destruction. In December 1945, he wanted to lead an anti-nuclear weapons rally in Hollywood, but was forbidden by Warner Brothers from doing so. In a 1986 meeting with General Edward Rowny, Reagan said, "I have a dream. I have a dream of a world without nuclear weapons. I want our children and grandchildren particularly to be free of these weapons."

George H.W. Bush (1989)

During Bush's time in the White House, the Iron Curtain and the Soviet Union collapsed. In 1991 he signed the START I treaty that eliminated ground-based tactical nuclear weapons and the United States withdrew them from Europe. In 1980, while running for president, he outlined how a nuclear war could be won to journalist Robert Scheer: "You have a survivability of command and control, survivability of industrial potential, protection of a percentage of your citizens, and you have the capability that inflicts more damage on the opposition than it can inflict on you."

Bill Clinton (1993)

The United States conducted its last nuclear test in November 1992, two months before Bill Clinton was inaugurated as president. In November 1996 Clinton signed the Comprehensive Nuclear Test-Ban Treaty, though Congress did not ratify it. In December 1997 his administration changed the nuclear weapons deployment policy, shifting focus away from how to wage nuclear war to how to deter the use of nuclear weapons.

George W. Bush (2001)

George W. Bush's administration is largely defined by the "War on Terrorism," or as it was later called, "the Global War on Terror." While there was substantial

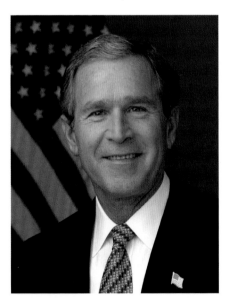

growth in the military-industrial complex during Bush's two terms, some of the administration's ideas for nuclear weapons were rebuffed, even by a Republican-controlled Congress. Bush asked Congress to fund the creation of "usable nuclear weapons," including what were known as "bunker busters," meant to destroy underground targets. They were never funded and never used. The Joint Chiefs of Staff tried to revise the rules about using nuclear weapons to include the right of preemptive strikes, though when this was leaked to the *Washington Post*, the Pentagon abandoned this revision.

Barack Obama (2009)

In 2010, shortly after winning the Nobel Peace Prize, Barack Obama revised the nuclear weapons use policy and heavily restricted when and how they should be used. That same year, he signed the latest START treaty that further reduced America's nuclear arsenal. Throughout his presidency and well before that, Barack Obama has committed to "seek the peace and security of a world without nuclear weapons." But in 2014, the Pentagon started spending less on containing nuclear weapons and reducing the nuclear arsenal, and more on new ballistic missiles and stealth bombers that could carry nuclear weapons.

PEACE, AT A PRICE

"My god, what have we done?"

> – Written in his logbook by Colonel Robert Lewis, the co-pilot of the
> *Enola Gay*, on seeing the Hiroshima mushroom cloud.

The first report that Hiroshima had been destroyed was sent by Oka Yoshie, a communications officer at the Chugoku Military District Headquarters half a mile away from the epicenter. Once she saw the explosion, she got on a special phone to Fukuyama Headquarters and told them, "Hiroshima has been attacked by a new type of bomb. The city is in a state of near-total destruction."

On the evening of August 9 – the same day that Nagasaki was bombed – the Soviet Union declared war on Japan. The Imperial War Council was deadlocked on whether to surrender, and they consulted Emperor Hirohito, who calmly told them to accept the terms of surrender. The cabinet agreed, and sent telegrams to the Allies, through the Swiss Political Affairs Office, of its intentions to surrender, requesting the Emperor remain Emperor.

The Allied response, primarily written by Secretary of State Byrnes, made no such promises. During a meeting between the Emperor and military officials, unlike many of his comrades the commander of the Second General Army, Hata Shunroku, advised against continuing the war. The Second General Army was based in Hiroshima and oversaw troops in southern Japan, and they had witnessed first-hand the devastation of the atomic bomb.

The War Cabinet unanimously approved surrender, prompting some radical military officials to occupy the Imperial Palace and attempt a coup. Hirohito recorded the surrender speech on a phonograph record and the rebels attempted to stop the recording from being broadcast, but they failed. The record eventually reached the offices of Radio Tokyo and was broadcast across Japan at 12 noon on August 15 – for many this was the first time they had heard the Emperor's voice.

Filmmaker Kurosawa Akira heard the announcement and recounted that day in his autobiography:

"On August 15, 1945, I was summoned to the studio along with everyone else to listen to the momentous proclamation on the radio: The Emperor himself was to speak over the air waves. I will never forget the scenes I saw

as I walked the streets that day. On the way from Soshigaya to the studios in Kinuta the shopping street looked fully prepared for the Honorable Death of the Hundred Million. The atmosphere was tense, panicked. There were even shop owners who had taken their Japanese swords from their sheaths and sat staring at the bare blades.

However, when I walked the same route back to my home after listening to the imperial proclamation, the scene was entirely different. The people on the shopping street were bustling about with cheerful faces as if preparing for a festival the next day. I don't know if this represents Japanese adaptability or Japanese imbecility. In either case, I have to recognize that both these facets exist in the Japanese personality. Both facets exist within my own personality as well."

Japan signed the official Instruments of Surrender on September 2 aboard the *USS Missouri*, anchored in Tokyo Bay. With that signature, World War II officially ended. The flag flown on the deck of the battleship was the same American flag flown by Matthew Perry when his fleet entered Tokyo Bay almost 100 years earlier.

Journalism and censorship in the aftermath

The use of the atomic bomb was officially announced in the United States at 11am on August 6 – 16 hours after being dropped on Hiroshima – in the form of a White House press release as well as a recorded message from Harry Truman. Now the atomic bomb was no longer a secret and reporters could talk about it openly. On the morning of August 7, the *New York Times* ran the first of a number of stories on the atomic bomb, many of them written by their chief science writer, William Leonard Laurence, who obtained leave, at the War Department's request, to explain the intricacies of the atomic bomb's operating principles in laymen's language.

As well as writing newspaper stories on the history of the atomic bomb, Laurence flew on the B-29 bomber *The Great Artiste*, which carried scientific measuring equipment on the bombing run of Nagasaki, as well as film cameras that captured the mushroom cloud. Laurence wrote an eyewitness account of the bombing which, along with 10 subsequent articles on the development and production of the bomb, earned him the 1946 Pulitzer Prize for Reporting.

Covering the events on board the *Missouri* on September 2 were hundreds of journalists, including George Weller of the *Chicago Daily News*. After signing the documents, SCAP (Supreme Command of the Allied Powers) authorities declared southern Japan "off-limits" to journalists, save for POW camps on Kyushu. The camps were being liberated and journalists could walk in and talk to the newly freed captives. Tokyo, six months after being firebombed, was also declared off-limits.

Censorship of journalists' reports on the atomic bombs only began after the signing of the Instruments of Surrender. Weller filed a dispatch from Tokyo on the effects of the bomb on August 31, which passed SCAP censorship, but the newspaper didn't run it:

> *"The atomic bomb holds first place over any other element as the cause of Japan's decision to surrender, according to Japanese civilians with whom I've talked. At first the authorities held down newspapers from announcing the bomb's effect on Hiroshima, but leakage began after four or five days...*
>
> *Actress Sonoi [Keiko], after Hiroshima, went to Kobe and telegraphed Tokyo, 'I am happy to have been saved.' She had only a small swelling of her wrist. But the swelling spread and soon covered her whole body. Her hair fell out. In approximately a week, she too died. These seemingly healthy persons who died many miles from Hiroshima many days afterward were the actual breakers of censorship, who compelled the military to allow the truth to be told about Hiroshima."*

The first reporter from a Western news agency to reach Hiroshima was Leslie Nakashima. The Hawaii-born Nakashima worked in United Press's Tokyo bureau before Pearl Harbor, and during the war went to work for the official Japan news agency Domei as a translator. On August 22, he entered Hiroshima by train:

> *"Alighting from the train I found that Hiroshima Station, which was one of the largest in western Japan, had gone out of existence.*
>
> *The only thing left was the concrete platforms. Fragmentary parts of the walls of the brick building that constituted the old section of the station also told of the severity of the destruction caused by the atomic bomb.*
>
> *Getting out into the open I was dumbfounded with the destruction before me. The center of the city immediately to the south and west of the station had been razed to the ground and there was a sweeping view to the foot of the mountains to the southeast and north of the city. In other words, what had been a city of 300,000 population had vanished."*

Nakashima sent his report to the United Press, which ran it on August 31 in its client newspapers. *The New York Times* ran the report, but cut some sections, including this one:

"Two weeks after the bomb was dropped I still found the devastated city to be deserted. No attempt has been made to restore the streetcar transportation system. And no attempt has been made to rehabilitate the city in any way. Warnings that people would take sick from the effects of uranium, which had seeped into the ground, kept people away from the destroyed area.

In this connection it has been reported that a number of soldiers doing salvage work have fallen ill, and therefore such work has been discontinued. From such developments a fear has risen among Japanese authorities that reports from American sources that such bombed areas will be impossible for human habitation for 75 years may well be true...

During this interval it is likely that I inhaled uranium because I'm still troubled with a loss of appetite and the least little exertion finds me tired.

The death toll was particularly heavy, I was told, because the governor of Hiroshima prefecture had issued a call for people on labor service to come out that day to haul away the lumber of buildings torn down to make fire escape routes in case of air raids. Thousands of middle school boys and girls were accordingly victims and the number of those missing is astounding."

Weller had felt the sting of General MacArthur's censors before – they killed a dispatch he wrote criticizing Roosevelt for conceding Eastern Europe to Stalin at the Yalta conference. Weller did not want to be pushed around. Disguising himself as a Colonel, Weller evaded military escorts and snuck into Nagasaki on September 6, 1945. Over the next three days he cabled eight dispatches to the authorities in Tokyo, requesting they forward them to his editors in Chicago. They included the following reports:

"The atomic bomb may be classified as a weapon capable of being used indiscriminately, but its use in Nagasaki was selective and proper and as merciful as such a gigantic force could be expected to be.

Such is the conclusion which the writer, as the first visitor from the outside world to inspect the ruins firsthand, has drawn after an exhaustive though still incomplete study of this wasteland of war."

......

"As one whittles away at embroidery and checks the stories, the impression grows that the atomic bomb is a tremendous but not a peculiar weapon.

The Japanese have heard the legend from American radio that the ground preserves deadly irradiation. But hours walking amid the ruins where the odor of decaying flesh is still strong produces in this writer nausea, but no sign of burns or debilitation. Nobody here in Nagasaki has yet been able to show that the bomb is different than any other, except in the broader extent of its flash and a more powerful knockout."

......

"The atomic bomb's peculiar 'disease,' uncured because it is untreated and untreated because it is undiagnosed, is still snatching away lives here. Men, women and children with no outward marks of injury are dying daily in hospitals, some after having walked around for three or four weeks thinking they have escaped. The doctors here have every modern medicament, but candidly confessed in talking to the writer – the first Allied observer to reach Nagasaki since the surrender – that the answer to the malady is beyond them. Their patients, though their skins are whole, are simply passing away under their eyes."

Weller's dispatches contained references to radiation sickness, which he called "Disease X," and doctors attributed to "X-ray poisoning." In a 1965 piece for the *Chicago Daily News* Weller recalled:

"I began to visit a city that was neither dead nor alive but dazed, stirring like a man emerging from a knockout blow. By day I paced the ruins, the hospitals, the harbor, the crushed Mitsubishi plant and the small Allied prison camp near it."

On September 9, a press junket led by Colonel John "Tex" McCrary landed in Nagasaki. McCrary volunteered to take Weller's dispatches and publish them, but Weller declined. The junket arrived from Hiroshima, where they'd been for a week. Among them was Homer Bigart of the *New York Herald-Tribune*, whose reporting on the Pacific War earned him a Pulitzer Prize in 1946:

"We walked today through Hiroshima, where survivors of the first atomic-bomb explosion four weeks ago are still dying at the rate of about 100 daily from burns and infections which the Japanese doctors seem unable to cure.

The toll from the most terrible weapon ever devised now stands at 53,000 counted dead, 30,000 missing and presumed dead, 13,960 severely wounded and likely to die, and 43,000 wounded. The figures come from Hirokuni

Dadai [sic], who, as 'chief of thought control' of the Hiroshima Prefecture, is supposed to police subversive thinking."

Also in that junket was W.H. Lawrence (not to be confused with William L. Laurence) of *The New York Times,* who would later have a prominent career at ABC News. In his report (which ran in the *Times* on September 5) he cites the same figures as Bigart, crediting them to "A Japanese official." He cites Dazai Hirokuni as well:

"While the Japanese still are staggered by the initial impact of this weapon and its lingering effects, their scientists still have not figured out whether the blast will have continuing harmful effects upon all who live in Hiroshima. They already have banned the drinking of city water because of chemical changes caused by the radioactive rays of the bomb, and they asked us whether we thought residing in the bombed area would be harmful."

......

"As a war correspondent in Europe and the Pacific I have never looked upon such scenes of death and destruction. It was enough to take your breath away when standing in the center of the area where the bomb fell. You could see nothing but rubble and the seared walls of a few earthquake-proof buildings that remained upright."

......

"A visit to Hiroshima is an experience to leave one shaken by the terrible, incredible sights. Here is the final proof of what the mechanical and scientific genius of America has been able to accomplish in war through the invention of the airplane, especially the B-29 Superfortress, and the atomic bomb. It should be the last evidence needed to convince any doubter of the need to retain and perfect our air offense and defense lest the fate of Hiroshima be repeated in Indianapolis or Washington or Detroit or New York.

Three Japanese newspapermen who interviewed us wanted to know the role of the atomic bomb in future warfare. We told them it was our purpose as one of the United Nations to make certain that peace is maintained throughout the world."

......

"We asked [Dazai Hirokuni] his opinion of the use of this type of bomb. He replied that he believed we had in our possession the ability to destroy every living thing of the civilization established by the gods."

W.H. Laurence, meanwhile, continued his series on the atomic bomb for the *Times*. To counter claims by Japanese officials of radiation sickness, the War Department invited him and other reporters to the site of the Trinity Test in New Mexico. On September 9, he submitted a report on the visit:

"This historic ground in New Mexico, scene of the first atomic explosion on earth and cradle of a new era in civilization, gave the most effective answer today to Japanese propaganda that radiations were responsible for deaths even after the day of the explosion, August 6 and that persons entering Hiroshima had contracted mysterious maladies due to persistent radioactivity...

'The Japanese claim,' General Groves added, 'that people died from radiations. If this is true, the number was very small. However, any deaths from gamma rays were due to those emitted during the explosion, not to the radiations present afterward. In the area where people could be killed by radiation they were killed by other causes, particularly blast. While many people were killed, many lives were saved, particularly American lives. It ended the war sooner. It was the final punch that knocked them out. Otherwise they might have kept on fighting for a longer period.'

The Japanese are still continuing their propaganda aimed at creating the impression that we won the war unfairly, and thus attempting to create sympathy for themselves and milder terms, an examination of their present statements reveals."

On September 10, Weller went to Omuta, where two POW camps had been liberated. He filed additional dispatches on the newly freed captives, which were not censored. Like most POWs sent to Japanese camps, the captives were put to work in nearby factories, mines and other centers of industry that relied on cheap labor. In the case of Camp No.17, near Omuta, many were put to work in a coal mine owned by Mitsui. Many of them saw the mushroom clouds from Hiroshima (217 miles away) and Nagasaki (50 miles away). Weller's dispatches from Camp No.17 consisted of quotes from captives, some of them held since the Battle of Wake Island in December 1941:

"I saw the atomic bomb over Nagasaki, when from a red ball suspended in the air it began to mushroom upward like an ice cream cone. The core stayed red for about 20 minutes. I got the impression that a fire was burning in the cloud. The Japs were very concerned, they kept pointing their swords toward

Nagasaki and jabbering. They knew about the first one at Hiroshima and were as worried as we were ignorant."
– Lieutenant Edward Little (Decatur, Illinois)

"Those flattened buildings made you want to cry, not on account of the lives lost, but because of the destruction involved."
– Corporal Lee Dale (Walnut Creek, California)
on the destruction of Nagasaki

Weller also interviewed British captives at Camp No.25 near Omuta who witnessed the mushroom clouds. The camp yielded 250 Britons, most of whom had worked in a zinc factory owned by Mitsui. Unlike their American counterparts, they were not briefed on what the bombs were after the camp was liberated:

"It seemed like a huge, ever-swelling mushroom-shaped whitish cloud, with a glowing center and stem reaching to the earth. I was queerly uneasy and very puzzled, and thought it was perhaps a new type of incendiary bomb."
– Captain Douglas Wilkie (Farlight, England)

"The bomb appeared like a growing ball of white smoke, with a red ball inside, giving me an impression of vague terror as an unaccountable phenomenon."
– Lieutenant William Miller (Glasgow, Scotland)

"I saw a flash – as if a mirror had shone into one's eyes – followed by a white puff in the sky spreading to a huge ball of cloudy fire. I felt uneasy and frightened at something unknown."
– Sergeant Albert Young (London, England)

Meanwhile, the War Department was trying to keep editors in the States at bay. It sent a note from President Truman on September 14 to editors of media outlets (including the *Chicago Daily News*) saying any information about the "operational use" of the atomic bomb should be kept secret unless quite specifically approved by the War Department. The same day, General Thomas Farrell traveled to Nagasaki and observed the destruction himself, concluding, "Summaries of Japanese reports previously sent are essentially correct, as to clinical effects from single gamma radiation dose."

On September 18, MacArthur shut down the Japanese state news agency Domei for 24 hours in retaliation for Domei printing stories about Allied forces raping and looting. SCAP authorities also issued new rules for the media, banning "anything… that would promote hatred or disbelief in the Allied forces."

When he returned to Nagasaki, Weller found medical staff from the US Navy had arrived. Weller hoped the Navy censors would approve his dispatches about Nagasaki, but the five he sent from there were heavily censored. Unlike the Tokyo authorities, the Navy did allow a few paragraphs through, which were eventually printed in newspapers that got the Daily News syndication like the *Miami Herald* and the *Los Angeles Times*:

> *"New cases of atomic bomb poisoning with an approximate 50 percent death rate are still appearing at Nagasaki's hospital six weeks after the blow fell, but United States Navy physicians who have examined them report that the death rate is falling off."*
>
> ......
>
> *"Whereas formerly 20 patients a day with dwindling hair and their bone marrow affected were coming to Japanese hospitals, the rate is now fallen to about 10. Death, which at the time of the writer's first series of dispatches were eight daily, are now about five or less."*

Weller took the opportunity to board a hospital ship to leave Nagasaki. While on board, he caught a medicine ball thrown by a staff doctor and injured his back. The ship took him to Guam, where he discovered MacArthur's censors had blocked nearly everything he had written.

According to Weller's son, Anthony, he was always infuriated that MacArthur prevented his dispatches from Nagasaki from being published. He wrote about his experience in essays for the *Chicago Daily News* in 1965 and for the anthology *How I Got That Story* (Overseas Press Club of New York, 1967). Anthony Weller discovered the original dispatches in an attic shortly after his father's death in 2002 and printed them in the book *First Into Nagasaki* in 2006.

John Hersey's *Hiroshima*

The readers who picked up the August 31, 1946 issue of *The New Yorker* saw a pleasant sight on the front cover: a cartoon drawn by Charles Martin of vacationing New Englanders frolicking. Inside, the issue began with this note from the editors:

> "The New Yorker *this week devotes its entire editorial space to an article on the almost complete obliteration of a city by one atomic bomb, and what happened to the people of that city. It does so in the conviction that few of*

us have yet comprehended the all but incredible destructive power of this
weapon, and that everyone might well take time to consider the terrible
implications of its use."

All 68 pages of the magazine were devoted to an article by John Hersey, who had
covered the war from Chongqing for *Time* magazine. In it, Hersey told the story of
six people in Hiroshima and followed their lives from the morning of August 6 to the
following year.

Hersey was commissioned to write the article by *New Yorker* assistant editor
William Shawn. When Hersey finished, he planned on having it published in four
parts, but Shawn felt it would be more effective if they were all published at once.
Shawn pitched the idea to *New Yorker* founder and editor Harold Ross to devote
the entire issue to the article. Ross was worried readers would be turned off that
their regular cartoons and features would be missing for a week. But he also knew
it would be jarring to have such lighthearted fare next to such a weighty piece of
journalism. Ross wrote to regular contributor E.B. White, telling him "Shawn wants
to wake people up, and he thinks we are the people to do it." After it was published,
Ross told Irwin Shaw, "I don't think I've ever got as much satisfaction out of anything
else in my life."

The August 31 issue of the magazine sold out, and was soon being scalped for
US$15 or US$20 (its cover price was 15 cents). *Newsweek* reported that Albert
Einstein was disappointed that he couldn't purchase 1,000 copies. By October,
Alfred A. Knopf had gained the rights to publish the article as a book, simply titled
Hiroshima.

In 1985, Hersey visited Hiroshima and followed up with the six survivors
featured in the original story. He wrote a follow-up article for *The New Yorker* that
was added to subsequent editions of *Hiroshima.* By the time "The Aftermath" was
added, the book had sold three million copies. When Hersey died in 1993, *The New
Yorker* called "Hiroshima" the most famous magazine article in history.

LIVING WITH THE PAST

On January 1, 1946, Emperor Hirohito issued a declaration that he was not a living god. This led the way to the creation of a new Constitution, written with the Allied Powers. This Constitution, approved May 3, 1947, is the basis of Japan's government today. The Emperor would still carry out the duties of the head of state, but would not participate in government. The Constitution also guaranteed a separation of church and state, abolished peerage (the House of Peers was replaced by the House of Counselors) and guaranteed the right to due process.

The most famous part of the Constitution is Article 9, which outlaws war as an instrument of policy. In keeping with it, Japan would be forbidden from maintaining armed forces. The article was inspired by the Kellogg-Briand Pact of 1928, which did much the same thing, and that pact also inspired the UN Charter, approved in 1945 in the wake of World War II.

The effects of the bombs on the national psyche

The bombings of Hiroshima and Nagasaki had a profound psychological effect on Japan (this was part of the US military's intention in keeping the bomb a secret until its use). Seven decades on the consequences can still be seen in Japanese culture, in its portrayal of the bombings themselves and allegorical representations of them.

One famous story tells of Sasaki Sadako, who as a two-year-old survived the initial blast in Hiroshima. Ten years later, however, she came down with leukemia and was hospitalized. A classmate told her that anyone who folded a thousand origami paper cranes would be granted a wish; Sadako began folding paper cranes, wishing to be cured of leukemia. She folded a thousand paper cranes, but died of the disease two months after starting her work. Her classmates raised money to erect a memorial to her, which was unveiled in 1958 as the Children's Peace Monument in Hiroshima's Peace Park.

As in Hiroshima, some partially damaged structures were preserved in Nagasaki to document what had happened. The Sanno Shrine was completely destroyed except for two *torii* gates. One gate was completely unharmed (it has since been demolished) but half the torii was destroyed on the second gate. The shrine was subsequently moved a short distance away. Two camphor trees within the shrine still stood after the bombing, but their bark, branches, and leaves were all burned away. They were originally assumed to be dead, but new life sprang from them and they are still alive today.

The Urakami Cathedral, one of the largest churches in East Asia, was a short distance away from the blast. Its bell tower rolled down a nearby hill where it still lies today. Parts of the old cathedral are now in the Nagasaki Atomic Bomb Museum, while a new cathedral has been built on the old site.

Despite full knowledge of the devastating effect nuclear bombs had on the environment and people, the Soviet Union soon began its own nuclear program in the steppe region of Central Asia, while the US continued its nuclear research. In 1946 it began nuclear testing at Bikini Atoll, part of the Marshall Islands in the central Pacific.

The most controversial test at the atoll was the Castle Bravo test on March 1, 1954, whose bomb had a yield of 15 million tons of TNT. Westerly winds sent the fallout across the sea where it fell on other atolls, whose inhabitants had to be evacuated. Even in 1985 radiation was still present on Rongelap Atoll more than 100km away, and the Greenpeace trawler *Rainbow Warrior*, at the request of locals, helped relocate inhabitants to safer islands.

Fallout from the Castle Bravo test also struck the *Daigo Fukuryu Maru* (Lucky Dragon Boat No. 5), a Japanese fishing boat. The entire crew came down with radiation sickness and the chief radio operator died of cirrhosis of the liver seven months after the bombing. The ship is now preserved at a museum in Tokyo.

The entire incident inspired filmmaker Honda Ashiro, who had also seen the devastation of Hiroshima and Nagasaki, to create *Gojira*, known in the west as Godzilla. In the original film, Gojira is created by a nuclear test and the first people to see him are fishermen on a boat. Gojira travels to Tokyo and devastates the city, a clear reference to the atomic bomb. Much of the anti-nuclear weapon subtext was removed from the English dub of the film.

In 1964 the writer Oe Kenzaburo traveled to Hiroshima and reported on the city and its *hibakusha* (atomic bomb survivors) 20 years after the bombing. The result was the book *Hiroshima Notes,* published in 1965. The previous year he'd written one of his most famous books, *A Personal Matter,* describing the birth of his son Hikari, who was born brain damaged in 1963 and was given little hope of survival by doctors.

In 1994 Oe received the Nobel Prize for Literature. In an interview with Sarah Fay for *The Paris Review* in 2007, he said:

"I saw many survivors of the atomic bomb write the name of someone who had died on a lantern and let it float on the river. They watched the lanterns

flow to the other side of the river – the souls of the dead going into the darkness. I wanted to participate. I wrote Hikari's name on a lantern because he was someone, I thought, who would be dying soon. At that time, I didn't have the will to live."

Cities of peace

In the immediate aftermath of the bombings, as Hiroshima and Nagasaki began the long, slow and acutely painful process of clearing and rebuilding, the two cities' mayors decided to become advocates for peace. On August 6, 1947, on the two-year anniversary of the first bombing, Hiroshima's mayor Hamai Shinzo delivered the first peace declaration:

"Today, on this second anniversary of the atomic bombing of Hiroshima, we, Hiroshima's citizens, renew our commitment to the establishment of peace by celebrating a Peace Festival at this site, and expressing our burning desire for peace.

The citizens of Hiroshima will never be able to forget August 6, 1945. On that morning, exactly two years ago today, the first atomic bomb to be unleashed on a city in the history of mankind fell on Hiroshima; it instantly reduced the city to ashes and claimed the precious lives of more than 100,000 of our fellow citizens. Hiroshima turned into a city of death and darkness. Yet as some slight consolation for this horror, the dropping of the atomic bomb became a factor in ending the war and calling a halt to the fighting. In this sense, mankind must remember that August 6 was a day that brought a chance for world peace. This is the reason why we are now commemorating that day by solemnly inaugurating a festival of peace, despite the limitless sorrow in our minds. For only those who most bitterly experienced and came to know most completely the misery and the guilt of war can utterly reject war as the most terrible kind of human suffering, and ardently pursue peace.

This horrible weapon brought about a 'Revolution of Thought,' which has convinced us of the necessity and the value of eternal peace. That is to say, because of this atomic bomb, the people of the world have become aware that a global war in which atomic energy would be used would lead to the end of our civilization and extinction of mankind.

This revolution in thinking ought to be the basis for an absolute peace, and imply the birth of new life and a new world. We know that, when in a crisis discover a new truth and a new path from the crisis itself, by reflecting deeply and beginning afresh. If this is true, what we have to do at this moment is to strive with all our might towards peace, becoming forerunners of a new civilization.

Let us join to sweep away from this earth the horror of war, and to build a true peace.

Let us join in renouncing war eternally, and building a plan for world peace on this earth.

Here, under this peace tower, we thus make a declaration of peace."

Through Hamai's efforts, Hiroshima was declared a "City of Peace" under Japanese law in 1949, and he reached out to peace activists during his long mayoralty, which lasted until 1955 and again from 1955 to 1967.

Since 1949, every mayor of Hiroshima has been a strong advocate for peace. In 1971, Japanese Prime Minister Sato Eisaku became the first Prime Minister to attend the Peace Ceremony. In a significant and admirable gesture, then-mayor Yamada Setsuo added the names of 12 American POWs held at Hiroshima when the bomb was dropped to the list of the dead.

In 1976 Araki Takeshi, along with Nagasaki mayor Morotani Yoshitake, protested an air show that imitated the bombings of the two cities. Two years later, Araki became the first Hiroshima mayor to speak at the United Nations, and in 1982 he founded the Mayors for Peace. In 2010, Akiba Tadatoshi became the first mayor of Hiroshima to meet a sitting US President, when he met President Barack Obama at the US Conference of Mayors in Washington.

Mayors of Nagasaki have been just as visible, but some of them have come under fire from nationalists for their views, often at the risk of their lives. In 1988, Mayor Motoshima Hitoshi suggested that Emperor Hirohito bore some responsibility for World War II. The Emperor died a month later at the age of 87. On January 18, 1990 a right-wing extremist shot Motoshima in the back, but he survived.

His successor, Itoh Iccho, was not as lucky. On April 17, 2007, a Yakuza gang member who held a personal grudge against the mayor, shot Itoh. He died the next morning. Two months later, Japan's Defense Minister Kyuma Fumio (whose representative district is part of Nagasaki Prefecture), said that in order to end the war quickly, the US "had to drop the bomb on Nagasaki." Itoh's successor (and current mayor of Nagasaki) Taue Tomihisa strongly criticized this statement and Kyuma resigned as Defense Minister a few days later, proving how deep feelings still run about that seminal moment in Japanese history.

Kazakhstan: an ally in anti-nuclear advocacy

Few can realistically understand the horrors experienced by victims of a nuclear attack, and most believe the citizens of Hiroshima and Nagasaki to be the only people to have suffered through it. However, the inhabitants of a region in Central Asia can claim to know intimately the appalling effects of nuclear blasts on the local population.

The Republic of Kazakhstan has been a leading advocate against nuclear weapons since it became an independent state in 1991, in large part due to its first – and current – president, Nursultan Nazarbayev. During the Soviet era, the government conducted hundreds of nuclear bomb tests in what is now Kazakhstan's northeastern steppe region, resulting in the destruction of the surrounding environment for the local nomadic Kazakhs, and appalling consequences for both them and the citizens of the nearby city of Semipalatinsk, who unknowingly suffered the effects of radioactive nuclear fallout for decades – above-ground tests took place from 1949 until 1963, and underground testing continued until 1989. Incredibly, the Soviet authorities and scientists were fully aware of what they were doing and kept the local populace in the dark in order to study the effects of radiation on humans.

On achieving independence, Kazakhstan immediately dismantled the nuclear weapons in its possession. President Nazarbayev was the driving force in getting rid of the nation's nuclear arsenal despite pleas from opposition party members – one of whom presented him with a letter from Libyan president Muammar Gaddafi asking him to keep the nuclear arsenal "in the name of Islam."

On August 29, 2012, the UN International Day Against Nuclear Tests, President Nazarbayev launched the Atom Project, an international initiative dedicated to stopping nuclear weapons testing and building greater awareness of nuclear weapons possession, testing and disarmament. Its ultimate goal is a nuclear-weapons-free world.

America's attitude to the "Atomic Age"

After the bombings of Hiroshima and Nagasaki, many of the scientists who worked on the Manhattan Project set up the *Bulletin of the Atomic Scientists*, still being published today from the University of Chicago, as a journal on nuclear weapons. In 1947 it introduced one of the most recognizable symbols of the atomic age, the Doomsday Clock, which tracks how close the world is to nuclear annihilation, expressed in the phrase "X minutes to midnight." When it was introduced, it was set at seven minutes to midnight and has been adjusted 23 times since then. As of 2015 it is two minutes to midnight.

Works in American culture have looked at the implications of nuclear power. The most famous example is Stanley Kubrick's film *"Dr. Strangelove, or How I Learned to Stop Worrying and Love the Bomb."* In that film, a bomber carrying two nuclear warheads (nicknamed "Dear John," and "Hi There") is not able to bomb its primary or secondary targets. It instead drops the bomb on the nearest target, and in an iconic shot Major T.J. "King" Kong (played by Slim Pickens) rides the bomb to oblivion, whooping and waving his cowboy hat.

Some of the most intense descriptions of such widespread destruction often come from people who have lived through similar experiences. Science-fiction author Kurt Vonnegut was an American POW who survived the firebombing of Dresden and used it as the inspiration for his novel *Slaughterhouse Five.* In a 2003 interview he said, "the most racist, nastiest act by this country, after human slavery, was the bombing of Nagasaki." Telford Taylor, one of the US lawyers who assisted chief prosecutor Robert Jackson at the Nuremberg Trials, was quoted as saying that the bombing of Nagasaki was a war crime.

Today, the American people remain conflicted about nuclear weapons. In 2004, polling showed that 60 percent believed that nuclear weapons should only be used in response to a nuclear attack against the US. In 2005 66 percent agreed with the statement "no countries should have nuclear weapons." Polls in 2007 showed that 73 percent of Americans wanted to eliminate nuclear weapons.

However, when it comes to the one time in history nuclear weapons have been used, most Americans believe it was the right decision. In 2009, 61 percent of Americans believed dropping the atomic bombs on Japan was "the right thing to do."

In 1995 the National Air and Space Museum (NASM) tried putting the *Enola Gay* in an exhibit that explored the consequences of the atomic bomb. Groups including the American Legion, Congress and *Enola Gay* pilot Paul Tibbets protested the exhibit as putting emphasis on the suffering of the Japanese, while leaving out descriptions of Japanese brutality. The museum ultimately dropped the exhibit and Smithsonian director Martin Hewitt resigned. The *Enola Gay* is now in the NASM's Steven Udvar-Hazy Collection at Washington's Dulles International Airport. The museum's description mentions the bombing and how it brought about Japan's surrender, but there is no mention of the 100,000-plus Japanese who were killed, and no mention of the atomic age that the bombing precipitated.

Japan's struggle with collective memory

Sadly, in Japan a similar phenomenon can be seen. The bombings of Hiroshima and Nagasaki, and many of the stories surrounding them, are known to every school-aged child. However, the atrocities committed by Japan during the Sino-Japanese War and the Pacific War (as World War II is called there) were whitewashed from school textbooks for many decades (although most of them do now include the Rape of Nanking, Unit 731, comfort women and other brutalities of the war). Conservative factions have tried unsuccessfully to remove these brutalities from history. China, Korea and Taiwan have weighed in heavily in this controversy, strongly condemning any attempt to remove references to the brutalities they faced during the war.

Despite the Nanking massacre being front-page news in Japan at the time, politicians to this day still say the massacre never happened, or that not as many were killed as is reported, a claim echoed by then-Governor of Tokyo Ishihara Shintaro in 2012.

As this book was being initiated, Japan's cabinet, led by Prime Minister Abe Shinzo, proposed re-drafting Japan's Constitution, specifically Article 9, to allow it to engage in conflicts, specifically "collective self-defense." In 2003, Japan's Self-Defense Forces participated in the US-led invasion of Iraq as one of the "coalition of the willing," but they were not allowed to fire on Iraqis and could only provide humanitarian assistance.

Then-Prime Minister Koizumi Junichiro made a point of visiting the Yasukuni Shrine in Tokyo, where Japanese casualties of war are enshrined, every year of his premiership. Visits to the shrine by Japanese politicians elicit strong responses from surrounding powers each time they happen, and are a thorn in the side of Japan's relations with its neighbors.

Despite these theatrics, most Japanese want the government to acknowledge the wrongdoings committed during World War II and earlier, and want to improve the relationship they have with neighbor countries. Most Japanese favor keeping Article 9 as it is, and oppose allowing "collective self-defense."

What next?

As of 2015 there are 16,000 nuclear weapons among the various nuclear nations. Half of them are in Russia, and most of the rest are in the United States. There are 4,000 active nuclear warheads with roughly the same distribution. This despite the fact that the major security threat to countries is not other nations with air forces, tanks and navies, but deranged terrorists with bombs hidden in suitcases or under their clothes. Nations with nuclear weapons have been slow to adapt their military to deal with these kinds of threats, and have remained convinced that the greatest threats can be dealt with through conventional means.

Since the end of the Cold War, the US Nuclear policy can be found in the *Nuclear Posture Review* (NPR), first issued in 1994. The first review stated that the main priority for the US is a reduction of nuclear weapons, though it would still use them as deterrents against nations who are hostile to either the US or its allies.

During the George W. Bush Administration, the Pentagon wanted to research Earth-penetrating nuclear weapons (known as "bunker-busters"), but Congress refused to fund the project. In 2005, the Pentagon proposed changing the NPR to allow preemptive use of nuclear weapons, but after this was reported in the *Washington Post*, they abandoned this idea.

The last change to the NPR was made in 2010 under the Obama Administration, which puts great emphasis on preventing nuclear proliferation and heavily restricts the number of nuclear weapons the US can have, and the circumstances under which they could be used.

Many issues related to the end of World War II remain unresolved, especially in Asia. It is for this reason that Japan and its neighbors still have regular flair-ups, whether over textbooks, disputed territories, or official apologies that are called insincere.

Meanwhile, the American people have still not fully come to terms with the introduction of nuclear weapons or their consequences. But there is hope – more and more Americans are beginning to question the official story and if it was necessary to drop such destructive weapons on Japan, in particular whether the second Nagasaki bomb, so soon after the first and not allowing the Japanese to fully comprehend the hopelessness of their situation, was a step too far.

At the end of World War II, the largest countries in Europe drew up an official history of the war and Germany fully accepted responsibility for the atrocities the Nazi Party committed. Now, Germany is an equal partner in the European Union and Western Europe has enjoyed its longest peace in centuries.

In contrast, within Asia each nation has its own version of the war, and oftentimes they conflict with each other. There has been peace in the Asia Pacific region, but many observers question how long that will last.

Nuclear weapons have been with us for more than 70 years, and are likely to be with us for a long time to come. Even if they are not used, their very existence is harmful to society and creates tension and strife. We can either accept they are a danger to all life on Earth or we can deny it. Ultimately our fate depends on whether we can come to a solution that benefits us all.

"That same rocket and nuclear and computer technology that sends our ships past the farthest known planet can also be used to destroy our global civilization. Exactly the same technology can be used for good and for evil. It is as if there were a God who said to us, 'I set before you two ways: You can use your technology to destroy yourselves or carry you to the planets and the stars. It's up to you.'"

– Carl Sagan, astronomer, science advocate, anti-nuclear activist

Dirge for the New Sunrise

And the ray from that heat came soundless, shook the sky
        As if in search of food, and squeezed the stems
    Of all that grows on the earth till they were dry
        And drank the marrow of the Bone.
    The eyes that saw, the lips that kissed, are gone
Or black as thunder lie and grin at the murdered sun,
    The living blind and seeing dead together lie
    As if in love… there was no more hating then,
    And no more love, gone is the heart of Man.

(Fifteen minutes past Eight o'clock of Monday
    the 6th August 1945, Dame Edith Sitwell)

FACTS FOR THE TRAVELER

"Though we travel the world over to find the beautiful, we must carry it with us, or we find not."

> – Ralph Waldo Emerson, American Transcendentalist writer and poet

Getting there
By air
All foreign nationals must have an onward/return ticket for visa-free stays. The usual price fluctuation tips apply when buying an air ticket to Japan: Thursdays are the best days to buy, Tuesdays are the best to fly, and the best time to book your ticket is 3-7 weeks before departure. Check discount airline ticket websites like Kayak.com for pricing patterns. Prices go up during Japanese holiday periods, especially during Golden Week (beginning of May) and the Bon Festival (in midsummer).

There is no airport tax levied in Japan, however as in most countries, passenger fees and facility charges (an additional US$15-20) are added to airline ticket prices.

By ferry
If you plan to visit Japan from a nearby country, ferries are a cheap alternative to flying – and an evocative form of travel that harks back to earlier times. Following is a list of ferries from ports in China and Korea, along with their offices in Japan:

China
Shanghai Ferry Company – Room BCF, 4/F The Panorama Shanghai, 53 Huangpu Road, Shanghai 20080; tel: +86 021 6537 5111 (5/F DAI Building, Midosuji, 4-1-2 Minami Kyuhoji-cho, Chuo-ku, Osaka 541-0058; tel: +81 06 6243 6345)

Japan-China International Ferry Company – 18/F Jinan No. 908 Dong Da Ming Rd, Shanghai 200082; tel: +86 021 6325 7642 (2/F San-Ai Building, 1-8-6 Shinmachi, Nishi-Ku, Osaka 550 0013; tel: +81 06 6536 6541)

China Express Line – No. 1 22/F Ocean Shipping Plaza, Hebei District, Tianjin; tel: +86 022 2420 5777 (4-5 Shinkocho Chuo-ku, Kobe 650-0041; tel: +81 078 321 5791)

Orient Ferry Ltd – Haitian Hotel, Room 1267/1268, 48 Xiang Gang Xi Road, Qingdao 266071; tel: +86 053 2389 7636 (1-10-64 Higashi Yamato-cho, Shimonoseki, Yamaguchi-ken 750-0066; tel: +81 08 3232 6615; orientferry-co.jp)

Korea

Kampu Ferry Company – 4-15 Jungang Dong, Jung-Gu, Busan; tel: +82 051 464 2700 (1-10-60 Higashi-Yamatomachi, Shimonoseki, Yamaguchi 750 0066; tel: +81 08 3224 3000)

JR Kyushu / Korean Marine Express – International Ferryport 15-3 4-Ga Jungang-Dong, Jung-Gu, Busan 600-014; tel: +82 051 465 6111 (3/F Hakata-ko Kokusai Terminal, 14-1 Nakahama-cho, Hakata-ku Fukuoka 812-0031; tel: +81 09 2281 2315)

Camellia Line Company – International Ferryport 15-3 4-Ga Jungang-Dong Jung-Gu, Busan 600-014; tel: +82 051 466 7799 (3/F Hakata-ko Kokusai Terminal 14-1 Nakahama-cho, Hakata-ku, Fukuoka 812-0031; tel: +81 05 1466 7799)

Visas

Citizens of 64 countries (including Australia, Canada, New Zealand, the UK and the US) may enter Japan without a visa and stay for 90 days or less for tourism purposes. Nationals from Thailand and Brunei may enter without a visa for 15 days or less. Nationals of countries that do not have "Reciprocal Visa Exemption Arrangements" with Japan must obtain a visa. For more details visit the Japan National Tourism Organization's website at www.jnto.go.jp/eng/arrange/essential/visa.html

Customs

Upon arrival in Japan, you must make a written declaration of your belongings. Import limits include two ounces of perfume, 500 grams of tobacco products and three bottles of alcoholic beverages – as well as 100kg of rice per year! Anything else must not exceed ¥200,000 in value.

On arrival, those aged 16 and older are electronically fingerprinted and photographed, which may be followed by a short interview conducted by an immigration officer. Entry will be denied if any of these procedures is refused.

General information
Cameras

Japan is the headquarters of many of the largest camera companies in the world (Nikon, Canon, and Sony, etc), so you'll have plenty of options to choose from if you want to buy a camera, but keep in mind that the devices sold in Japan are meant for domestic customers, so they'll run on 100V plugs. Like all electronic devices, check the voltage range they'll tolerate before buying them.

Climate

Both Hiroshima and Nagasaki have a humid, subtropical climate, with mild winters and hot and muggy summers. In the wintertime, daytime temperatures hover around 10°C/50°F. In summer, the average high daytime temperature is 28.7°C/83.7°F. Rainfall is highest during June and July. Nagasaki is one of the wettest cities in Japan, receiving approximately 2,000mm (78 inches) of rain per year.

Typhoon season lasts from May to October, with peak activity occurring in August and September. During a typhoon, take the following precautions:

- Do not go outside unless you have to
- Listen to weather warnings issued by the Japan Meteorological Agency (JMA)
- Stay away from flooded streets
- Stay away from downed power lines

The JMA also issues warnings regarding volcanic ash activities and has an early warning system for tsunamis and earthquakes. For details visit www.jma.go.jp

Clothing

Bring clothes appropriate to the season. Both Hiroshima and Nagasaki have subtropical climates with dry, mild winters and hot, humid summers. August is the warmest month.

It is important to wear clean socks without holes in them if you are visiting someone's home, as you will be asked to take off your shoes and given a pair of house slippers.

Business dress is conservative, and as such necklines and any tattoos should be covered. Modern Japanese typically wear Western clothing (*yofuku*) in their day-to-day lives, and traditional Japanese clothing (*wakufu*) only for ceremonies, festivals and other special events. Kimonos are easy to buy and there are stores everywhere that specialize in traditional Japanese clothing.

If you want to buy clothes in Japan, it is best to buy one size up from what you normally wear (if you buy "medium" normally, buy "large" instead).

Currency and credit cards

The Japanese currency is the Yen and is designated using the symbol "¥". Yen come in ¥1, ¥5, ¥10, ¥50, ¥100 and ¥500 coins and ¥1,000, ¥2,000, ¥5,000 and ¥10,000 notes. The coins have a wide variety of patterns, weights and sizes, so they are easy for people with visual impairments to tell apart.

The daily exchange rate between various international currencies can be checked at www.xe.net/ucc; as of mid-2015 US$1 equalled approximately ¥120.

Hotels and high-end restaurants accept most overseas credit cards. Retail stores may have a set requirement for credit card purchases and most small shops will not take any. Overseas-issued debit cards can only withdraw cash at Seven Bank, Japan Post Bank and Citibank. Seven Bank ATMs can be found in 7-11 stores and other locations.

Tipping is uncommon in Japan, though most professionals will appreciate tips. It's a good idea to tip bus/taxi drivers as long as their companies do not ban it. Handing money directly to a person is considered rude in more traditional circumstances, but professionals in the tourism/hospitality industry will take them without issue.

Bargaining is not a custom in Japan, though some shops that cater to tourists allow it.

Electrical accessories

Voltage in Japan is 100 Volts, less than North America (120V) and most other regions (220-230V). Japanese electrical outlets (sockets) resemble North America's outlets, but North American plugs may not work in Japan's outlets. Japanese outlets don't accommodate plugs with grounding pins either.

NB: Buy enough plug adapters for your gadgetry requirements *before* you leave for Japan, as they are not widely sold in the country.

Health

Some over-the-counter medications are prohibited in Japan, including inhalers and some allergy medications. Medications that contain stimulants or Codeine are prohibited. Up to two months' supply of allowable OTC medications and up to four months' supply of approved vitamins can be brought into Japan duty free.

Japan is a developed country, and there are no outstanding health hazards, though the Centers for Disease Control (CDC) still advises a checkup with your doctor before traveling. Routine vaccinations should be up to date, as should vaccines for Hepatitis A and B. You can still get Hepatitis A in Japan from contaminated food or water, or Hepatitis B through sexual contact or contaminated needles.

The CDC recommends getting a vaccination for Japanese Encephalitis if your trip lasts more than a month and especially if you plan on visiting rural areas or will be spending a lot of time outdoors. Rabies is not present in dogs in Japan, but it is found in bats. A vaccine is recommended for travelers involved in outdoor activities in remote areas.

For more information, consult the CDC website at www.cdc.gov/travel/destinations/traveler/none/japan

Luggage

Pack light when traveling to Japan. There is little space for bulky luggage on trains and in train stations. Coin lockers can be found in every train station, but they might not fit larger luggage sizes – prices range from ¥300-500 per day (midnight-midnight). Luggage storage facilities can be found at airports and some large train stations and charge ¥500-1,000 per piece per day.

According to JR (Japan Railway) regulations, passengers may bring up to two pieces of luggage onto trains, not including smaller items. Each piece must not weigh more than 30kg, and its dimensions should add up to no more than 250cm x 200cm (98 x 78 inches).

Mobile phones

Japan has always been in the vanguard of mobile phone technology, and has one of the highest phone-to-user ratios in the world. Travelers can rent a phone with a Japanese number and are charged for use by the day. A variety of companies can be found in major airports (especially Tokyo's Narita). Purchasing a phone requires getting an Alien Registration Card or a friend willing to front for you.

2G phones from anywhere else in the world do not work in Japan. 3G phones with a SIM card and that use UMTS 2100 will work, though countries in North and South America (with the exception of Aruba, Brazil, and Costa Rica) are not on this standard.

Time

All of Japan is on Japanese Standard Time (JST), which is nine hours ahead of Coordinated Universal Time (UTC+9). JST is maintained by the National Institute of Information and Communications Technology (NICT). Japan does not observe daylight savings time.

Toiletries

Most toiletries can be found readily in Japanese grocery stores or drugstores. Deodorants, hair and skincare products are abundant. Most toothpaste in Japan does not contain fluoride, and the water is not fluoridated. Sunscreen is expensive for small bottles, so it is recommended that you bring your own, especially the waterproof types.

Useful websites

Consult the following websites for useful information regarding Japan in general or either city in particular:

- Japan National Tourism Organization – www.jnto.go.jp
- Japan Travel Guide – www.japan-guide.com
- Japan Travel – en.japantravel.com
- Official Hiroshima Prefecture Tourism site – www.visithiroshima.net
- Hiroshima Navigator – www.hiroshima-navi.or.jp/en
- Nagasaki Official Visitor Guide – www.visit-nagasaki.com
- Official Tourism Website for Nagasaki City – www.travel.at-nagasaki.jp
- Japan Rail Pass – www.jrpass.com

Hiroshima
Getting there
Air

Hiroshima Airport (HIJ) is located 31 miles east of Hiroshima. ANA flies from Tokyo (both Haneda and Narita), Sapporo, and Sendai, while Japan Airlines provides a service from Sapporo and Tokyo Haneda. There are international flights from Beijing (Air China), Shanghai (China Eastern Airlines), Taipei (China Airlines) and Seoul (Asiana Airlines).

A bus service runs between the airport and the Hiroshima Bus Center, taking 45-50 minutes and costing ¥1,340 one way. For more details visit www.hij.airport.jp/english

Rail

The most common route to Hiroshima for visitors is by rail. JR West owns most of the passenger lines running through Hiroshima Station, the most prominent route being the Sanyo Main Line (Kobe-Kagoshima). Regional lines like the Kabe and Kure lines connect the greater Chukogu region to the city, and the Geibi Line connects Hiroshima Prefecture with the city.

The Sanyo Shinkansen that runs from Osaka to Fukuoka stops in Hiroshima. At Osaka one can transfer to/from the Tokaido Shinkansen that connects the station to Tokyo and Nagoya. The Hikari service runs from Tokyo to Fukuoka and stops in Hiroshima.

The JR Japan Rail Pass is highly recommended for travelers who plan to use the country's railway network extensively. It grants free passage on most JR lines anywhere in Japan for a set period of time. However, it is not usable on all Shinkansen so check first. Travelers must purchase it before they arrive in Japan, as it is not available domestically. The Japan Rail Pass can be purchased from Japan Airlines at the following international airports:

- Terminal 5, Chicago O'Hare International Airport
- Honolulu International Airport
- Terminal 1, JFK International Airport, New York
- International Terminal, San Francisco International Airport
- Tom Bradley International Terminal, Los Angeles International Airport
- Guam International Airport

Passengers on ANA flights can purchase a Japan Rail Pass from ANA's overseas sales office in Los Angeles (tel: 1 800 826 0095). Selected travel agents throughout the US and Canada sell the pass. Consult www.japanrailpass.net for a complete list.

The JR West issues the ICOCA smart card, which behaves similarly to the SUICA card issued by JR East. Both cards can be used on JR West lines, which is especially useful if you're traveling from Tokyo.

Bus
Intercity buses arrive and depart from Hiroshima Station and the Hiroshima Bus Center. The New Breeze overnight bus departs from Hiroshima and Tokyo at 9pm and arrives in the destination city at 8am the next morning. A one-way ticket costs ¥11,600 and it's ¥21,000 for a round trip. There are five daytime express buses to and from Osaka (¥5,500 one way, ¥9,000 round trip). There are also discount buses like Willer Express (www.willerexpress.com/en) that offer bookings online and in English.

Around town
Tram
The best and most scenic way of seeing Hiroshima is riding the tram. It's also the cheapest – there's a flat fee of ¥160 if you travel within the city. Enter through the back door and exit out the front, handing your fare to the driver, or the conductor if the car has one. Line 2 (red) goes as far as Miyajima and the rates go up to ¥260 the farther out you go from the city. Tickets can be paid in cash or by the PASPY card. Trams also accept ICOCA cards.

Most tram lines go through the city center, where they connect with the underground Astram metro. The metro was opened for the 1994 Asian Games and goes from the city center to the suburbs. Most tram lines also stop at Hiroshima Station. For the locations covered in this book, the nearest tram stop is listed.

Bike

Hiroshima is a great city for biking. Most locations are within reach of a short ride, the terrain is mostly flat and there are plenty of day excursions for the really active cyclist. The Shimanami Kodo (a toll road near Hiroshima) is highly recommended for cyclists. The route is 43 miles long, going from Onomichi in Hiroshima Prefecture to Imabari in Ehime Prefecture on Shikoku Island, and crosses a series of islands along the way with great views of Hiroshima Bay.

Eta-jima Island is also popular for cyclists. It can be reached by ferry from Hiroshima port. The ride takes 30 minutes. For beginner cyclists, Tobishima Kaido in Kure goes along the Seto Island Sea.

All of these routes offer bicycle rentals for ¥500 per day plus ¥1,000 warranty, which is returned if you return the bike to the same terminal.

Hotels

Western properties

In 2011 Sheraton opened its first hotel in western Japan at Hiroshima (www. starwoodhotels.com/sheraton). Located just outside the Shinkansen gate of Hiroshima Station, the hotel offers everything expected of a Western-style hotel. Across the parking lot is the Hotel Granvia (www.hgh.co.jp/english). Both hotels have rooms at Western-equivalent prices.

Within the city, the Grand Intelligent Hotel (www.intelligent-hotel.co.jp/grand) and Grand Intelligent Hotel Annex run to about ¥6,300 per night. Comfort Hotel (www.choicehotels.com), the Japanese branch of Comfort Inn, has a location near the Peace Park for roughly the same price.

Hostels and guesthouses

These establishments offer similar accommodation to hostels around the world, with a few variations. Bunk beds boast futons in place of a spring mattresses, towels can be rented and the shower facilities are coin-operated (usually ¥500 for five minutes of water). It's a great way to get a mix of Western and Eastern hospitality, combining the Western expectations of a hostel with more traditional elements like tatami floors and a futon to sleep on.

The following hostels are a part of the Hiroshima Peace Hostel Network, a program run by the city's tourism division. Unless otherwise noted, they all accept Visa and Mastercard credit cards:

J-Hoppers Trad Guesthouse – 5-16 Dobashi-cho, Naka-Ku; tel: +81 82 233 1360. From ¥2,500. Tram: Dobashi-cho (2, 3, 6, 8).

Reino Inn Hiroshima Peace Park – 3-7-3 Otemachi, Naka-Ku; tel: +81 82 236 7003. From ¥2,400. Tram: Chuden-Mae (1, 3, 7).

Hiroshima International Youth Hostel – 4-17 Kakomachi, Naka-Ku; tel: +81 82 247 8700. From ¥3,690. Does not accept credit cards. Alcohol is prohibited. Tram: Shiyakusyo-mae (1, 3, 7) or Funairi-cho (6, 8).

Ikedaya Bekkan – 5-6 Dobashi-cho, Naka-Ku; tel: +81 82 296 8880. From ¥3,150. Visa is accepted. Tram: Dobashi-cho (2, 3, 6, 8).

The following guesthouses are located slightly farther away:

Akicafe Inn Guesthouse – 2-7 Enkobashicho, Minami-ku; tel: +81 70 5525 6971, website: www.akicafe.co.jp. From ¥2,500. Does not accept credit cards. Tram: Hiroshima Station.

Guest House Lappy – 1-7 Wakakusacho, Higashi-Ku; tel: +81 82 569 7939. From ¥2,200. Tram: Hiroshima Station.

Guest House Carpe – 1-5-18 Koinaka, Nishi-Ku; tel: +81 70 6693 8090. From ¥2,500. Tram: Hiroden-nishi-hiroshima (2, 3) or JR station Nishi-Hiroshima.

K's House – 1-8-9 Matoba-cho, Minami-Ku; tel: +81 82 568 7244. From ¥2,600. Tram: Matoba-cho (1, 2, 5, 6).

Hana Hostel – 1-15 Kojinmachi, Minami-Ku; tel: +81 82 263 2980. From ¥2,500. Tram: Hiroshima Station.

Hiroshima Peace Hotel – 2-6-14 Yokogawa-cho, Nishi-Ku; tel: +81 82 532 1121. From ¥1,580. Tram: Yokogawa 1-chome tram stop (7, 8) or JR station Yokogawa.

Ryokan

For an authentic Japanese experience, *ryokan* are the places to stay. Ryokan are a traditional travelers' inn that developed during the Edo period. They feature tatami floors, communal baths and visitors sleep on a futon that is rolled up and stowed away during the day. They are more expensive than traditional hotels and while most ryokan are in scenic places away from cities, there is one in Hiroshima. The Aioi Ryokan is right next to the Peace Park and costs ¥21,000 per night.

Other ryokan located near the Peace Park (prices are per person) include:

Chizuru Ryokan – 4-12 Fukuromachi, Naka-ku; tel: +81 82 247 3346. From ¥4,200. Credit cards not accepted. Tram: Fukuro-machi (1, 3, 7).

Kasugan Ryokan – 3-6-23 Otemachi, Naka-ku; tel: +81 82 241 5482. From ¥3,000. Visa accepted. Tram: Chuden-mae (1, 3, 7).

Ikawa Ryokan – 5-11 Dobashi-cho, Naka-ku; tel: +81 82 231 5058. From ¥4,725. Meals must be booked in advanced. Tram: Dobashi-cho (2, 3, 6, 8).

Sansui Ryokan – 4-16 Koami-cho, Naka-ku; tel: +81 82 239 9051. ¥4,200 for one person, ¥7,500 for two people, ¥10,500 for three people. Meals not included. Tram: Koami-cho (2, 3).

Minshuku are less expensive alternatives to ryokan, and the Minshuku Ikedaya, also close to Peace Park, is available for around ¥4,200-5,775 per night for a single room. For more details on accommodation go to www.visithiroshima.net/accommodations

Sightseeing

Peace Park

The focus of most tourists who come to Hiroshima is the Peace Park. The Hiroshima A-Bomb Dome is probably the most iconic structure in the park, and one of the most notable structures anywhere in the world. The park is arranged so visitors can look through the Cenotaph across a reflecting pool and the eternal flame straight at the dome.

The target of the bomb, the Aioi Bridge, was heavily damaged but remained standing despite the blast. The current bridge replaced the old one in the 1980s. There are monuments to companies that lost all of their employees in the blast,

The Hiroshima A-Bomb Dome seen through the cenotaph.

like the Chugoku-Shikoku Public Works Office, the Hiroshima District Lumber Control Corporation, the Hiroshima Post Office and the Coal Control-related Company. Historically, the Peace Park was the site of the city's lumber yards, which collected stock from upstream.

There are also tributes to students from local schools who were killed clearing fire lanes. They were let out of school to clear lanes in case the city was targeted for firebombing and the work continued up to the morning of August 6. Their remains, as well as all unidentified remains, are interred beneath a grassy mound in the northwest corner of the museum.

The Hiroshima Peace Museum has a permanent exhibit on the bombing, what led up to it, the aftermath and nuclear weapons. The mayor periodically sends letters to world leaders on nuclear issues and these are posted in the museum as they are sent. It also contains burned items recovered from the destruction like a charred tricycle, a burned lunch box and watches whose hands stopped at 8.15am. There

Above: The top of the Memorial Mound in Peace Park, which covers the ashes of 70,000 unidentified victims of the Hiroshima bomb. Opposite: A poignant photo in the Hiroshima Peace Museum of two children who died in the blast, here playing joyfully with their kitten.

is an explanation of the physics behind nuclear weapons and a brief history of the anti-nuclear movement. Towards the end of the permanent exhibit are the signatures of various dignitaries who have visited the museum over the years, and visitors are encouraged to add their own.

There is a ¥50 entrance fee (children and seniors enter free). There are also recorded tours in 17 languages available on portable devices for ¥300 per recorder. A theater near the gift shop shows two A-bomb documentaries from Japan (available in English as well): "Hiroshima: A Mother's Prayer" and "Hiroshima and Nagasaki: The Harvest of Nuclear War."

Just north of the museum is the Hiroshima National Peace Memorial Hall for the Atomic Bomb Victims, where visitors can see a panorama of the destroyed city created from US Army photos. Underneath the panorama are 140,000 tiles, representing the number of people estimated to have been killed by the atomic bomb. A special exhibition area shows the names, photographs and stories of victims. Admission is free.

Tram: Genbaku Dome-mae (2, 3, 6, 7).

Peace Ceremony

On August 6, the anniversary of the bombing, a Peace Ceremony is held in front of the Cenotaph. There is a moment of silence at 8.15am, followed by the mayor giving a peace declaration, which is published in various languages in media outlets soon after. As soon as the speech is finished, doves are released into the air. The Prime Minister of Japan and the President of Hiroshima's City Council also give speeches.

If the government in Tokyo engages in efforts counter-productive to peace, the mayor and City Council President will include critical remarks against these efforts in their speeches. As this book was being written, Prime Minister Abe Shinzo's cabinet was looking to expand the role of the Self-Defense Forces and the mayor in his declaration criticized this plan.

The rebuilt keep of Hiroshima Castle.

The Peace Lantern ceremony takes place on the banks of the Motoyasu-gawa River, across the river from the A-bomb dome. Lanterns are for sale all day for ¥600, which includes a piece of paper on which you can write a message for peace. The ceremony begins at 6pm and lasts for roughly 3-4 hours (when the organizers run out of lanterns).

Live music, story readings, prayers and film showings happen throughout the day (and in preceding days). The Tourism Division gives out brochures with a complete schedule of events related to the ceremony.

A tricycle buried with its owner, three-year-old Shinichi Tetsutani, in the backyard of the house where he was playing when the bomb dropped, and donated to the Hiroshima Peace Museum 40 years later when his bones were reburied in a formal grave.

Hiroshima Castle

Built by Mori Terumoto between 1589 and 1591 after he moved his headquarters from Yoshida to Hiroshima, the castle served as a military facility after feudal domains were abolished in 1871, and the Emperor Meiji resided here during the first Sino-Japanese War of 1894-95. The original castle grounds extended as far west as the Honkawa River and as far south as Aioi Dori Avenue (where the trams now run), but during the Meiji and Showa eras the moats were filled in and the land was given away. The current grounds are the main compound (*honmaru*) and the second compound (*ninomaru*).

The original castle was destroyed in the atomic bomb blast. A new castle, built with concrete, was built in 1958 and is a museum dedicated to the history of Hiroshima before the bombing. There are several fascinating exhibits on Mori Motonari and his grandson, the Sengoku period and the Edo period. There are also some fascinating exhibits on the economic activities of the city and the daily life of its citizens. It all builds up to the top floor, which provides a decent view of the city.

Around the grounds are the foundation stones of the original castle tower, collected next to the stone steps leading to the new castle. Nearby is the site of the Imperial Headquarters from 1894-95. The Hiroshima-Gokoku Jinja Shrine, in the southwest corner of the main compound, is a reconstruction of the shrine destroyed in the bombing. Adjacent to the shrine are the remains of the war office communications bunker where the first dispatch reporting the atomic bomb was sent.

The nearest station is Kencho-mae on the HRT Astram line. Admission to the main keep costs ¥370, but the rest of the castle grounds are free.

Art museums

Hiroshima has three art museums boasting very different collections. Half of the paintings in the Hiroshima Museum of Art are by masters from the Romantic, post-Impressionist, and Cubist eras through the 20th century. They include works by Claude Monet, August Renoir, Édouard Manet, Eugène Delacroix, Edgar Degas, Vincent Van Gogh, Henri de Toulouse-Lautrec, Pablo Picasso, and others. The other half is by Japanese artists of the Yoga school (Western-style), like Asai Chu, one of the pioneers of the school. Other leaders of the movement like Kuroda Seiki and Saeki Yuzo are on display as well. The museum's other great strength is in paintings

of the Nihonga (Japanese-style) school, contemporaneous to the Yoga but which embraced more Japanese techniques than the Yoga. Leaders of the movement include Yokoyama Taikan, Shimomura Kanzan, Umemura Shoen and Murakami Kagaku, all of whom have work on display. The museum is close to the Kencho-mae station on the HRT Astram line. Admission is ¥1,000 for adults.

Above: Van Gogh's *Daubigny's Garden*, painted in 1890.
Opposite top and bottom: Henri Matisse's *La France*, painted in the country's tricolor in 1939;
the entrance to the Hiroshima Museum of Art, where both these paintings are on display.

The Hiroshima Prefectural Art Museum focuses on local artists and temporary exhibits, but it does have 4,000 objects in its possession. Most of these items are related to Hiroshima Prefecture, Asian crafts, and art of the 1920s-30s. The Kenmin Gallery in the basement displays work from local artists. It is also attached to the Shikukkein Garden and a ticket to both costs ¥260. Admission to the museum only is ¥410 for adults. Tram: Shukkeien-mae (9).

The Hiroshima Museum for Contemporary Art features contemporary Japanese artists. It is located in Hijiyama Park not far from the Hiroshima City Manga Library, which houses 100,000 volumes of Manga and serves as a venue for artists of this form to present their work. There are brochures in English giving a brief history of manga, but the vast majority of their holdings are in Japanese.

Shikukkein Garden

Located next to the Hiroshima Prefecture Art Museum, the Shikukkein Garden is
a quiet spot in the middle of the city where you can relax and enjoy the beauty of
a traditional Japanese garden. It was built in 1620 by Ueda Soko, the principal
retainer of Asano Nagaakira, who became Daimyo of Hiroshima the previous year.
Entrance costs ¥260. Tram: Shukkeien-mae (9).

Mazda Museum

Mazda has been based in Hiroshima since 1920. Its main production facility is close to its corporate headquarters and you can go through it in a daily English tour that takes about 90 minutes. During the tour you visit a museum showcasing notable cars made by the brand. A highlight of the tour is the Mazda 787B car that won the 1991 24-hour Le Mans race. To date, Mazda is the only Japanese car manufacturer to win the race.

The tour is free, though you need to sign up beforehand (www.mazda.com/en/about/museum/reservations) and it requires a short train ride from the city center to the JR Mukainada Station (Sanyo line).

1975
COSMO
AP

Above top and bottom: Motoring exhibits in the Mazda Museum.
Opposite: The peaceful haven of Shikukkein Garden.

Excursions

Miyajima

Not to be missed is this island about 13 miles away from Hiroshima. The Itsukushima Shrine and the floating *torii* in the bay were described by Confucian scholar Shunsai Hayashi as one of the three most scenic spots of Japan in 1643. The Shrine is dedicated to three goddesses of the sea, traffic safety, fortune and accomplishments and was finished in 1168. The torii is 54.5 feet (16.6 meters) tall and 79 feet (24 meters) across. It is the eighth such torii since the Heian period and was erected in 1875.

Nearby is the Senjokaku Hall. Literally "the hall of a thousand tatami mats," the hall can accommodate as many people. The building was commissioned by Hideyoshi in 1587 as a hall to pray for dead soldiers during his conquest of Japan and Korea. Construction was stopped at his death and it remains unfinished to this day. Next to it is a five-story pagoda that incorporates Japanese and Chinese architecture.

Mount Misen was visited by Kukai, the founder of Shingon Buddhism, in the year 806, and since then it has been an important religious pilgrimage site.

Above: The floating *torii* gate at Miyajima, constructed in 1875. Opposite: Deer are considered messengers of the gods in Shinto mythology. For this reason they are allowed to roam free on Miyajima.

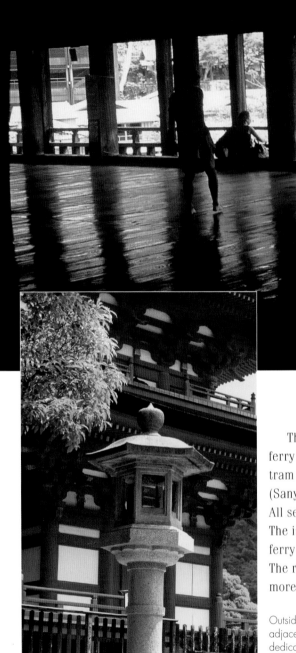

The island can be reached by ferry from nearby Miyajima-guchi tram station, accessible via JR trains (Sanyo) and the Hiroshima tram (2). All services from here are frequent. The island can also be reached by a ferry that berths at the Peace Park. The ride takes 50 minutes and is more expensive (¥1,900 one way).

Outside the Gojunoto (five-storied pagoda), adjacent to Senjokaku. Built in 1407, it was dedicated to the Buddha of Medicine.

The interior of Senjokaku Hall, built on the orders of Hideyoshi in 1587 to commemorate the souls of those who died during his unsuccessful invasion of Korea.

Tomonoura

The second largest city in Hiroshima Prefecture is Fukuyama, which includes the former port town of Tomonoura. Tomonoura is one of the oldest towns in Japan, having been mentioned in the 8th-century collection of poems the *Man'yoshi*. It has since been an attractive place for artists, most recently the world-renowned animator Hayao Miyazaki. The setting of his film *Ponyo* is based on Tomonoura, where he stayed for two months in 2005.

Kusado Sengen, a medieval town that's been excavated since the 1960s, has a museum on objects found at the sight and exhibits on medieval Japanese life.

JR: Fukuyama Station (Sanyo Main, Sanyo Shinkansen, Fukuen Line).

Kure

Kure was the sight of the largest shipbuilding yards in Japan for many decades. The yards built the largest battleship in the Japanese Navy, the *Yamato*. Admiral Yamamoto Isoroku, the Commander-in-Chief of the Combined Pacific Fleet used the *Nagato* – also constructed at Kure – as his flagship before transferring to the *Yamato* shortly after Pearl Harbor. There is a museum dedicated to the *Yamato* and a history of the shipyards. It is also one of the headquarters of the Maritime Self-Defense Forces.

JR: Kure Station (terminus of the Kure Line).

Iwakuni

The Kikkawa family were retainers of the Mori clan, and some of their members helped Hideyoshi during his conquest of Kyushu. For their service, they became Daimyo of the region Iwakuni is a part of. Their castle at Iwakuni is one of the 100 Great Castles of Japan. The nearby Kintai Bridge and Kikko Park are popular tourist spots – the bridge has five arches and looks like a snake.

JR: Iwakuni Station (Sanyo Main Line, Gantoku Line terminus).

Takahashi

The Raikyu-ji temple is well-known for its Japanese garden, which is maintained by the abbot. The Bitchu Matsuyama castle is one of the oldest in Japan, though the existing structure was built more recently.

JR: Bitchu-Takahashi (Habuki Line).

Kurashiki

The eight-mile-long Great Seto Bridge goes from here across the Seto Inland Sea to Sakaide, one of three bridges between Honshu and Shikoku and the only railway bridge. Kurashiki is also home to the oldest art museum in Japan dedicated to Western art, the Ohara Museum of Art.

JR: Kurashiki (Sanyo Main Line, Habuki Line).

Shimonoseki

Sitting right at the southern tip of Honshu, Shimonoseki has always been a crucial port city in Japan. It was bombarded by Western powers in 1864 and was the site of the Treaty of Shimonseki that ended the first Sino-Japanese War in 1895. It is the largest pufferfish harvester in Japan, and is nicknamed the "Fugu capital."

JR: Shimonoseki (Sanyo Main Line).

Izumo and Matsue Castle

The Izumo-Tahisa is the oldest Shinto shrine in Japan, and is considered the second most important shrine in the religion (the shrine at Ise is the most important). JR: Izumo-shi (Sanin Main Line).

Very close to Izumo, Matsue Castle is one of the oldest in Japan. Author Laifcadio Hearn taught here from 1890-91. His former house is now a museum of his life.

JR: Matsue (Sanin Main Line).

Opposite top and bottom: A large model of the battleship *Yamato* in the Kure naval museum.

Sake

Sake has been brewed in Japan for thousands of years. References to it show up in the earliest written records of the islands. Sake is usually called "rice wine" in English, though the brewing process is closer to beer. It is usually about 16 percent alcohol, which is stronger than most wines and beers. For centuries it has been used in Shinto ceremonies, court activities, and Kamikaze pilots used to drink it before missions.

Saijo, now a part of Higashihiroshima, is famed throughout Japan for its sake breweries. October 1 is officially Sake day in Japan and there's a Sake festival in Saijo around the same time each year. JR: Saijo.

Baseball

Baseball was introduced to Japan by Horace Wilson, a Union Army veteran who taught English at what is now Tokyo Imperial University. In 1872 he introduced the game, believing his students needed more exercise. The first team was organized in 1878 and baseball has been popular in Japan ever since.

Hiroshima is home to the Hiroshima Toyo Carp baseball team, who play at Mazda Stadium. Mazda has a large share of the team and the Matsuda family who founded the company owns a significant share as well. The team was formed in 1949 in Hiroshima and is a member of the Nippon Central League. It has won the Japan Series three times, in 1979, 1980, and 1984. Baseball seasons in Japan start in April and the championship series takes place at the end of October.

Among its more notable players is Sachio Kinugasa, nicknamed "Tetsujin" ("Iron Man"), who held the world record for consecutive games played until Cal Ripkin Jr. (also nicknamed "Iron Man") surpassed him in 1996. Some of its players also have careers in MLB teams like Hiroki Kuroda (now with the NY Yankees) and Colby Lewis (now with the Texas Rangers).

The Hiroshima Toyo Carp baseball team plays a game at the Mazda Stadium.

Nagasaki
Getting there
Air
Nagasaki Airport (NGS) is 11 miles northwest of Nagasaki Railway Station in the town of Omura. ANA flies to Nagasaki from Nagoya Centrair, Osaka Itami and Tokyo Haneda airports, while Japan Airlines provides flights from Osaka Itami and Tokyo Haneda. China Eastern Airlines flies from Shanghai's Pudong Airport and Jin Air has a route from Seoul.

Several bus companies provide shuttle services to and from Nagasaki Airport. From Nagasaki Station the ride takes between 45 and 60 minutes and costs ¥800 one way or ¥1,200 round trip. For more information visit www.nabic.co.jp/english

Rail
Chances are you'll be coming into Nagasaki via Nagasaki Railway Station. Nagasaki is the terminus for the Nagasaki Main Line, which runs to Tosu Station (Saga Prefecture) and is the terminus for the Kamome Limited Express, which runs to Hakata Station (Fukuoka). The Kyushu Shinkansen is being expanded to run between Hakata and Nagasaki and is scheduled for completion in 2023. The Nagasaki Main Line is run by JR Kyushu, which issues the SUGOCA card. Other JR smart cards are accepted by JR Kyushu like the SUICA (East), ICOCA (West) and TOICA (Central). The SUGOCA card is also usable on JR West lines.

The nearest station to Nagasaki Railway Station on either route is Urakami, which is within walking distance of the Peace Park, Hypocenter and Atomic Bomb Museum.

Bus
Kosoku buses connect Nagasaki to Fukuoka. They are run by JR Kyushu Bus and other private companies, but none of them have English-language websites and are consequently difficult for foreigners to use.

Around town
Tram
Like Hiroshima, the cheapest and most scenic way to get around Nagasaki is riding the tram. Fares are ¥120 for adults and ¥60 for children. If you need to transfer from one route to another, tell the driver "transfer" and they'll give you a small transfer sheet. Drop this in the slot when you leave the system. You can also purchase a daily tram pass from most hotels for ¥500. The Nagasaki Smart Card is

similar to other smart cards and can be used on trams and bus companies that run in the city and throughout Nagasaki Prefecture.

Bikes

Bikes can be rented from Nagasaki Station for ¥500 for two hours or ¥1,500 per day. There's a 40 percent discount if you have a JR Rail Pass. Nagasaki's streets are narrower than Hiroshima's, but bike excursions from the city are just as pleasant.

Hotels

Western properties

Western-style hotels are concentrated around Peace Park, the JR Nagasaki Station and Oura. The only Western-brand hotels in Nagasaki are the Comfort Hotel (www.choicehotels.com) and Crowne Plaza (www.ihg.com/crowneplaza), while the rest are chains based in Japan. Business hotels are concentrated near Nagasaki Station.

The Hotel Monterey near Oura (www.hotelmonterey.co.jp) has a Portuguese theme to it, in honor of the Portuguese traders who passed through the city 500 years before.

Hostels and guesthouses

The family-owned AKARI hostel (www.nagasaki-hostel.com) is probably the most prominent such establishment in Nagasaki. It is located near the Kofukuji Temple and Siebold Museum, and prices are reasonable (¥2,600 per night for a dorm bed). They have a rolling job offer for cleaners at the hostel: you must stay longer than 10 days and will not be paid a salary, but you will get free accommodation.

Ryokan

Most ryokan are in less populated areas, and the only one in Nagasaki is the Fujiwara Ryokan, near City Hall (www.nagasaki-fujiwara-ryokan.jimdo.com). The Nagasaki Kagamiya has kimono rental and is located within a shrine.

Nagasaki's efficent and convenient tram system is the best way to see the sights.

For more information on accommodation in Nagasaki and its surrounding area consult www.visit-nagasaki.com

Sightseeing

Atomic Bomb Museum

Like the Hiroshima Peace Museum, this museum focuses on the bombing of its home city – what happened, the science behind the bomb and efforts to reduce nuclear weapons after 1945.

A spiral hallway leads from the front door to the main exhibit. One of the first objects of note is a clock whose hands have stopped at 11.02am, the moment of the explosion. The remains of the Urakami Cathedral are strewn throughout the exhibit, including a preserved wall, damaged statues and other pieces of the building. This section of the exhibit is dimly lit, with ominous ambient noise making it all the more haunting. The museum also displays some rosary beads that were being held by parishioners in the building at the moment of the explosion.

There is some discussion of the development and mechanics of the Fat Man bomb, including a life-size replica of the bomb casing. Also displayed are copies of the leaflets dropped on Japan by American planes describing the destruction of Hiroshima and demanding they leave the city or risk being destroyed. Like the Hiroshima museum, fragments of everyday items recovered from the blast site like lunch boxes, helmets, and clothes are on display.

Outside stands a statue of a teacher and a student, commemorating the approximately 5,800 elementary school students, 1,900 mobilized students and 100 teachers killed by the explosion. There is also a white pine, dedicated by a returning Japanese soldier who found his home and entire family destroyed by the bomb.

Admission to the Atomic Bomb Museum is ¥200, free on August 9.

Nagasaki National Peace Memorial Hall for the Atomic Bomb Victims

Connected to the Atomic Bomb Museum and across the way from the Nagasaki City Peace Hall, the highlight of this building is the Remembrance Hall Atrium, with six tall beams of light on either side. At the front, a list of the names of the Atomic Bomb victims is kept, encouraging visitors to pray for the souls of those who died. The memorial has a library with portraits, personal memoirs and testimonials of victims. On the upper level is a basin that holds fresh water. Underneath, 70,000 optical fibers light up at night, representing the estimated number of victims to have died by the end of 1945.

Downstairs is the Museum of History and Folklore, which has many objects from early Nagasaki history (unfortunately all of the signage is in Japanese). The hall also hosts the Yataro Noguchi memory museum, which displays the paintings of Yataro Noguchi, one of the city's great oil painters.

Hypocenter

Between Peace Park and the Atomic Bomb Museum is the Hypocenter Park. A large monolith stands at its center – the exact point above which Fat Man exploded at an altitude of 1,650 feet. Nearby is a section of the Urakami Cathedral's south wall, moved from its original location. Beside it is the Shimonokawa River, where a plaque notes that many people died drinking water from the river in 1945. Across the street from the park is a brick from the old Hamaguchi-Machi streetcar station destroyed by the bomb. Many poets are commemorated near the Hypocenter Park, including Sumako Fukuda, Takami Oyama, Yoshiho and Haruto Kuma. Washington D.C. donated one of the cherry trees it had originally received from Japan, and this is located at the top of the steps leading from the Peace Memorial Hall to the Hypocenter Park.

Peace Park

Across the street and up a hill from the Hypocenter, this is where the Peace ceremony takes place each year. At 11.02am on August 9, air-raid sirens sound throughout the city and there is a moment of silence in the park. Then the mayor reads his peace declaration in front of the centerpiece of the park: a 10-meter-high statue by Seibo Kitamura representing peace. Beside it are towers of folded paper cranes, similar to the towers in Hiroshima.

Opposite top: Inside Nagasaki's Peace Memorial Hall. Opposite bottom: The monolith at the center of the Hypocenter Park. Above: A colorful mural outside the Peace Memorial Hall.

Throughout the park are statues donated from various places including Nagasaki's sister cities. The oldest Sister City relationship in Japan is between Nagasaki and St. Paul, Minnesota. Lewis F. Hill Jr. (grandson of railroad tycoon J.J. Hill) visited Japan often and when President Eisenhower proposed the Sister Cities Initiative, Hill was the first to answer the call and proposed a relationship between his hometown of St. Paul and Nagasaki. In 1992 St. Paul donated the sculpture "Constellation Earth" by Paul Granlund to the people of Nagasaki and it sits in the Peace Park.

The hill to the park is quite steep, but thankfully there are escalators. The nearest tram stops to the Peace Park are the Matsuyama-Machi and Hamaguchi-Machi stops (1, 3). The JR Urakami station is farther away.

Urakami Cathedral

The original cathedral was built by exiles who returned to Urakami after the ban on Christianity was lifted in 1871. When the building was completed in 1925, it was the largest Catholic Church in East Asia. Fat Man exploded 1,645 feet from the cathedral and it was mostly destroyed. One of the bell domes rolled down a nearby hill, where it still sits today. The remains of the original church have been moved to the Atomic Bomb Museum and the Hypocenter Park. In 1959, another cathedral was built on the same location, and this still holds services today.

Nyokodo

Not far from Peace Park, Nyokodo was the home of Dr. Nagai Takashi, a physician specializing in radiology – and bomb survivor himself – who helped victims of the bombing until his own death. Adjacent to it is the Nagai Takashi Memorial Museum, showing photographs, handwritten manuscripts and personal possessions.

Kofukuji Temple

The first Chinese temple built in Japan for Chinese traders, the Kofukuji Temple dates to 1620. Many Buddhist temples were built by Chinese residents during this period as a way of asserting their faith in the Buddha. The temple has a fish motif, since many of the traders worshipped the goddess of the sea, Matsu, praying for safe passage across the ocean. In 1654, the Zen Master Ingen came to Nagasaki from China and became the resident priest at Kofukuji. He founded Obaku Buddhism, which became greatly influential in Japan in the ensuing centuries, and is also credited with introducing the kidney bean to Japan.

Tram: Kokaido-Mae (4, 5). Admission costs ¥300.

A Confucian statue at Sofukuji Temple.

Sofukuji Temple

Built a few years after the Kofukuji Temple, this Chinese temple was also built for Chinese traders and also contains a statue of Matsu, enshrined for her worshippers.

Tram: Shokakuji-Shita (1, 4, Terminus). Admission ¥300.

Chinatown

The oldest Chinatown in Japan (officially Shinchimachi), this used to be an artificial island where Chinese traders would stay. At its peak as many as 10,000 Chinese traders lived here. It's almost twice the area of Dejima, though it is still a working Chinatown, with restaurants and trinket shops. Like Dejima, land reclamation projects have filled in the surrounding sea and it's no longer an actual island.

Chinatown is very close to the Nagasaki Bus Terminal, which has bus services to Nagasaki Airport and elsewhere.

Tram: Tsuki-Machi (1, 5).

Dejima

The old Dutch trading post has been reconstructed on the site of the fan-shaped island (though like Chinatown, land reclamation projects have filled in the sea around it). The original buildings are long gone, but historical replicas roughly recreate the trading post as it might have looked. Entrance costs ¥510.

Tram: Dejima (1) or Tsuki-Machi (1, 5).

Siebold Museum

Opened in 1989, this museum on the life of Phillip von Siebold is one of the oldest museums dedicated to a Westerner in Japan. It is next to his former residence and tells the story of his life, his family and contributions to science in Japan. It is the only museum dedicated to Siebold in Japan – there are two in Europe (Leiden and Munich) that also have objects related to Japan.

Tram: Shin Nakagawa-Machi (3, 4, 5).

Two surviving camphor trees outside the Sanno Shrine.

Sanno Shrine

Originally located closer to the Urakami Highway, the original shrine was destroyed in the bomb blast. Its two torii gates remained standing – the first was completely preserved, but one pillar of the second gate (the one closer to the bomb) collapsed. The first gate was demolished some time during reconstruction, but the second one is preserved, known as the half-torii. The remains of the other half are strewn on the ground nearby.

The shrine was moved farther away from the highway, behind two camphor trees that survived the bombing. Originally thought dead, they sprouted leaves and branches months after the bombing and have become symbols of the rebirth of the city.

Tram: Urakami Eki-Mae or Daigaku Byoin-Mae (1, 3).

Museum of History and Culture

Like Hiroshima Castle, the Nagasaki Museum of History and Culture tells the history of the region before the bombing. It has many objects related to trade with China and the Dutch from the Edo Period and earlier. Many of the exhibits are interesting, though not all of the signage is in English. There's a section about the contents of a traditional Japanese home where you are required to take off your shoes. Another section recreates the Magistrate's Office (*bugyosho*) that helps visitors understand the life of samurai warriors during the period.

Admission is ¥600 for adults. Tram: Sakura-machi (3).

Oura Cathedral

When this cathedral was built in 1864, underground Christians flocked to its services. When news reached the Pope, he called it a miracle. Today, the cathedral is a historical monument, and was for many decades the only Western building

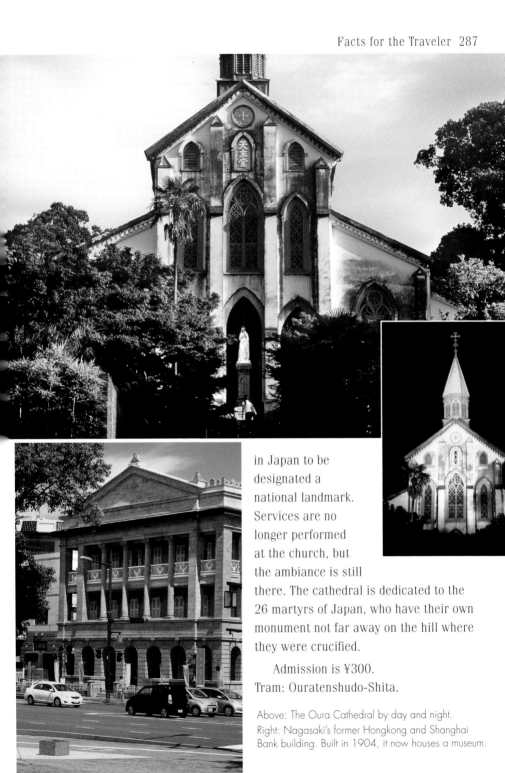

in Japan to be designated a national landmark. Services are no longer performed at the church, but the ambiance is still there. The cathedral is dedicated to the 26 martyrs of Japan, who have their own monument not far away on the hill where they were crucified.

Admission is ¥300.

Tram: Ouratenshudo-Shita.

Above: The Oura Cathedral by day and night.
Right: Nagasaki's former Hongkong and Shanghai Bank building. Built in 1904, it now houses a museum.

Glover Garden

Thomas Glover's house was far enough away from the bomb blast to be undamaged. The site is a historical area and many historic houses have been moved from other parts of Oura to the site, such as William Alt's house and the Mitsubishi Quarters, which were originally farther away. (Alt made huge profits from exporting tea from Kyushu along with Oura Kei, who came from a family of wealthy oil merchants. William Alt's home was designed by Hide Koyama, who was also the architect of the Oura Cathedral.)

The Glover Garden gives an immersive look at life in Nagasaki's foreign settlement in the 1870s. The Glover house was called the "Madame Butterfly house" by US troops during the Japanese occupation, and for this reason Glover is often incorrectly cited as the inspiration for the opera. Not far from a statue of Puccini stands another statue and a special exhibit on Tamaki Mura, a Japanese soprano who gained worldwide fame for her portrayal of Cio-Cio-San.

Above: One of the entrances to Thomas Glover's house.
Left: The Mitsubishi Dock House, built in 1896 to serve as a resthouse for ships' crews docked in Nagasaki.

Robert Neil Walker helped establish the first beverage manufacturer in Japan, while his older brother Wilson established the Japan Brewery Company with Glover, which later became Kirin. Walker's house was built next to Oura Cathedral, but has been moved to the grounds of the Glover Garden. The Glover house also has a room dedicated to Thomas Glover's son Thomas Albert ("Tomisaburo") Glover, who wrote a fish atlas, one of the first for Japan and one of the most comprehensive. He also established the Unzen Golf Course, the first public course in Japan.

Unfortunately, because he was half-Scottish, friends of Tomisaburo distanced themselves from him during World War II, fearing the authorities would harass them. The windows of the Glover house were blown out by the atomic bomb, but it survived further damage.

Tram: Ouratenshudo-Shita (5). Admission is ¥610.

Mt. Inasa
The top of this 1,093-foot mountain offers a spectacular view of Nagasaki. It is accessible by cable car from Fuchi Jinja station. It is popular with tourists and you can see all of Nagasaki stretching from Urakami to Oura. A round-trip ticket on the ropeway costs ¥1,230.

Magome Church, dedicated to Saint Michael, was originally built in 1890 but was destroyed by a typhoon in 1930. It was rebuilt in 1931 and stands on Iojima Island near Nagasaki port (photo by Hiroaki Misawa).

Excursions

Hashima

Also known as Gunkanjima ("Battleship island") due to its silhouette, this island was the site of a Mitsubishi-owned coal mine starting in the 1890s. The mine was closed in 1974 and the island was abandoned. The remains of the mine and the surrounding town are still intact, and the Gunkanjima Concierge tour company offers tours. The tour comprises a ferry ride from Nagasaki to the island with a brief landing on the island itself; it lasts around three hours and costs between ¥3,600 and ¥3,900 for adults. Website: www.gunkanjima-concierge.com/en

Goto

The Goto islands are accessible by ferry from Nagasaki's Port Terminal (not to be confused with Nagasaki Harbor, where luxury cruise liners occasionally dock). Among the highlights are the Dozaki Church, built by French missionaries and now a museum on Christians in Japan and their suppression. The ferry to Goto from Nagasaki is either a Jetfoil (85 minutes, ¥6,300) or a normal ferry (3.5 hours, ¥2,520). Tel: +81 2095 822 9153.

Iki

There are many beach resorts on Iki Island, but the largest and most popular is the Tsutsuki-hama beach on the southeast side. A dolphin park puts on shows and preserves the animals in natural coves.

Opposite: Shimabara castle, its imposing walls surrounded by a now-dry moat.

There are flights from Nagasaki Airport, but a ferry from Karatsu is the more common access point. An express bus runs from Nagasaki to Karatsu and the ferry to Iki takes 75 minutes. Alternatively, a ferry from Fukuoka takes 2 hours and 15 minutes. For more information on points of interest visit www.iki-island.net

Mount Unzen

Not far from Shimabara, Mount Unzen is a series of active volcanoes. The highest peak is Heisei-shinzan at 4,875 feet. The peak emerged during its most recent active period, from 1990 to 1995 (during the Heisei era, hence its name). It is one of 17 Decade Volcanoes around the world, which are noted for their proximity to populated areas and large destructive activity. The worst volcanic disaster in Japanese history occurred in 1792 when Mt. Unzen erupted and created a tsunami that killed 15,000 people. The region is famous for its hiking potential and in nearby towns like Obama and Shimabara there are many hot spring spas (*onsen*).

Sasebo

Once one of the largest shipbuilding yards and naval bases in Japan, most was destroyed in World War II and the Americans have kept a base here since the occupation. There is some American influence in the city as a result, though the highlight of the city is Huis ten Bosch, a Dutch-themed park. The park is a recreation of a Dutch town, but the highlight of the park is a replica of the *Liefde*, the first Dutch ship to arrive in Japan.

Shimabara

The site of the Shimabara rebellion. The rebel stronghold was Hara Castle, and one can visit the ruins. The town is close to Mt. Unzen, an active volcano, and like many Japanese towns near volcanoes there are lots of natural springs around town.

Hirado

Hirado was the original port of trade with the Dutch and English before Nagasaki became the main port. The Dutch and English factories have been preserved and much like Dejima it is a great walking history tour. Hirado is connected to Kyushu via a suspension bridge that looks similar to the Golden Gate Bridge, though it's half as long.

Tabira Church in Hirado, dedicated to the 26 Martyrs of Japan (photo by Hiroaki Misawa).

Tsushima

Halfway between Kyushu and Korea, the lords of the island of Tsushima often played both sides against each other to gain riches. In 1615 they built the Banshoin Temple, which is a highlight of the trip. Tsushima can be reached from Fukuoka and Busan by plane or ferry.

Saga

Saga castle is one of the few remaining castles in Japan to be surrounded by a moat. Disgruntled samurai occupied the castle during the Saga rebellion against the Meiji Government in 1874. In late October/early November, the city is the site of the Saga International Balloon Fiesta, when 15 million hot-air balloon enthusiasts from all over the world convene and fly here.

Arita in Saga Prefecture has been a center of porcelain wares for centuries. Much of it was exported to Europe during the Edo Period by the Dutch. Porcelain craftsmen still work in the town, carrying on their ancestors' craft.

Fukuoka

The largest city on Kyushu, flying into Fukuoka Airport puts you right in the middle of Hiroshima and Nagasaki. Hakata Bay was the landing point of the Mongol armies during their two invasions – the Hakozaki Shrine near the coast has an anchor from one of the Mongol ships. The Hakata Machiya Folk Museum focuses on life in Fukuoka from the 1860s to the 1920s.

Dazaifu

This was the Imperial headquarters in Kyushu during the Heian Period, and the target of both Mongol invasions. The government house is now a historical park and none of the buildings remain standing. The Kyushu National Museum showcases the development of Japanese culture through interaction with the rest of Asia. It is five miles south of Fukuoka.

Beppu

Beppu is renowned for its hot springs – tourism authorities call it one of the three great hot springs of Japan (the others are Atami and Shirahama). The springs are multicolored volcanic pits known as the "eight hells of Beppu." They are too hot to be used as onsen (hot spring baths), but plenty of them are located throughout the city.

Kumamoto

Kumamoto Castle is one of the largest in Japan, named one of the country's three greatest castles according to tourist authorities. It was established in 1496, though the keep was replaced by a concrete replica in 1960.

Takachiho

Located a short bus ride from Kumamoto (and completely inaccessible by train), this small town is in the middle of a deep gorge which contains the Ama-no-Iwato cave, where Amaterasu supposedly hid and where in legend Jimmu descended from the heavens. There is a shrine at the cave, but no one is allowed to enter. You can rent a boat and paddle down the gorge for some spectacular views. The Miyazaki Jingu shrine in Miyazaki celebrates a festival dedicated to Jimmu every autumn.

Miyazaki

In 1940, Miyazaki city built the Hakko Ichiu monument on the legendary site of Jimmu's original palace. *"Hakko Ichiu"* was the slogan Japan used in promoting its Greater East Asia Co-Prosperity Sphere during World War II. The monument is still there, with the phrase carved on its side. The city is also known as a great surfing destination and has many golf courses in the surrounding area. David Duval runs a golf academy and Tom Watson designed one of the courses. The Phoenix Country Club hosts the Dunlop Phoenix Tournament each year, and many prominent golfers have won it, including Tiger Woods.

Usuki

Located in Oita Prefecture, this castle town is most famous for its 59 Buddhas carved in stone. Carved between the 11th and 14th centuries, the Buddhas range in height from two to nine feet tall. The rock was created by eruptions from nearby Mount Aso, the largest active volcano in Japan and the highest mountain on Kyushu. It is slowly becoming popular with hikers, though park officials are vigilant on the volcanic activity and will turn away visitors if it becomes particularly active. Like Mt. Unzen, there are many onsen resorts close to the volcano, most notably the Beppu Hatto in Beppu City.

Kagoshima

Some of the first contact between Japan and the West took place in Kagoshima. The British bombarded the city in 1863 in retaliation for the murder of Charles Lenox Richardson a year earlier. It was also the site of the Satsuma Rebellion in 1877. Admiral Togo Heihachiro, the hero of the Russo-Japanese War (the British called him the "Nelson of the Orient") was born in Kagoshima. The city today is known throughout Japan for its *shochu,* a distilled beverage usually made from sweet potato. Its alcohol content is stronger than wine and sake, but not as strong as vodka. In 2003, exports of shochu exceeded sake for the first time.

Just outside Kagoshima City stands a monument at the approximate spot where St. Francis Xavier landed in Japan for the first time.

The Kagoshima Prefectural Museum of Culture and History details the folklore, arts and crafts of the prefecture. The Museum of the Meiji Restoration explains that period as well as the Satsuma Rebellion.

Kagoshima's most interesting museum is the Chiran Peace Museum for the Kamikaze Pilots, which has various materials and mementoes of the 1,000 Kamikaze pilots based in Chiran.

The cover of the August 31, 1946 issue of *The New Yorker*, which featured a bucolic image filled with irony considering the horrific story of Hiroshima's decimation that was told within its pages by John Hersey.

RECOMMENDED READING

Agee, James, *Dedication Day* (Politics, 1946)

Akizuki, Tatsuichiro, *Nagasaki 1945: The First Full-length Eyewitness Account of the Atomic Bomb Attack on Nagasaki* (Quartet Books, 1982)

Alden, Dauril, *The Making of an Enterprise: The Society of Jesus in Portugal, Its Empire, and Beyond, 1540-1750* (Stanford University Press, 1996)

Alperovitz, Gar, *The Decision to Use the Atomic Bomb* (Vintage, 1996)

Bernstein, Barton J., *The Atomic Bombings Reconsidered* (Foreign Affairs, 1995)

Bix, Herbert P., *Hirohito And The Making Of Modern Japan* (Harper Collins, 2009)

Boorstin, Daniel J., *The Discoverers* (Vintage, 1985)

Boxer, Charles Ralph, *The Christian Century in Japan, 1549-1650* (Carcanet Press Ltd, 1993)

Bundy, McGeorge, *Danger and Survival: Choices about the Bomb in the First Fifty Years* (Random House, 1988)

Burchett, Wilfred, *Shadows of Hiroshima* (Verso Books, 1983)

Burke-Gaffney, Brian, *Nagasaki: The British Experience, 1854-1945* (BRILL/Global Oriental, 2009)

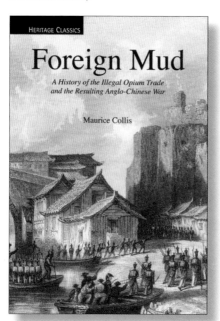

Chang, Iris, *The Rape of Nanking* (Basic Books, 1997)

Coerr, Eleanor, *Sadako and the Thousand Paper Cranes* (Puffin Modern Classics, 2004)

Collie, Craig, *Nagasaki: The Massacre of the Innocent and Unknowing* (Allen & Unwin, 2012)

Collis, Maurice, *Foreign Mud: Being an Account of the Opium Imbroglio at Canton in the 1830's and the Anglo-Chinese War that Followed* (New Directions Publishing, 1946)

De Bary, William Theodore (editor), *Sources of Japanese Tradition* (Columbia University Press, 1958)

Ebert, Robert, *Seven Samurai* (2001)

Eden Lynn, *Whole World on Fire: Organizations, Knowledge, and Nuclear Weapons Devastation* (Cornell University Press, 2006)

Feis, Herbert, *Japan Subdued: the Atomic Bomb and the End of the War in the Pacific* (Princeton University Press, 1961)

Field, Norma, *In the Realm of a Dying Emperor* (Vintage 2011)

Fitzhugh, William W., Rossabi, Morris and Honeychurch, William, *Genghis Khan & the Mongol Empire: Mongolia from pre-history to modern times,* (Odyssey Books & Maps, 2013)

Ford, Kenneth W., *Building the H Bomb: A Personal History* (Amazon Digital Services, Inc., 2015)

Frank, Richard B., *Downfall: The End of the Imperial Japanese Empire* (Random House, 1999)

Gerson, Joseph, *Empire and the Bomb: How the U.S. Uses Nuclear Weapons to Dominate the World* (Pluto Press, 2007)

Grace, Richard J., *Opium and Empire: The Lives and Careers of William Jardine and James Matheson* (McGill Queens Universtity Press, 2014)

Grousset, René, *The Rise and Splendour of the Chinese Empire* (University of California Press, 1964)

Ham, Paul, *Hiroshima Nagasaki* (Black Swan, 2013)

Hawley, Samuel, *The Imjin War: Japan's Sixteenth-Century Invasion of Korea and Attempt to Conquer China* (Royal Asiatic Society-Korea Branch, 2005)

Hearn, Lafcadio, *Writings from Japan: An Anthology* (Penguin Classics, 1995)

Heller, Joseph, *Closing Time* (Simon & Schuster, 1995)

Hersey, John, *Hiroshima* (New Yorker/ Conde Nast, 1946)

Hiroshima Peace Memorial Commission, *The Spirit of Hiroshima: An Introduction to the Atomic Bomb Tragedy* (City of Hiroshima, 1999)

Extraordinary Regeneration

Even though the wreckage had been described to her, and though she was still in pain, the sight horrified and amazed her, and there was something she noticed about it that particularly gave her the creeps. Over everything up through the wreckage of the city, in gutters, along the river banks, tangled among tiles and tin roofing, climbing on charred tree trunks, was a blanket of fresh, vivid, lush, optimistic green; the verdancy rose even from the foundations of ruined houses. Weeds already hid the ashes, and wild flowers were in bloom among the city's bones. The bomb had not only left the underground organs of plants intact; it had stimulated them.

Everywhere were bluets and Spanish bayonets, goose-foot,
morning glories and day lilies, the hairy-fruited bean,
purslane and clotbur and sesame and panic grass and feverfew.
Especially in a circle at the centre, sickle senna grew in
extraordinary regeneration, not only standing among the charred
remnants of the same plant but pushing up in new places,
among bricks and through cracks in the asphalt.
It actually seemed as if a load of sickle-senna seed
had been dropped along with the bomb.

(John Hersey, *Hiroshima*)

"Our house collapsed, completely burying my father, my two-year-old sister, and me. I don't know how much time passed. As my mother watched, a section of roof tiles began to rattle and move. As they parted, my father arose, clutching my sister and me under his arms." – A Zuroku A-bomb drawing by a survivor, Hiroshima Peace Museum.

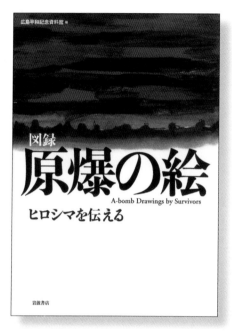

Inazo, Nitobe, *Bushido: The Classic Portrait of Samurai Martial Culture* (Tuttle Classics, 2004)

Jansen, Marius P., *The Making of Modern Japan* (Belknap Press, 2002)

Kang, Jae-eun, *The Land of Scholars: Two Thousand Years of Korean Confucianism* (Homa & Sekey Books, 2005)

Keene, Donald, *Emperor of Japan: Meiji and his World 1852-1912* (Columbia University Press, 2002)

Keiji, Nakazawa, *Barefoot Gen* (Last Gasp, 1973-74)

Keiji, Nakazawa, *I Saw It* (Educomics, 1972)

Lao Tzu (translated by Arthur Waley), *The Way and Its Power: Lao Tzu's Tao Te Ching and Its Place in Chinese Thought* (Grove Press, 1994)

Laurence, William L., *The Story of the Atomic Bomb* (Knopf, 1946)

Laurence, William L., *The Hell Bomb* (Knopf, 1951)

Levi, Primo (translated by Woolf, Stuart), *If This Is a Man and The Truce* (Little, Brown Book Group, 1991)

Lidin, Olof G., *Tanegashima-The Arrival of Europe in Japan* (Nordic Institute of Asian Studies, 2002)

Lifton, Robert Jay and Mitchell, Greg, *Hiroshima in America: Fifty Years of Denial* (Grosset/ Putnam, 1995)

Lovell, Julia, *The Opium War: Drugs, Dreams and the Making of China* (Picador, 2012)

Luttwak, E.N., *Give War a Chance* (Foreign Affairs, 1999)

Maroncelli, James M. and Karpin, Timothy L., *The Traveler's Guide to Nuclear Weapons: A Journey Through America's Cold War Battlefields* (Historical Odysseys Publishers, 2002)

Milton, Giles, *Samurai William: The Englishman who opened Japan* (Penguin, 2003)

Mirsky, Jonathan, *Okinawa: Why They Chose Death* (New York Review of Books, 2014)

Mitchell, David, *The Thousand Autumns of Jacob van Zoet* (Sceptre, 2010)

Mitchell, Greg, *Atomic Cover-up: Two U. S. Soldiers, Hiroshima & Nagasaki and the Great Movie Never Made* (Sinclair, 2012)

Murdoch, James, *A History of Japan* (K. Paul Trench Trubner & Co. Ltd., 1926)

Murdoch, James, *A History Of Japan During The Century Of Early Foreign Intercourse, 1542-1651* (Nabu Press, 2011)

Norris, Robert S., *Racing for the Bomb: General Leslie R. Groves, the Manhattan Project's Indispensable Man* (Steerforth Press, 2003)

Oe, Kenzaburo, *Hiroshima Notes* (Grove Press, 1965)

Perrin, Noel, *Giving up the gun: Japan's reversion to the sword* (David R. Godine, 1988)

Quan, So, *Japanese Piracy in Ming China during the 16th Century* (Michigan State University Press, 1975)

Richie, Donald, *The Films of Akira Kurosawa* (University of California Press, 1965)

Ryuku, Shimpo (translated by Ealey, Mark), *Descent into Hell: Civilian Memories of the Battle of Okinawa* (Merwin Asia, 2013)

Sadler, A.L., *Shogun: The Life of Tokugawa Ieyasu* (Tuttle Classics, 1937)

Sato, Hiroaki, *Legends of the Samurai* (Overlook Duckworth, 1995)

Schell, Jonathan, *The Fate of the Earth* (Alfred A. Knopf, Inc., 1982)

Sui, R.G.H., *The Portable Dragon: The Western Man's Guide to the I Ching* (The MIT Press, 1971)

Takaki, Ronald, *Hiroshima: Why America Dropped the Atomic Bomb* (Back Bay Books,1996)

Takaki, Ronald, *Strangers From a Different Shore: A History of Asian Americans* (Little, Brown & Co., 1998)

Taylor, Jay, *The Generalissimo: Chiang Kai-Shek and the struggle for modern China* (Belknap Press of Harvard University Press, 2009)

Terkel, Studs, *"The Good War"* (Pantheon, 1984)

Terkel, Studs, *P. S.: Further thoughts from a lifetime of listening* (The New Press, 2009)

The City of Hiroshima, *A-bomb drawings by survivors* (Iwanami Shoten, Publishers, 2007)

Theodore, William, *Zen & Japanese Culture* (Princeton University Press, 1973)

Tokayer, Marvin and Swartz, Mary, *The Fugu Plan: The Untold Story of the Japanese and the Jews During World War II* (Gefen Publishing House, 2004)

Vonnegut, Kurt, *Cat's Cradle* (Dell Publishing, 1963)

Vonnegut, Kurt, *Slaughterhouse Five* (Delacorte, 1969)

Wardega, Artur K. (editor), *Portrait of a Jesuit: Alessandro Valignano* (Macau Ricci Institute, 2013)

Weller, George (edited by Weller, Anthony), *First Into Nagasaki: The Censored Eyewitness Dispatches on Post-Atomic Japan and its Prisoners of War* (Broadway Books, 2007)

White, Theodore H., *In Search of History: A personal adventure* (Harper & Row, Publishers, 1978)

Wiley, Peter Booth and Ichiro, Korogi, *Yankees in the Land of the Gods: Commodore Perry and the opening of Japan* (Viking Penguin, 1990)

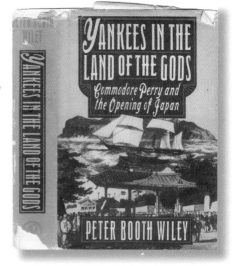

Wranovics, John, *Chaplin and Agee: The Untold Story of the Tramp, the Writer, and the Lost Screenplay* (Palgrave Macmillan, 2005)

Yamazaki, James N. and Fleming, Louise B., *Children of the Atomic Bomb: An American Physician's Memoir of Nagasaki, Hiroshima, and the Marshall Islands* (Duke University Press, 1995)

Young, John Russel (edited by Fellman, Michael), *Around the World with General Grant (abridged)* (Johns Hopkins University Press, 2002)

Yuki, Tanaka and Young, Marilyn B. (editors), *Bombing Civilians* (The New Press, 2010)

PHOTOGRAPHY AND ILLUSTRATION CREDITS

Grateful acknowledgement is made to all individuals and organizations whose images/illustrations are used in this book. The publisher has made every effort to obtain express permission of all copyright holders and to give proper attribution wherever possible; any omission of credit in whole or in part is unintentional. In the event of errors or omissions with respect to attribution kindly direct our attention to these by contacting Odyssey Books & Maps and we will make every effort to correct them for future editions. All photography/illustrations remain the property of their respective copyright holders as indicated below:

Photography/illustrations courtesy of:

Pieter van der Aa (page 87); Archivo di Stato di Firenze (91); Asian Collection Internet Auction (142); Jan van Baden (64); Magnus Bartlett (264, 265, 269 bottom, 271 top and bottom, 272, 273, 274 bottom, 274-75, 280, 282 top, 283, 285, 286, 287 top and bottom, 288, 289); British Museum (123); Anne S.K. Brown Military Collection, Brown University (32-33, top); Bundesarchiv/CCAS3.0 Germany License (41, 145); Center for Creative Photography (2); Church of Gesu, Rome (81); ehagaki-nagasaki.com (128); Alfred Eisenstadt/Getty Images (53); Department of Energy (194); Dutch National Archive (94); John Gast (27); Gifu History Museum (84-85); *Harper's Weekly* (144); Hayakawa (46); Hiroaki Misawa (290, 292); Hiroshima Museum of Fine Art (269 top); Hiroshima Peace Museum (6, 16, 56, 214, 267, 298); Mats Hjertson, Museum of Evolution, Uppsala University, Sweden (102); Huntington Library (149, 152); *Illustrated London News* (38 top, 131 bottom); Imperial Japanese Navy (156 top); Johann Caspar Horner (176); japanfocus.org/CCAS2.0 Generic License (202 inserts); Kawahara Keiga (109 top and bottom, 110); Ishikawa Koyo (204 bottom); Kobe City Museum (68, 69, 72, 99); Kyoto University (74); *Le Monde Illustre* (131 top, 132); Library of Congress (26, 38 bottom right, 40, 66, 111, 118, 122, 126, 153 top, 159, 181, 182 top, 186, 207); Lázaro Luis (23); Massachusetts Institute of Technology (165); Wolfgang Michel, University of Fukuoka (100-101); Moriyasu Murase (170); Museum of Fine Arts, Boston (120); Museum of Imperial Collections, Tokyo (62-63); Nagasaki Museum of History and Culture (55); National Archives (4, 5, 12, 185, 209); National Army Museum (156 bottom); National Diet Library (161, 162); *The New Yorker*/Condé Nast (295); New York Historical Society (32-33 bottom, 139); Robert O'Connor (263, 266, 270, 282 bottom, 287 middle); Office of War Information (193 top); Oregon Historical Society (105); Osaka Museum of Fine Art (78); Peabody Essex Museum (150); Perry-Castañeda map collection, University of Texas (83); psywarrior.com (211 top); Punch Limited (167, 179); Rory Export S.A.S./charliechaplin.com (163); F.B. Schell (137); Philip Franz von Siebold (89); Staatliche Museum, Berlin (58);

Ignacio Stafford (93); Marky Star/Japan This! (134); Christer Strömholm (213, 216); I.W. Taber (112); Tokyobling (276 top and bottom); University of Adelaide (191); U.S. Army (9, 193 bottom, 200, 202-203 main image); U.S. Army Air Force (49, 51, 203 insert, 205, 211 bottom, 212, 217); U.S. Army Corps of Engineers (196); U.S. Holocaust Memorial Museum (183); U.S. Navy (47); Utagawa (124); Utagawa Kunisada (104); Utagawa Yoshimori (133); Vincent Van Gogh Museum, Amsterdam (119, 121); VisitNagasaki.com (291); War Department (201, 204 top); War Relocation Authority (197, 198); Wikimedia Commons (35, 71/CCAS2.0, 75, 90, 97, 171, 172, 187, 189, 190, 268, 278, 318); and Yosuke Yamahata (21, 221).

The images on pages 95, 98, 107, 108, and 125 are from *Nagasaki Ukiyo-e* by Hiroshi Higuchi (Tokyo: Mito Shooku, 1971). Despite our best efforts we could not find more information about the current owners of this work.

Literary extracts are copyrighted as follows:

Page 3 "The Interlude, III" *Poetry*, March 1944, (c) 1944, 1971 by Karl Shapiro, used with permission of Harold Ober Associates Incorporated; pages 7, 18, 57, 215, 299 *Hiroshima* (c) John Hersey, used with permission of Penguin Random House; p24 *The Discoverers* (c) 1983 by Daniel J. Boorstin; p24 *Travels with Herodotus* (c) 2007 Ryzard Kapuscinski; pp26-28 *Memories, Dreams, Reflections* (c) 1963 by Carl Jung; p42 *The Memories of Marshal Zhukov* (c) 1971 Delacorte Press; p45 *The Atomic Bombings Reconsidered* (c) 1995 by Barton J. Bernstein, Foreign Affairs; pp46-48 *Japan Subdued* (c) 1961 Princeton University Press; pp50-52 *In Search of History* (c) 1978 Theodore H. White; p59 *The Fate of the Earth* (c) 1982 Jonathan Schell; p80 *St. Francis Xavier* (c) 1956 James Brodrick, S.J.; p124 *Narrative of the Expedition of an American Squadron to the China Seas of Japan* (c) 1856 United States Navy, Matthew Perry; pp136-138 *Around the World with General Grant* (c) 1880 James Russell Young; pp165-66, 168-173 *The Rape of Nanking* (c) 1998 Iris Chang, used with permission of Basic Books; p184 "The Eighth of December" (c) 1941 Takamura Kotaro; pp197-99 "A Challenge to American Sportsmanship" (c) 1943 Eleanor Roosevelt, used with permission of her estate; p210 "Atomic Bomb Blues" (c) 1946 by Homer Harris, used with permission of Alfred Publishing Company; p217 *Black Rain* (c) 1965 Masuji Ibuse; p218 "Here is New York" (c) 1949 E.B. White; pp234-35 *Something Like an Autobiography* (c) 1981 Akira Kurosawa; pp237, 238, 240-41, 242 *First Into Nagasaki* (c) 2006 Broadway Books, used with permission of Anthony Weller; p253 "Dirge for the New Sunrise" in *Cantile of the Rose Poems 1917-1949* (c) 1949 Vanguard Press, used with permission of Peters Fraser & Dunlop.

INDEX

The Perfect Way knows no difficulties except
that it refuses to make preferences. Only
when freed from hate and love does it reveal
itself fully and without disguise
A tenth of an inch's difference
And heaven and earth are set apart.
If you wish to see it before your own eyes,
have no fixed thoughts either for or against it.
To set up what you like against what you dislike
this is the disease of the mind.
When the deep meaning of the Way is not understood
peace of mind is disturbed to no purpose...

Pursue not the outer entanglements,
dwell not in the inner void;
Be serene in the oneness of things,
and dualism vanishes of itself,
When you strive to gain quiescence by stopping motion
So long as you tarry in such dualism,
how can you realize oneness?
And when oneness is not thoroughly grasped
loss is sustained in two ways:
The denying of external reality is the assertion of it,
and the assertion of Emptiness, the Absolute,
is the denying of it.

Transformations going on in the empty world
that confronts us
appear to be real because of ignorance.
Do not strive to seek after the True, only cease
to cherish opinions.

The two exists because of the One
but hold not even to this One.
When a mind is not disturbed
The ten thousand things offer no
offense...
If an eye never falls asleep,
all dreams will cease of themselves;
If the Mind retains its absoluteness
The ten thousand things are of one
substance.
When the deep mystery of one suchness
is fathomed all of a sudden we forget
the external enlargements.
When the ten thousand things are viewed
in their oneness we return to the origin
and remain where we have always been...
One in all all in one
If only this is realized
When Mind and each believing mind are
not divided.
And undivided are each believing
mind and Mind, this is where words fail,
for it is not of the past
present or future.

(Xinxin Ming, often attributed to the "Third Patriarch"
Sengcan, translated by D.T. Suzuki)

The Happiness of Mankind

My first wish is to see the whole world in peace, and the Inhabitants of it as one band of brothers striving who should contribute most to the happiness of mankind

(George Washington, 1732–1799)

Praise for other Odyssey Books & Maps...

"Like the colorfully layered matryoshka doll, this indispensable travel guide is packed with style and character. It not only provides a cornucopia of practical information and cultural insight, but takes the traveler on a splendid journey through the extensive map of the Russian soul."
—Isabel Allende

"...As the designer of Russia's first ever golf course in Moscow, I and my international crew had the pleasure of using Ms Nordbye's guide extensively as we placed the Reds on the Greens! A definite 'Don't Leave Home Without It! '..."
—Robert Trent Jones, II

"Thorough and beautifully illustrated, this book is a comprehensive—and fun—window into Afghan history, culture, and traditions. A must-have for travel readers and a gripping read for anyone with even a passing interest in Afghanistan."
—Khaled Hosseini, author of *The Kite Runner*

"It is one of those rare travel guides that is a joy to read whether or not you are planning a trip."
—New York Times

"Don't leave home without *Angkor* by Dawn Rooney."—*San Francisco Chronicle*

"The bible of Bhutan guidebooks..."—*Travel & Leisure*

"Odyssey fans tend to be adventurous travelers with a literary bent. If you're lucky enough to find an Odyssey Guide to where you're going, grab it."
—National Geographic Traveler

"Quite excellent... No one should visit Samarkand, Bukhara or Khiva without this meticulously researched guide."—Peter Hopkirk, author of *The Great Game*

"A beautiful book..."—Peter Hessler, author of *River Town*

"...poetic prose that captures the very essence of the brave, proud people of Afghanistan..."
—*New York Times*

"The Odyssey guide is a good read, full of historical background; the one to read before you go..."—*Times* (London)

"I especially recommend *The Silk Road*"—*Forbes Magazine*

"For coverage of Chongqing and the Gorges, and of the more placid and historically notable sites below Yichang and downriver to Shanghai, [this book] is unrivalled."
—Simon Winchester

"Nothing is as insightful as a comprehensive guidebook. Correspondents I know rely on them, but few of us like to admit it. The best one I've encountered on *Georgia* is Roger Rosen's Georgia published by Odyssey."
—Robert D. Kaplan, in *Eastward to Tartary*